T0272552

The Men Who Made
MANCHESTER
UNITED

'At a time when money is king in football, this is an important insight into just how humble the beginnings of Manchester United were.

'These are human football stories but they also provide a slice of Manchester's social history.' – **John Murray, BBC Football Correspondent.**

'A fine book with incredible attention to detail as Robinson unearths and examines long forgotten United stories.' – **Andy Mitten, founder and editor of United We Stand.**

'So much of the history of Manchester United is widely documented from the Busby Babes to Sir Alex Ferguson.

'Harry's book shares the stories of the less-documented characters that came before and who instilled values in the club that have gone on to define it in youth, courage and success.

'A great background spanning almost a hundred years on the men who made everything that followed possible. A must-read for any Manchester United fan.' – **Gary Neville, 602 appearances for Manchester United, 20 major trophies.**

The Men Who Made

MANCHESTER UNITED

The Untold Story

HARRY ROBINSON

First published by Pitch Publishing, 2023

Pitch Publishing
9 Donnington Park,
85 Birdham Road,
Chichester,
West Sussex,
PO20 7AJ
www.pitchpublishing.co.uk
info@pitchpublishing.co.uk

A CIP catalogue record is available for this book
from the British Library.

ISBN 978 1 80150 085 2

Typesetting and origination by Pitch Publishing
Printed and bound in India by Thomson Press

Contents

Acknowledgements 9
Introduction 11
Timeline 17
Prologue 21
Part One: Origins, 1874–1902 23
  1. Meredith and coal 25
  2. Stafford and rail 30
  3. Meredith's inspiration 33
  4. Rocca and gelato 36
  5. Meredith and City 42
  6. Stafford and Newton Heath 46
  7. Stafford's reinvention 50
  8. Stafford, Boers and beers 53
  9. Newton Heath's bazaar 59
10. Roberts and iron 65
11. The end for Newton Heath 69
Part Two: Birth of United, 1902–07 77
  1. John Henry's innovation 79
  2. A new secretary 87
  3. Falling short 93
  4. Meredith and scandal 99
  5. Roberts, the captain 103
  6. United and riots 107
  7. Promotion promises 112
  8. Blue to Red 117
Part Three: Success, 1907–11 121
  1. Charlie's league leaders 123
  2. Meredith's union 125
  3. Meredith in excelsis 130
  4. United enter Europe 136
  5. John Henry's day in the sun 144
  6. One lucky horseshoe 147
  7. Red and white rosettes 155
  8. Cockney Reds 159
  9. United's cup final 163
10. To Sandy 166
11. See the Conquering Heroes Come 168
12. Outcasts 171
13. Will there be football? 181
14. A legacy in Stretford brick 184
15. One-man show 189
16. United's finesse 192

Part Four: A Slow Demise, 1911–32 199
1. Stafford's exit. 201
2. Red to Blue. 205
3. Pastures new 208
4. War. 212
5. Futility 219
6. Crickmer's fight 226
7. Freedom 229
8. Football's return 235
9. Crickmer's new job. 240
10. Davies's unique offer 243
11. Meredith's farewell tour 248
12. Mangnall's ambition 257
13. Old Trafford's curses 261
14. Barson's hotel. 267
15. Meredith's film. 271
16. Funeral 278
17. A threatening love 282
18. An Old Trafford boycott 286
19. Dire straits 292
20. United's Christmas turkeys. 298
Part Five: Youth, 1932–39 307
1. The first 100 days 309
2. Gibson's cornerstone 313
3. Rocca's train supper 317
4. Railway. 321
5. Motor car of the year 326
6. Youth 332
7. The World Cup. 338
8. History 342
9. Magnificent MUJACs 349
10. Gibson's mission statement. 355
11. An era's end. 358
Part Six: Courage, 1939–48 361
1. A little dynamo. 363
2. Little Italy's horror 368
3. The Luftwaffe 373
4. The essence of opportunism 377
5. The Goslings. 381
6. Rocca's old pal 385
7. The Busby secret 390
8. Crickmer's final 392
9. Busby's final 396
Epilogue 404
Bibliography 410

For Patricia Markus (1929–2023).
An inspiring woman.

Acknowledgements

THANKS MUST first go to a member of this book's supporting cast, Manchester United great Stan Pearson, for helping my dad, and therefore me, become a Red. And thanks, Dad, for being the most well-meaning ruthless reviewer of work possible; Mum, for your unerring support and encouragement, and for listening to any concern, or discovery, no matter how boring a 19th-century census find might be; Alice, for being equally encouraging and offering incisive advice for every single page of this book; Romi, for *always* listening, supporting and providing a pick-me-up whenever I needed it; and Will, for talking things through, those valuable late edits, inspiring me to pursue writing and ensuring I developed the sickness of Manchester United. Rocca All Over The World.

This book is the consequence of the *United Through Time* podcast and my work as a freelance football journalist over the last few years. Thanks to anyone who listened to or shared that podcast, or the *Manchester United Weekly Podcast*. Thanks particularly to those who financially supported those shows and thus the research of this book.

In the realm of journalism, I have to thank a select few who offered encouragement to me as a young journalist when they didn't have to, some of these people, just with one comment or a friendly hello in a press box or office that no doubt meant very little to them, but a great deal to me. Particular gratitude to Andy Mitten for the constant backing, and also Paddy Barclay, Joe Brewin, Adam Crafton, Andy Exley, Oliver Kay,

Jon Mackenzie, John Murray, Simon Peach, Jim Proudfoot, and Jim White, and to Steve Bartram, Adam Bostock, Sam Carney, Paul Davies, Mark Froggatt, Joe Ganley, Charlie Ghagan, Adam Marshall, Ian McLeish, John Murtough and Gemma Thompson at Manchester United.

Thanks to everyone at Pitch Publishing for the opportunity and their endless patience, and to Duncan Olner for a wonderful cover.

Research-wise, grateful acknowledgements to anyone who has made any contribution to the British Newspaper Archive, an incredible resource, and to Dr Alexander Jackson at the National Football Museum and to Katie at the Greater Manchester Police Museum. Thank you to John Harding, Ean Gardiner, Gary James, Mark Metcalf and Tony Park for their crucial assistance, both in conversation with me and via their excellent books. Thanks also to Joe Armstrong's grandson Mark Armstrong, John Henry Davies' great-granddaughter Jo Jones, members of Louis Rocca's extended family Patricia Blount, Andy Routledge, Tony Rocca and Paul Rivers, Ancoats expert Tony Rea, Newcastle United historian Paul Joannou and Darlington expert Chris Lloyd. Thanks to James Gibson's relatives Alan and Andrew Embling for their wonderful stories, and to Matt Johnson for sharing information on his great-grandfather Harry Stafford. To Ted Roberts, grandson of Charlie Roberts, and your son, Bill, thank you for your encouragement, information and guidance. I hope you feel this book does your grandfather's story justice.

And thank you for reading. It's been a pleasure to write.

Introduction

WHAT IS Manchester United? Ask around the world and some will say Ronaldo, Beckham or Best. Others will say Ferguson or Busby. This book tells the fascinating, oft-forgotten story of United before Ferguson or Busby, or Cantona, or Robson, or Charlton or Edwards. This is the story of how United got its name and its colours; of the club's first successful team and its iconic Old Trafford stadium; of its first great manager, and player, and captain; of its 1920s demise and of its 1930s renewal; of its academy, and its heart; of youth, courage and success.

Those three principles have drawn countless generations, from both the city itself and the farthest reaches of the globe, to Manchester United Football Club.

Youth. Not just a tradition, but the heartbeat of United; a well-established blueprint for success defined most famously by two teams: Sir Matt Busby and Jimmy Murphy's Babes of the 1950s and Sir Alex Ferguson and Eric Harrison's Class of '92. These were the ultimate expression of a brilliant ideal.

Courage. When eight United players perished in the Munich snow – along with 15 others, including sporting journalists, club staff and one supporter – Manchester despaired, England mourned, and the world grieved with them. The phoenix-from-the-ashes revival after the 1958 Air Disaster attracted football fans worldwide to a brave and indomitable institution. Jimmy Murphy kept the flag flying at Old Trafford, a stadium scarred for eternity by the untimely deaths of eight players who had the world at their feet. A new team was built

11

on the same principles. In 1963, the FA Cup was won. Titles followed in 1965 and 1967 and then, finally, that holy grail of the European Cup in 1968, a symbolic decade on. But the courage of that team was not limited to times of tragedy. Courage, in fact, was the very principle on which the side was built. Club president James W. Gibson gave a fresh-faced Matt Busby the power to be an omnipotent manager, going against the precedent set in the half-century before. In turn, Busby and Murphy trusted and believed in young talent, and, with success achieved, defied the Football Association and Football League by entering the European Cup in 1956. Those same stubborn, defiant and courageous traits of Busby's were mirrored by Sir Alex Ferguson, who in 1995 sold his best players and promoted United's best young prospects. Told 'you can't win anything with kids', he soon lifted another double before conquering Europe himself in 1999. Having done so, he entered the Club World Cup, to the great fury of the Football Association and the English media. Those are the managers; then there are the players, most recently Marcus Rashford, who, in 2020, put his head above the parapet and spoke up for what he believed in. Before him, in wildly different ways, but all with courage and conviction: Beckham, Neville, Cantona and many more.

Success. Trophies, victories; put simply, playing attractive, entertaining football with the world's best players. The result? A record 20 English titles, 12 FA Cups and three European Cups.

This book is the story of how those three principles – youth, courage and success – came to define Manchester United *before* Matt Busby, and of the people responsible. These are **The Men Who Made Manchester United**.

Formed as Newton Heath L&YR Football Club in the late 1870s, years of inconsistent success, accompanied by far more consistent financial strife, saw the old club replaced by a new one: Manchester United.

This book tells the story of the eight pioneers who, over 45 years, salvaged from the ashes that Newton Heath club and laid the foundations for one of the world's biggest sporting institutions – today a quasi-religion. They include the grittily determined saviour of 1902: a womanising, beer-loving full-back turned disgraced footballer, pub landlord and hotel owner. The man who, along with his St Bernard dog, is responsible for United's very existence: **Harry Stafford**.

There is **John Henry Davies**, a portly, prosperous brewer who discovered Newton Heath via Stafford's dog, a piece of steak and an accountant knocked off his bike, saved the dying club and ambitiously drove it forward for the next quarter of a century.

Only three managers have guided United to the English title, and the first was **Ernest Mangnall**, a Bolton-born fitness fanatic who led United on their first European tour, where they were chased out of Budapest by stone-throwing hooligans, and into a gleaming new stadium: Old Trafford.

Two players are featured because of their off-pitch significance as much as their undeniable brilliance on it. **Billy Meredith** was football's first superstar, the boy miner who became a global celebrity, who played four months shy of his 50th birthday and who holds legendary status at both United and rivals Manchester City. He founded the Players' Union – the predecessor to the Professional Footballers' Association – with his great friend **Charlie Roberts**, a footballing pioneer in more sense than one: his style of play paved the way for future generations and inspired Italy's World Cup-winning sides of the 1930s. When Gary Neville led a potential England national team strike in 2003, he was following in the footsteps of Meredith and Roberts a century before.

Second-generation Italian immigrant **Louis Rocca** began life at Newton Heath as an eager teaboy and over a 60-year career fulfilled the roles of kitman, groundsman, fixer, chief scout and assistant manager. He is the man who brought Matt Busby to United and created one of England's first organised scouting networks. As the Great Depression struck in the 1930s, he worked tirelessly with the ravenously determined football fanatic **Walter Crickmer**, the mastermind of the club's world-famous academy who almost single-handedly dragged United through a six-year global war, leaving Busby to inherit a side ready for success. And it was with the money and ambition of **James W. Gibson**, visionary businessman and clothing magnate, that Crickmer and Rocca could lay the foundations for the modern United to become the behemoth we know today.

This story is necessarily set against the ever-changing social setting of Victorian, Edwardian and interwar Britain. It cannot be told without acknowledging the major historical forces changing the lives of the men on whom it focuses. And so you will see explored the themes of trade unionism, industrialisation, railways and plenty more. Do not be surprised even by regular references to Manchester City – at one point the employer of two of our main characters – and to Eton and Harrow, to Vienna and Prague, to both football and society.

These are the men who made Manchester United. There were, of course, so many women who played their parts. You'll find references to wives whose hotpot suppers and baths played a vital role, and to suffragettes, whose protests in this era laid the foundations for women to be considered more than additions to their husbands. But even by this book's end, James Gibson's wife was kept off United's board after his death simply due to her gender. The focus of this story reflects that injustice.

This book includes the transfer fee of two freezers of ice cream, the death of a young footballer and his forgotten family, the fight for the right to unionise, the joy of cup glory and the pelting stones of the angry residents of Budapest. It includes devout loyalty and the greatest act of betrayal from womanisers and family men alike. It includes stories of northerners invading London, Edwardian Cockney Reds and, of course, some thrilling football matches along the way.

With the help of the descendants of these eight men, original research and new-found archives, this book is the story of United's early days, sprinkled with the great tales that make it so entertaining. I hope you enjoy reading it as much as I have relished telling it.

Timeline

Newton Heath/Manchester United

1878: Newton Heath L&YR formed, primarily as
a cricket club

1880: First recorded football match

1888: Enter the Football Combination | Football
League founded

1889: Enter the Football Alliance

1892: Enter the Football League's Division One

1893: Move to Bank Street

1894: Relegated to Division Two

1901: Fundraising bazaar

1902: Refounded and renamed 'Manchester United'

1906: Promoted to Division One

1908: Division One champions | Embark on the club's first
overseas tour

1909: FA Cup winners

1910: Move to Old Trafford

1911: Division One champions (2)

1922: Relegated to Division Two

1925: Promoted to Division One

1931: Relegated to Division Two

1932: United's 'A' Team is founded

1936: Promoted to Division One

1937: Relegated to Division Two

1938: Promoted to Division One | Manchester United
   Junior Athletic Club (MUJAC) is founded
1941: Old Trafford destroyed in German bombing raid
1948: FA Cup winners (2)
1949: United return to Old Trafford after seven years
   at Maine Road
1952: Division One champions (3)
1956: Division One champions (4) | United enter the
   European Cup (first English side to do so)
1957: Division One champions (5) | United reach the
   European Cup semi-finals
1958: The Munich Air Disaster

The Men Who Made Manchester United
1864: John Henry Davies born
1866: Ernest Mangnall born
1869: Harry Stafford born
1874: Billy Meredith born
1877: James W. Gibson born
1882: Louis Rocca born
1883: Charlie Roberts born
1892: Harry Stafford's Crewe Alexandra debut | Billy
   Meredith's Chirk AAFC debut
1894: Billy Meredith joins Manchester City
1895: Billy Meredith's Wales debut
1896: Harry Stafford joins Newton Heath
1899: Raymond Walter Crickmer born
1900: Ernest Mangnall becomes Burnley FC secretary
1902: John Henry Davies takes over Manchester United |
   Charlie Roberts joins Bishop Auckland
1903: Ernest Mangnall becomes Manchester
   United secretary |
   Charlie Roberts joins Grimsby Town

1904: Charlie Roberts joins Manchester United

1905: Charlie Roberts's England debut

1906: Billy Meredith joins Manchester United

1907: Billy Meredith and Charlie Roberts form the Players' Union

1911: Harry Stafford emigrates to the USA

1912: Ernest Mangnall leaves Manchester United for Manchester City

1913: Charlie Roberts leaves Manchester United for Oldham Athletic

1920: Walter Crickmer joins Manchester United as a clerk

1921: Billy Meredith leaves Manchester United for Manchester City | Charlie Roberts becomes Oldham Athletic manager

1922: Charlie Roberts resigns as Oldham Athletic manager

1926: Walter Crickmer becomes Manchester United secretary

1927: John Henry Davies dies after 25 years as Manchester United president | Louis Rocca becomes United's assistant manager

1928: Billy Meredith and Charlie Roberts get involved with new club Manchester Central

1931: Walter Crickmer assumes managerial responsibility at United | Billy Meredith becomes United's reserve team coach

1932: James W. Gibson takes over Manchester United | Ernest Mangnall dies | Walter Crickmer returns to his role as secretary

1937: Walter Crickmer assumes managerial responsibility at United (second time)

1939: Charlie Roberts dies

1940: Harry Stafford dies

1944: Louis Rocca writes to Matt Busby

1945: Walter Crickmer returns to his role as secretary as
    Matt Busby becomes United manager

1950: Louis Rocca dies

1951: James W. Gibson dies after 19 years as Manchester
    United president

1958: Walter Crickmer is killed in the Munich Air Disaster
    | Billy Meredith dies

Prologue

April 1909

'To Sandy,' Charlie Roberts toasts, his normally pale cheeks flushed by an afternoon of celebratory drinks. Billy Meredith mumbles a joke. Sandy Turnbull, as ever his partner-in-crime, sniggers. Roberts smiles and gestures for glasses to be raised. Inside the Trocadero Restaurant in London's West End, Manchester United's captain is delivering a short speech to his team-mates, their families, and friends. It is a grand setting for the grandest of achievements, and a little different from the hotpot suppers at the Merediths' house in north Manchester where United's players normally muse over tactical plans.

The Reds are English Cup winners thanks to Sandy Turnbull's first-half goal that afternoon. Almost 80,000 watched United beat Bristol City, many of them coming to the Crystal Palace sports ground just to see Roberts and Meredith, two of their generation's finest players.

Charlie's speech is brief. He pays tribute to **Harry Stafford**, the old club captain who saved Newton Heath; to **John Henry Davies**, the club president; to **Ernest Mangnall**, the secretary; and to the many volunteers. With that, he nods at **Louis Rocca**, the amiable groundsman and kitman. The Italian has changed from the red and white pyjamas he wore to the cup final. The Trocadero is no place for pyjamas.

Roberts makes a subtle reference to the football world's brewing unrest. A month ago, the Meredith and Roberts-founded Players' Union met officials from the General Federation of Trade Unions. The Football Association's fury was instant, and within weeks of Charlie's jovial speech at the

Trocadero, the entire United team will be suspended without pay. Add in last season's English title, Charity Shield and a first European tour and it has certainly been quite the year.

As the night begins to run away with itself, Roberts is reminded that United have promised famous stage performer George Robey they will appear at his nine o'clock performance at the Alhambra Theatre. Charlie tells everyone to finish their drinks but still leaves with only half the squad in tow.

When they arrive at the Alhambra, Roberts is with a smattering of team-mates, bolstered necessarily by several friends from home. Robey, who gifted United their magnificent white cup final kits, presents England's finest football team to his audience, who respond with an enormous ovation. Roberts, though, has an uncontrollable giggling fit. When he looks from side to side, he sees not the English Cup winners, but his mates: a sheepish-looking butcher, poultry dealer, bookmaker, builder, and greengrocer.

The next morning, the cup's lid is missing. It's found in Sandy Turnbull's jacket pocket where Meredith, ever the prankster, has placed it the night before. United return home to Manchester to the adulation of tens of thousands of delighted supporters.

Part One: Origins, 1874–1902

1

Meredith and coal

*'The football commentator cannot do justice
to the footballing genius of Meredith. Had
he lived in earlier years he would've been the
subject of an epic poem and been immortalised
with Achilles, Roland and the Knights of the
round table.'*

– Manchester United programme, 1912.

July 1874 – 'I'm putting him in the oven,' Grandmother calls out. **William Meredith**, born minutes earlier, is weak, feeble and unready for the world. His parents, recently moved north from Trefonen, a Welsh-sounding town in the English county of Shropshire, scuttle around Chirk enlisting help from their new neighbours. They are just inside the Welsh border. Had he been born 200 metres south, little Billy – who will be proudly capped 48 times by Wales – would be an Englishman. Whether it's his grandmother's warm oven or a natural determination, Billy survives. His initial deficiencies are quickly overcome even though, as one of ten kids, he elicits little direct attention from his parents, James and Jane.

Billy watches his father and his elder brothers trudge through Chirk's grassy fields, the tips of which are browned by colliery smog, and disappear over the lip of the hill to the Black Park pit. Every Chirk man works in one of the town's two coal mines. A month after Billy's birth, Parliament's

Factory Act establishes a 56-hour working week and prevents children from being used as chimney sweeps, but it will not prevent Billy from an education in coal. The chief guzzler of Chirk's produce is Manchester. As Cottonopolis throbs with the pulsating beat of industrial growth, Chirk is one of a glut of small towns providing it with the resources it needs to blossom into the heart of the country's Industrial Revolution.[1]

Mining, religion and sport define the Meredith family. Two of Billy's six sisters become nurses, inspired by their Primitive Methodist faith, while his brother will be a lay preacher. Away from the pits and the church, the vast expanse of Welsh valleys and hills provides plenty of space to play, although when Billy Meredith is born, exactly what football is remains unfixed and unclear. It has been played for centuries in one form or another, as it is in Chirk, where Billy falls in love with the game alongside his brothers, Sam and Jim. In larger towns and cities, newspapers regularly report on 'football' games with scores varying from 1-0 to 43-40 and two tries to one. The organisation of what is to become England's national sport has only just begun. The Football Association (FA) was founded 11 years ago, in 1863, and England's first international match was played against Scotland seven years later. In the summer of 1871, exactly three years before Billy's birth, Parliament legalised trade unions and three weeks later, the English Cup was born.[2] A painfully close relationship will form between these two events for Billy Meredith, but not for another 38 years.

British sport overall is finding its feet. The first England versus Australia Test cricket match is held in 1877, two months before the first Wimbledon Championship at the All England Lawn Tennis and Croquet Club. Its victor is Spencer Gore, the Harrow-educated great-grandson of an earl. Football's 'English Cup' features similar public school

---

1 Manchester is known as Cottonopolis as it's the city at the centre of Britain's globally dominant cotton industry.

2 Now known as the FA Cup.

dominance. The 1873 final is moved to 11am to allow the players to attend the afternoon's Oxford versus Cambridge boat race. A 'games cult' has overtaken England's public schools, whose teachers believe team sports will produce good men suitable to fight for the Empire, men who are courageous and athletic but also unselfish, gentle, fair, restrained and unpretentious. At Harrow, boys are made to play football with the direct intention of producing good warriors. Old Harrovians dominate the Wanderers Football Club, who win five out of the first seven cups.

With most prestigious public schools located in England's south, the north is playing catch-up football-wise until a wave of new Lancastrian teams are founded in the 1870s. Included amongst these is the predecessor to Manchester United.

In Newton Heath, just north-east of Manchester's city boundaries, signs of grass to play football on are hard to find. Once a Lancashire farming town, the area has been rapidly industrialised. It is now criss-crossed by the lines of the vast Lancashire & Yorkshire Railway Company, which employs a couple of thousand local men. The company's Dining Committee has begun to put on 'Improvement Classes' which include opera but are primarily sport-based. The result is the formation of various clubs including Newton Heath L&YR, formed by the Carriage & Wagon Department in 1878 to develop team spirit and social skills. While they usually play cricket against other departments of the railway company, hence their predominantly white strip with blue trim, they do dabble in 'soccer' and football soon takes precedence over cricket. Teenager Sam Black buys a football from a Market Street shop in Manchester's city centre and soon, in November 1880, the team are playing their first recorded match, a 6-0 defeat to Bolton Wanderers' second XI.

The Heathens play friendlies against varied opposition which includes Hurst – the pioneers of Mancunian football – Manchester Arcadians, Blackburn Olympic's reserves and St Mark's. The latter, who will undergo three name changes before settling on Manchester City, played their first recorded match one week before Newton Heath, who triumph 3-0 in the sides' first encounter.

They face off at Newton Heath's North Road, a just-about-suitable patch of ground immediately next to the Carriage & Wagon Works in which the team's players are employed. The ground is owned by the Manchester Cathedral authorities and the Lancashire & Yorkshire Railway company agree to pay a small rent on behalf of their employees. In the summer months, North Road is uneven, stony and cracked. In winter, it's muddy and swamp-like. All through the year, passing trains cast a thick fog of steam across the pitch. The players change in the nearby Three Crowns pub on Oldham Road and walk up to play. As crowds begin to develop and grow, the 'Coachbuilders', as the team becomes known due to their occupations, have to jostle through their own supporters to get access to their pitch, bursting randomly out of the mass of people on the touchline like corn kernels do in Charles Cretors' newly invented popcorn machine in Chicago.

Football is receiving increasing focus in Manchester as many northern sides flourish, Newton Heath L&YR included. The *Manchester Guardian* still prioritises rugby, but the *Manchester Courier* brings on a dedicated football reporter named 'Dribbler'. A 10,000 crowd at the neutral Whalley Range ground for an English Cup semi-final in March 1882 certainly helps the status of the game and while Manchester's teams are not yet at the level of those in neighbouring towns, important sporting events are common within the globally renowned city's boundaries. In late 1882, the International Football Association Board (IFAB) is founded in Manchester, perhaps the most powerful governing body in the game.[3] In the same season, Blackburn Olympic's FA Cup victory represents the sudden wrestling of football power away

---

3 It remains football's most powerful governing body, ranking ahead of FIFA in that regard.

from the public school alumni and towards the northern professional classes.

Months later, the Manchester and District FA is founded, comprising 16 clubs. Meetings are well-attended and, after campaigning from Hurst, Newton Heath and West Manchester, a Manchester Cup is begun. This will be the making of both Mancunian football and Newton Heath L&YR, whose side's diversity reflects that of its birthplace. Newton Heath is typical of Manchester in that its community is an ever-changing mosaic of 'locals' and immigrants. The Railwaymen's key organiser is Frederick Attock, a 36-year-old Carriage & Wagon Works superintendent who lives with his two sons, elderly mother and two servants, none of whom are Manchester-born. They have moved from Essex for work. Vice-president Thomas Gorst, 53, is a Liverpool-born railway clerk who lives with railway workers born in Ireland, Scotland and Wales.

Back down in north Wales, 12-year-old Billy Meredith has joined his father in Chirk's Black Park mine. Due to his slight frame, he's employed to unhook the tubs at the pit's bottom. It's a risky business, one of many roles down the mines that lead to all-too-common deaths of children who should be playing in the fields, or getting a good education. Stories are regularly told of children's heads crushed between the tubs and doors, underneath horses or enormous cages, but Billy survives and enjoys himself. Unwashed, grimy and with blackened faces, he and his mates sprint off at the end of the working day and out on to the fields where they play football, the light dying behind the rolling hills.

2

Stafford and rail

*'Crewe is at the heart of rail, and rail is at
the heart of Crewe.'*

– Dr Kieran Mullan MP, Houses of Parliament,
29 March 2022.

January 1884 – Harry Stafford, the future captain of Newton
Heath and Manchester United is, like Billy Meredith, a
boy worker.

Crewe, like Chirk, was a small town before the Industrial
Revolution grasped it, shook it about and spat it out. Its
inhabitants numbered a mere 200 when the Grand Junction
Railway line opened in 1837. By Harry Stafford's birth in
late November 1869, 18,000 people lived around him. Just
south of Manchester, this bustling workshop is a fantastically
connected place producing reliable locomotives that traverse
the length of the country.

Harry's father, George, is a railwayman but, at the mercy
of Crewe's entirely dominant employer, the London North
Western Railway (LNWR), workers can endure irregular
earnings in times of recession, so he is also a part-time hatter.
Aged 14, young Harry joins the LNWR as an apprentice
boilermaker, earning four shillings a week for 54 hours of
labour. He'll need to work for 35 weeks to afford an overcoat.

On days off, Stafford plays with his brother Walter, and
his best mate: another Walter, surname Cartwright. Stafford
shows an aptitude for athletics and football, the organisation
of which remains slapdash and clumsy despite its rapid recent

growth. The greatest debate is over professionalism. FA officials believe footballers should play for honour, pride and self-improvement, not financial reward. An admirable goal, it may be, but it prevents working-class participation and as working-class footballers grow in numbers, the long-fought and bitter dispute becomes acute. In the end, the threat of 25 first-class clubs breaking away to form a new association forces pragmatic conservatism to prevail and professionalism is reluctantly legalised in 1885. This is a bonus for Newton Heath L&YR who can offer jobs in the attached company as payment for players.

Football's rules are now also overwhelmingly agreed upon. Teams of all abilities play in the 2-3-5 formation that will prevail for decades more. It features two defensive 'backs', three half-backs – the most central of which is the heart of the team – two wingers, known as outside-right and outside-left, and a centre-forward flanked by two inside-forwards.

So, a generally coherent and organised sport exists, but ill-matched, cancelled and clashing fixtures are a common bane. The railwaymen of Newton Heath and Crewe adhere to a strict and organised timetable, and yet football's fixture list is as eccentric and non-uniform as a Picasso painting. Victorian Britain is a place of timekeeping, where workers stamp in and out of their factories and trains, buses and trams fulfil their timetables. Victorian football is not. Successful sides frequently find themselves needing to fulfil two fixtures on the same day. Newton Heath L&YR's first Lancashire Cup match is played against Blackburn Olympic's second-string team because the visitors also have an FA Cup game that day. Conversely, less successful outfits are fixture-less for weeks when knocked out of cup competitions early on and those smaller teams who do unexpectedly progress are ruthlessly decimated by much stronger opposition. Hyde concede 26 times against Preston North End in one FA Cup match. The *Lancashire Post*'s reporter has the unenviable task of fitting all 26 goals into a two-paragraph match summary.

Thus in the spring of 1888, following Blackburn Olympic's symbolic FA Cup win and the advent of professionalism, football's third seminal change of the decade takes place.

3

Meredith's inspiration

*'Every year it is becoming more and more
difficult for football clubs. I beg to tender the
following suggestion: that the most prominent
clubs in England combine to arrange home-
and-away fixtures each season.'*

– The 1888 letter, by William McGregor.

January 1889 – Billy Meredith, hands stuffed in pockets, as
they always are except when playing football, skips forward
to keep pace with his elder brother, Elias, who left Chirk to
become a railway engine driver. Permitted to take Billy on
free trips, Elias and his brother roam about watching football.
Today, they travel to Liverpool to watch the as-yet-unbeaten
Preston North End at Everton.

It is North End's penultimate match of the new Football
League, founded last spring by the 12 leading Lancashire-
and Midlands-based clubs. Football's power base has moved
north; the pioneering sides who formed the FA in 1863 were
all from London.

The league's founder, William McGregor, was likely
inspired by two sports with leagues already established:
baseball, which he is involved with himself, and cricket, with
which several fellow Aston Villa committee members are
associated, including Alf Albut, a name worth remembering.
Football and cricket remain intrinsically linked, and
McGregor's idea was certainly well-received. After initial

discussions in London before the 1888 English Cup Final, the Football League was created in a decisive second meeting in Manchester.

Despite the location of its foundation, Billy Meredith and his brother Elias cannot visit Manchester to watch league football. McGregor's elite selected few excludes Manchester's two most prominent clubs, Ardwick and Newton Heath – later to become City and United. The latter enter an alternative set-up: The Combination, which is more of a loose trade agreement than a sporting division. Mild chaos ensues compared to the immediately esteemed Football League, which generates incredible excitement.

Changing trains at Chester, the Meredith brothers head to Birkenhead in a cattle-like third-class carriage, cross the Mersey and find their way to Everton's home ground at Anfield, joining a mass of people all afflicted by the new football craze.

It's a predominantly male crowd, although there are some groups of women. Half a decade earlier, Preston welcomed women free of charge to their home ground, Deepdale. When 2,000 girls turned up for one game, they abandoned that particular strategy on economic grounds. The men wear hats – stiff bowler, derby, homburg, felt, billed, flat, whichever – and their work clothes from the Saturday morning shift, or a suit if they've come from home, underneath heavy winter coats. The smoke of pipes wafts upwards into the crisp air, heated by the breath of the cramped thousands below, and Billy rides with the motion of the crowd. Elias used to have to shoulder-lift him to achieve a view of any sort, but Billy can stand freely now, despite his slim frame, and he takes inspiration from what he sees: Jack Gordon. The Preston winger is unorthodox in his style, but brilliant.

Preston win. Of course they do. They are already confirmed as champions, having won 16 of their 20 games before this one. The rest are drawn. Jimmy Ross, who plays just inside Billy's new hero Jack Gordon, scores North End's first goal. A second is added before the close of play. Billy returns to Chirk tired and inspired. When he leaves the Black Park Colliery at dusk on Monday, he takes to the hills to try out what he's seen at the weekend.

North End's final game of this inaugural league season is at second-placed Aston Villa on an intensely cold Birmingham night. Alf Albut 'umpires' in front of an immense attendance. Another Preston victory means they have achieved an invincible season. Soon, they are holders of the double. Their rise has been rapid. Like many clubs, they took some time to turn to association football, first playing cricket, then rugby briefly before adopting the association game in 1881. Now, 20,000 people greet the double-winners upon their return. Hats and handkerchiefs are waved rapidly; boys and men hang from lampposts, shouting themselves hoarse. Shawls, jackets, aprons – in fact, any piece of clothing which can be removed – are swung in the wildest manner. Lancastrian football is well and truly alive.

Beneath the League, which attracted an astonishing total attendance of 600,000, football remains messy. The Combination failed. When Newton Heath played away at Darwen in January, a 6-0 loss was accidentally telegrammed back to Manchester the wrong way round. 'Imagine the state of affairs at the Bird in Hand when they found out it was a defeat instead of a victory,' the *Cricket and Football Field* mused. The competition disbanded without a winner.

Newton Heath subsequently make an ambitious bid to join the Football League but, when spurned, help to form another new alternative: the Football Alliance. Its foundations are far sturdier than The Combination and it's not long before fixtures in this division are attracting league-esque bumper crowds too.

4

Rocca and gelato

'Ancoats ... is to Manchester what
Manchester is to England.'

– *Morning Chronicle*, 21 December 1849.

March 1892 – Ten-year-old **Louis Rocca** lifts up a loose board in the fence and beckons his friend, who runs blindly into a mass of burly Newton Heath-supporting men. Louis follows, but too slowly. He's dragged up by his collar, yelping.

'I was promised a hiding.' Said I to the man who caught me – 'Never mind the walloping; please can I watch the match?'

'He was so taken with the cheek or enthusiasm which backed the request that he gave me a job.'[4]

Young Louis is soon making the players' half-time tea and cleaning out the baths, and very proud of it he is, too. His parents are immigrants. Luigi Rocca left a small northern Italian town aged 27, seeking work in Manchester's slum-like industrial suburb, Ancoats. Even by Victorian Britain's mucky standards, Ancoats then was a dusty, noisy, smoky, exhausting, appalling place. Once a hardly populated hamlet in Manchester's extreme east, with views over green woodlands and a clear river, by 1851 here was somewhere so densely packed with factories, mills and people that, were it a town in its own right, it would have been one of England's most populous. And so it stank. Smoke from its endless chimneys intermingled above narrow streets, the droppings of humans

---

4   Louis, writing in 1935.

and horses alike encrusted into the gaps between the cobbles. First came the canals, then the mills, then the factories, and soon American cotton via Liverpool, Baltic timber through Hull, Ashton coal and Pennine stone.

Those factories. Eight or nine stories high, and revolutionary. Described by one German visitor as 'the miracles of modern times', by another as 'monstrous shapeless buildings', by Friedrich Engels as 'colossal and towering' and later by Sylvia Pankhurst as the 'blight' of a district. Cotton dominates, and other industries rise to service it: machine construction, workshops for nuts, bolts and screws, glass-making, silk mills, chemicals and dye production. When Louis' parents arrived, Ancoats was remarkable. Fluff floated off the cotton and into the smoggy air, drifting on to hair and clothing like an unmelting snowflake. A glance into a dusty and screeching glass factory exposed chalky-faced men standing at troughs, grinding, smoothing and polishing delicate and dazzling objects of glass; beauty amongst squalor.

* * *

Ancoats' first immigrants were Irish. By the mid-1800s, nearly half the population was Irish-born. Then came the Italians. They brought lively street talents, music, a new culture and, eventually, ice cream, just as the recently formed Manchester City Council intervened to prevent Ancoats from one day sinking beneath the weight of its own shit. The Ancoats that Louis grows up in is thankfully cleaner than the one into which his father arrived.

The Rocca household is busy. In Louis' youngest years, the Roccas host as many as 14 lodgers at a time. Working-class families sublet rooms to single men and women; the poorest even sublet beds. Louis often shared a bedroom with ten others, but his father's ice cream business grows so the number of lodgers decreases until it's only Abraham, aged 43, who works as an assistant in the shop. Instead, 64 Rochdale Road is filled by friends of the Rocca children as often as

Luigi's own kids, who help the family business. Louis works in the basement as Rocca's Ices becomes a cornerstone of the area, except on Saturdays, when he heads to Newton Heath, to make the tea, empty the filthy baths, guard the players' belongings and carry their bags.

A little over a decade old, Newton Heath long ago swapped white-with-blue-trim kits for red and white. Their team is good, not great. The Heathens have dominated the Manchester Cup since its inception, but English Cup ties are the most attractive occasions at North Road, the imperfect ground which Louis snuck into.

Crisis is closely averted in the spring of 1892 when 17 committee members are sued for unpaid goods supplied by two local printers. In court, they all deny knowledge of quite literally anything. The judge is unimpressed by this farcical tactic, but they get off, nevertheless. Come the season's end, Newton Heath – the association with the L&YR now dropped – becomes a limited liability company, allowing the club to raise capital. Several prominent local gentlemen promise to purchase shares because, despite controversy over unpaid bills, this is a successful club with a series of Manchester Cups in its past, a recent second-place finish in the Football Alliance and a potentially bright future. Indeed, Newton Heath are immediately voted into the Football League as it expands into two tiers. In fact, they will assume a spot in Division One.

Their pilot to these new heady heights is Alf Albut, an experienced and well-liked Aston Villa committee member whose loyalties are split between cricket and football. Alf's hometown of Bromsgrove – south-west of Birmingham – is another small market town transformed by the Industrial Revolution. Bromsgrove's workers produce nails, though Alf's father avoided this industry, floating anywhere that'd make him a quick quid, selling coal, china, glass and groceries. Alf emulated his father but devoted much of his time to playing and administrating cricket. His organisational skill and devotion saw him warmly accepted on to Aston Villa's committee.

When Football League members convene in July 1892, the meeting's chair is Alf's old friend, William McGregor. Albut attends, but now representing Newton Heath. The Heathens had wanted a full-time secretary and, having served a long apprenticeship at Villa where he was 'instrumental in bringing that club to prominence', Albut is an excellent choice for Manchester's leading football club.[5]

Alf had reason to leave Birmingham. He let his margarine business slip through his fingers. A travelling man robbed him of £140 and then killed himself a week later, leaving Albut bankrupt in August 1891. A fresh start seems sensible.

Running an average football club such as Newton Heath requires careful financial manoeuvring and Albut devises several fundraising schemes, but a supporters' social club soon ends when some scally nicks the billiards cues. On the pitch, Newton Heath hint at an ability to cope with the big boys early on, but heavy losses soon follow. One anomaly sticks out, a quite ridiculous 10-1 home thrashing of Wolverhampton Wanderers.

'The Wanderers could not stand, much more kick the ball,' concludes the sympathetic *Birmingham Daily Gazette*.

Unfortunately for Albut, muddy home advantage is far from sufficient when you fail to win away from home all season. With no chance of emerging from the table's bottom, Albut dedicates his spring to finding two things: new players and a new home.

As Newton Heath's tenancy on their North Road ground ends, its owners, the Manchester Cathedral, demand the club allow spectators in for free, on ideological grounds. This would deprive Newton Heath of their only source of income, and so they plead with their former benefactors, the Lancashire & Yorkshire Railway Company, to curry favour

---

5 *Clarion*, 1 October 1892.

on their behalf. Their argument is sound, that the increased rail traffic from the club playing at North Road will make it worthwhile, but no solution is found. Aware that losing their ground could compel them to disband and lose their new Football League status, Albut and the committee members endure a stressful time.

In June, Albut finally secures new premises at Bank Street, a small ground owned by the Bradford and Clayton Athletic Company. It has no stands and Albut quickly gets to work. He advertises in local papers, asking for 'cheap, old timber' and 'a large quantity of second-hand tongue-grooved boards' – again, with a real emphasis on 'cheap'. The stadium is accessible by tram and rail, but the pitch is once again poor. Whereas North Road was stony and muddy, Bank Lane is dry with an awkward rise in the centre.

As September comes, sporting ears still tingling with the crack, thump and cheers of bat and ball, the noises of Britain's new passion spread nationwide, ready for a new football season. Newton Heath's new home brings no new playing style, as the *Birmingham Gazette*'s reporter, Jephcott, scathingly explains after his West Bromwich Albion are beaten 4-1.

'It was not a football match, it was simple brutality … Next week Newton Heath have to play Burnley, and if they both play in their ordinary style it will perhaps create an extra run of business for the undertakers.'

Albut duly responds in the newspapers, attaching a response from the referee which he believes shows his team's innocence, and the matter even ends up in court, but Jephcott is hardly the only man to complain of Newton Heath's brutish style. They are aggressive and the unpleasant antidote to the 'scientific' football played by Aston Villa, Preston North End and any other successful team. These tactics earn neither fans nor points. At the end of their second Football League season, the Heathens are relegated to little fanfare. Liverpool take their place.

***

Future Heathens captain **Harry Stafford** represents an equally brutish team: Crewe Alexandra. He is quick, as demonstrated by his athletic prowess during the summer months in the 100 yards, half-mile and hurdles, and he is broad, a natural consequence of manual labour. He makes for a good full-back. After making his senior debut for Alexandra shortly before his 21st birthday – which brings a small pay rise from the London North Western Railway company – he becomes a regular.

It is not passion or commitment that inhibits Harry's Alexandra team, but the dictatorial influence of Frank Webb, a legendary railwayman, locomotive designer, LNWR superintendent, alderman and mayor. In essence, Crewe is his town. He opposes professional football and threatens to sack anyone who wishes to engage in it. With few non-rail employment opportunities, Stafford and his team-mates have little choice but to remain amateur. Perhaps frustration at the instability of employment drives the Alexandra players to an aggressive style. As Newton Heath end their first Division Two season in third, Crewe finish bottom. They concede 113 goals in 36 games and take the much-merited title of the Football League's worst-ever side.

Also amateur but better resembling the era's successful, 'scientific' sides is a little team in north Wales: Chirk. Gangly with quick feet and a patience to his play, Billy Meredith's football career has blossomed.

5

Meredith and City

'Nature has certainly endowed him
with advantages above the common. An
awkward customer to tackle, slippery as an
eel with shooting powers extraordinary, he
is a real gem.'

– *Athletic News*, 9 December 1895.

October 1894 – The Meredith brothers played football constantly throughout their childhood despite the protestations of their mother, frustrated by the insatiable need for new shoes as the Meredith boys came back with scuffs, rips and tears from their evenings on Chirk's hills, to-ing and fro-ing from one goal to the other.

This north Wales strip has produced a whole generation of talented international players. Local schoolmaster Thomas E. Thomas is a long-time teacher of the association game and a significant participant in the Welsh FA. His tutelage provided drive and impetus to Billy's football. William Owen, who made his Wales debut a decade earlier, is another Meredith mentor. From his September 1892 debut for Chirk, Meredith's frontline performances alongside Owen earn him rave reviews. His dribbling ability and thunderous shot help Chirk to the Welsh Cup Final, where they are defeated by Wrexham.

His second full season of senior football is punctuated by mining strikes which force Chirk to drop out of the semi-professional Combination League due to decreased attendances. The team's talented squad, Meredith included, thus turn out for nearby sides Wrexham and Northwich Victoria, picking up much-needed extra money as the miners picket against a wage cut. Significantly, the saga temporarily forces Billy into the professional game. When a resolution is eventually reached, the Chirk team is reunited in full and they continue to excel, reaching a sixth Welsh Cup Final in eight years.

Billy loves playing and feels fulfilled at Chirk. He enjoys home life, his work at the pit and his appearances across a selection of local teams. But his brother Sam – now a player himself at Stoke City – Thomas E. Thomas, William Owen and plenty of other impressed team-mates and spectators are not content leaving Billy's potential untapped. Di Jones, a fellow Chirk graduate, one-time Newton Heath player and long-serving Bolton Wanderers full-back, tells his club of Billy's talents but they deem his frame too small for top-flight football. Others think the same, but not Manchester City – recently renamed from Ardwick AFC – who receive recommendations from their forward Pat Finnerhan, who played alongside Billy at Northwich Victoria, and Lawrence Furniss, ex-Ardwick secretary and now trusted advisor behind the scenes, who has refereed Meredith's games.

**

When City representatives Joshua Parlby and John Chapman arrive in Chirk, they are unwelcome. English railways, mines and culture have already pierced the Welsh border, and things are no different in football. Billy's mother, for one, resents professional football.

'A mother thinks of other things besides money,' says Jane.

'Our boys are happy and healthy, satisfied with their work and innocent amusements. You gentlemen come and put all kinds of ideas into their heads. You tell them they can get more money for play than they can for hard but honest work. If Billy takes my advice he will stick to his work and play football for his own amusement when work is finished.'

The Chirk locals are no more cordial.

'It was said that representatives from Manchester City were chased by local people and ducked in the village pond; that they had to disguise themselves; that they had to entertain Meredith's fellow miners in the local pub before they could be allowed to speak to him.'[6]

Parlby and Chapman finally sit down with Billy in Chirk's only hotel. They order lunch, and Meredith puts away pork chop after pork chop with astonishing speed. Parlby whispers to Chapman: 'If he can play football in the manner in which he can consume chops, he must be our man.' They will soon discover he can do both, but it takes Parlby's silver tongue to convince a reluctant Meredith. He signs but only on amateur terms and with a stubborn commitment to continue living and working in Chirk. It's unfortunate, then, that Billy's debut is away at Newcastle. He leaves Chirk at 2am on Saturday morning for the 11-hour trip to England's north-east – which he modestly describes as 'somewhat strenuous' – and will not return until mid-morning the next day. The 90 minutes of football is the easy part. He sets up two goals in a 5-4 defeat, playing alongside Pat Finnerhan on the right wing. A home debut with a slightly easier trip follows. City are beaten 5-2 by local rivals Newton Heath but Meredith is applauded off after scoring both of his side's goals.

City's supporters adore their new signing. There is a swagger about him. As an outside-right, he plays on the wing of a five-man attack. His job is to support the centre-forward and inside-forward with penetrative runs and crosses. Good stamina is essential, intelligence and technique non-negotiable. Meredith keeps the chalk beneath his heavy boots, stepping inside to receive the ball and isolating defenders. His speed is unremarkable but his acceleration excellent and his ability to

---

6   As relayed in John Harding's biography of Meredith.

keep defenders on their heels means he doesn't rely on a bolt of pace. He can ride challenges and sit defenders down, and he very quickly becomes City's best player. The *Athletic News* soon declare there is 'no man playing better football'.

Eventually, Meredith turns professional and reluctantly gives up his full-time job at the Black Park Colliery, but he remains determined to head home after matches. He quickly and quietly packs his bags and boards a train back towards tranquillity. This must be baffling to his team-mates, the majority of whom traipse into one pub or another, often the City headquarters, the Hyde Road Hotel. City's owner, chairman and secretary are brewers and publicans. For a teetotaller like Meredith, City isn't the Cinderella fit, but he flourishes and his beloved nation soon comes calling.

Billy is enthralled at the chance to represent his country because his enormous Welsh pride is further exaggerated by his distaste for English arrogance. Military battles are long in the past, but the Industrial Age has seen Welshmen work on railways and in mines largely under the direction of what they perceive to be greedy, miserable English bosses.

Although the Irish Sea's swell makes him deeply uncomfortable en route to Belfast in spring 1895, Meredith plays well in a 2-2 tie with Ireland and, two days later, starts in a draw against England at London's Queen's Club.

Back at his club, Meredith's City and neighbours Newton Heath are both in Division Two. Both sides require additional oomph to progress through the tough promotion play-off matches. Now assisting the Heathens in that endeavour is Walter Cartwright, an impressive half-back who bonds with recently married club secretary Alf Albut over a shared cricketing passion. Cartwright is a wicketkeeper from Nantwich, near Crewe, where he soon returns for a word with an old mate.

6

Stafford and Newton Heath

'The back play of Stafford for Newton Heath
was excellent.'

– Sheffield Daily Telegraph, 5 October 1896.

March 1896 – A knock on Alf Albut's door jolts the Newton Heath secretary. Is it that time already? The venerable Brummie has spent the morning trying to balance the club books, an unenviable task. He lifts himself from the rickety wooden chair and releases the door from its fairly comprehensive selection of bolts, the locking of which is a habit Albut has yet to let go, having put them in place years ago to prevent the bailiffs charging in unexpectedly when the club coffers were at their worst.

Outside, on the tumble-down cottage's stone-paved passage waits Walter Cartwright, the moustachioed 5ft 8in man from Crewe who joined the Heathens last summer. Albut whips his coat off its hook, locks up the small hutch at the end of the Bank Street pitch, and walks with Cartwright to take the tram into town, from where they head south to Crewe.

When they arrive at Harry Stafford's house, their host is delighted to see his old friend Walter and Stafford is quickly convinced to leave the sinking Crewe Alexandra and join Newton Heath. He'll still work in his hometown and although Frank Webb's dictatorial amateurism policy means a wage is out of the question, a few quid can no doubt be slipped his way here and there. Stafford dons a green and gold shirt for his debut,

46

the Newton Heath kit recently changed from red and white, inspired by a search for uniqueness, either to attract supporters or simply comply with FA regulations preventing kit clashes.

Harry is a full-back who knows if he can't win the ball, he can at least stop someone else from getting to it. Fast and strong, he proves popular at Newton Heath, who conclude the 1895/96 season sixth-placed in Division Two. Billy Meredith's Manchester City finish second, losing out in the Test matches between the two top-placed second-tier sides and Division One's bottom two teams. Meredith has scored 12 goals from the wing but needs more support if City are to finally earn top-flight promotion.

Billy's uniquely named Wales team-mate Caesar Augustus Llewelyn Jenkyns joins Newton Heath's rank of brutes over the summer.[7] Jenkyns left Small Heath last year, released for assaulting two spectators. Newton Heath have never had a player sent off, but Caesar will soon see to that. It's another shirt change for Albut's lads, too. Green and gold is gone, white shirts with blue shorts is in.

Stafford, effortlessly settled into his new club, plays every game of the 1896/97 season until Christmas Day, which proves a particular highlight as the Railwaymen triumph 2-1 over Manchester City at home and thus move three points clear of their neighbours and into second. Around 18,000 watch on and a select few order celebratory pints for Stafford in the Shudehill bars later on. It is an inescapably lively and eccentric part of town. Street performers dance, artists toil, sellers yell, young scruffs pick pockets, bookmakers take illicit bets, felons loiter, beggars sit alongside pretenders, drunks fight and pocket knives are drawn. Amid the madness are beautifully carved arches and cavernous structures, covering sellers of fish, fruit, vegetables, bread, beef, flowers, jewellery, stationery, furniture, books and everything else. The market is so large it one day gets its own police force. As evening

---

7   His brothers are called Jenkyn Jenkyns and Plato Jenkyns. Brilliant.

descends, a strange mingling of characters begins, as Harry Stafford and company join the masses searching for a drink in this sometimes charming and often absurd area. The pubs rarely close. There's always someone to serve in Shudehill.

Harry's joy continues when in March, 366 days after signing for Newton Heath, he is finally permitted to turn professional. Frank Webb of the London North Western Railway relents from his sanctimonious devotion to amateurism, just as the Football Association did in 1885. The forcing factor this time is not a group of clubs threatening to quit, but the realisation that Crewe's rail traffic has declined compared to that of Preston – where the great North End play – or Birmingham, where the great Villa play, or even Bank Street, Clayton, where the mediocre Newton Heath play. Football brings crowds.

Not long ago, the Newton Heath committee met by candlelight, sticks rammed in ginger beer bottles because the gas company had cut them off over unpaid bills. Stafford's side have now finished second. Albut's knack for pulling off unlikely schemes has got them through it. Even when regular court papers were coming through the Bank Street letter box, he had something up his sleeve. He once heard a goalkeeper he wanted to sign hadn't been paid by his club for several weeks. He duly instructed his recruit to take one of Newton Heath's court orders – recognisable for the blue-coloured paper – and wave it in his club secretary's face, demanding a transfer. The player soon joined Newton Heath, and with his wages paid too. Young Louis Rocca hears these scheming tales and picks up a trick or two.

Second place secures not automatic promotion but the chance to play Division One's bottom sides to earn the rise. Defeat at Sunderland deprives Stafford and his team-mates of promotion and a £10 bonus. Football is a cruel game, although satisfaction can be taken in progress.

Harry spends a week over the summer on the annual Railway Engineer Volunteers trip to the coast. The Crewe railway boys do military engineering while in Rhyl, enjoying their evenings in several public houses, especially the Victoria Inn, but Stafford's merriment is curtailed. His long-time partner, Frances Annie Wood, is suffering from tuberculosis, a cruel, unpreventable illness with harrowing symptoms preceding a slow and painful death.

This hangs over Stafford's head even while his club begin the new campaign in bouncing fashion, scoring nine goals and conceding none in their opening two games. The directors prematurely speak of a championship-winning season but despite a raucous beginning, the team picks up only 11 points from 11 games. Player discipline is poor and captain Caesar Jenkyns is sold as punishment. Stafford is Newton Heath's Tiberius, crowned Caesar Augustus's successor.

A Christmas Day derby victory sparks excitable celebrations and more Shudehill drinks. This time there is another cause for festivity: captain Stafford is to be married, his wedding hastened by his fiancée's illness. Walter Cartwright is best man four days later at St Paul's Church in Crewe, after which the gaiety dissipates into pain. The rest of Stafford's season is draining. He misses several games, including the Lancashire Cup Final at Goodison Park. While the Heathens triumph over Blackburn, Harry can only watch on, sidelined by injury and grief. His wife dies in May, aged 29.

In July, a grieving Stafford heads once again with the Railway Engineer Volunteers on their annual coastal trip, this time to Blackpool. Amongst the heavy drinking and boisterous tale-telling, he saves a drowning boy stuck out at sea, wading in while others stood by. It's a mark of his bravery, and supposedly that of his valuable rescue assistant, a St Bernard dog named Major.

7

Stafford's reinvention

*'Newton Heath do some brilliant things, and
at times fail horribly.'*

– London Evening Standard, 5 December 1898.

July 1898 – As Harry Stafford hoists out this spluttering child, he is himself hauled out of mourning by the thrill of the occasion on the Lancashire coast. He undergoes a self-revolution, returning to his jack-the-lad charismatic self, donning spectacularly colourful waistcoats and a white top hat. His father was once a part-time hatter, after all.

Harry quickly finds a new partner, too. Mary Evans works at her father's Victoria Inn in Rhyl, which Harry frequented the summer before and now returns to on weekends throughout July and August. He needs little excuse to escape Crewe, so he and Mary waste no time getting acquainted.

Harry Stafford and Billy Meredith are now captains of Manchester's two leading football sides. In the new season's first derby, played in splendid September weather, fans spill on to the pitch early on, allowing Newton Heath to reorganise after balanced opening stages. Stafford crosses for the team's opening goal, and two more follow in the second half, including one by star striker Joe Cassidy who nets in all three opening games. By November's end, Cottonopolis threatens to dominate the division, Newton Heath sitting first and City third.

Life has eased for Stafford. An FA resolution allows him to train with Crewe Alexandra during the week, saving him an arduous journey to Clayton and back. There are consequences, though. Harry is captain, but seen only on matchdays. He would hardly be the most restrictive influence on the drinking of Newton Heath's unruly players were he there, but perhaps things wouldn't get quite so out of hand, quite so often. Missing players, sometimes due to drink, prevent the Heathens from developing the necessary consistency. *Sporting Life* deems the team 'erratic'. They lose 5-1, win 3-1, lose 1-0, win 9-0, lose 4-0 and then win 6-1. Erratic. Too right.

Crucially, that 4-0 defeat comes away to now top-of-the-table Manchester City in front of 25,000 Mancunians at Hyde Road. Billy Meredith scores his 13th goal in as many games in this Boxing Day demolition of Newton Heath, whose status as Manchester's leading club is thus quivering. Meredith looks better than ever, now ably assisted by new sidekick Billy Gillespie, a prolific, goal-hanging, goalscoring Scottish centre-forward. A brilliant pairing on the pitch, the duo are acutely different off it, but good friends. Welshman Billy is a teetotaller, a man built for the quiet life. Scottish Billy can put away as many pints as he can goals, loves a night out and, occasionally, turns out for City a little drunk. Aware of his own shortcomings, Gillespie gives Meredith custody of part of his wage each week to limit his alehouse spending. On other occasions, Meredith takes Gillespie angling to keep him out of trouble. Meredith appreciates country life and loves to fish. While on a Derbyshire training camp once, he caught breakfast down at the river every morning. As an early riser, he often brought back a catch for his team-mates, too. So plentiful was his success, the village policeman visited City's secretary, insisting 'something would have to be done if the man who looked like a footballer didn't stop in bed a little later in the morning'.

Continued inconsistency ushers Newton Heath down the table, eventually to fourth, three points off the all-important second spot. The club directors bemoan player misconduct, and they have a right to. Three were suspended in March. Two are sold.

While Newton Heath fail, Manchester City prevail. Billy Meredith is a champion and his brilliant talent will finally be shown in the country's premier league. Beyond jealousy, it's an economic concern for Alf Albut. Derby days are, by some distance, the club's most profitable.

On-pitch disappointment aside, Heathens captain Stafford enjoys a far more joyful end to this season than last. A year on from his first wife's death, Stafford is wedded again, to Mary Evans, but personal trouble is brewing anew.

8

Stafford, Boers and beers

*'The morning broke dull and grey, but just
as her Majesty left Buckingham Palace, the
sun broke through, and a wave of light spread
over the capital of the Empire. Not since
the Coronation had London witnessed such
a scene of general joy and enthusiastic and
unbounded loyalty.'*

– *The Freeman's Journal*, 23 June 1897.

October 1899 – Gaiety and hysteria greeted Queen Victoria's
Diamond Jubilee three years before the turn of the century
because the celebration of another landmark for the United
Kingdom's longest-serving monarch offered an opportunity
to relentlessly glorify the Empire. But, in truth, the Victorian
Age was already heading towards its conclusion. The true
extent of England's cruel poverty was becoming uncovered
with greater speed, questions were asked if Britain's imperial
prowess could last into the new century, Victoria's influence
on daily life and politics had long diminished and the British
economy was undergoing relative decline compared to the
USA and Germany, whose Reichstag would soon permit
massive naval expansion to compete with Britain. Irish
nationalism was rising, as was the power of Japan and Russia,
while a rebellion was brewing in China.

Fearing imperial decline, Britain's politicians committed
further to colonial assertiveness and expansion. After a

failed British raid into gold-rich Transvaal in 1895, tensions strained sufficiently between the governments of Britain and the two Boer Republics for war to begin in October 1899. Highly mobile and well-equipped Boer forces, fighting to preserve their independence, initially outnumber Britain's underprepared, headstrong troops fighting merely to add another small section of land to an already enormous global mass.

As a Railway Volunteer through his work, Harry Stafford follows these developments nervously. He could soon find himself travelling to southern Africa. The *Athletic News* writes, 'If all the men who are to fight under England's flag possess [Stafford's] pluck and nerve then the war will not last long,' the emphasis on 'pluck and nerve' harking back to the public school vocabulary which defined football in its early days.

Pluck and nerve England's soldiers have, but knowledge of African topography and the Boer Republic's forces they do not. The war shall last far, far longer than anticipated. In December's 'Black Week', significant reverses are suffered at Stromberg, Magersfontein and Colenso. The new century arrives and before its first month is out, further ignominy ensues at Spion Kop.[8] 'Bloody Sunday' follows at Paardeberg and Britain, it is declared, has 'forfeited our reputation before the world'.[9] News travels back fast. Volunteers are hardly found queueing up.

Stafford thus travels not to this blood-thirsty conflict, but instead – with his wife, her father, a little Welsh terrier and a massive St Bernard – to the beer-gulping town of Wrexham and a new job. Harry has recently clocked out of Crewe's

---

8   Meaning roughly spy hill, or lookout hill. The battle gains notoriety back home and Spion Kop soon becomes a byword for a steep terrace in British football. Woolwich Arsenal's Manor Ground will first be likened to this place of death, in 1904, and later, and most famously, Liverpool's Anfield terrace.

9   H.W. Wilson, *With the Flag to Pretoria* (London: Harmsworth Brothers, 1900), p.207.

LNWR works for the final time. Having first followed in his own father's footsteps, Harry now takes the example of his retired publican father-in-law in taking charge of Wrexham's Bridge House Inn. He, Mary, Robert, and two nieces will live at the pub, the latter two put to work in the bar. Formerly home to Billy Meredith's swerving skills, the north Wales town is a famous brewing hub, being one of the first places in Britain to serve lager, a new form of beer that gained popularity after a series of baking 1860s summers. German immigrants introduced it as a lower-alcohol, thirst-quenching, exhilarating, summer tonic drink.

Few know better of beer's 19th-century explosion in popularity than a portly, mid-30s Manchester man called **John Henry Davies**. In his hometown, a new beer house opened once a week between 1830 and 1850, much to the government's delight. Concerned by the nation's gin consumption, spirit regulations were made stringent while tankards of beer were tipped back at new 'beer houses', cheap to set up with lenient regulation because beer is harmless, maybe even nutritious, including for kids. It's safer than dirty water after all.

Born in Staffordshire in 1864, the son of a Welsh engineer and a Cheshire girl, John Henry Davies developed into a good mathematician when educated in Manchester. After success as a cashier, a well-respected job, he became an accountant just as he met and was besotted with Amy Cattrall, niece of wealthy sugar magnate Sir Henry Tate. Within two years, the 23-year-old John Henry and Amy were married at St Matthew's Church in Ardwick, just a hundred yards from Manchester City's Hyde Road football ground. A daughter, Elsie Amy, was soon on the way.

With self-earned wealth, necessary because the enormously rich Sir Henry Tate has taken a rather significant dislike to his niece's partner, Davies pulled together a property portfolio that stretched all across Manchester. Although not exclusively buying pubs and beer houses, in the early 1890s Davies purchased and rented out such properties in Salford,

Hulme, Exchange, St Ann's, Piccadilly, Oxford Road and Rochdale Road. Beer flowed through Manchester's streets just as smog and fog floated up from the city's bellowing chimneys and passing trains.

Davies's competition was not other individuals, but breweries who were, with increasing frequency and effectiveness, tying beer houses exclusively to their products. It is why, for example, the Chesters Brewery invested in Manchester City: to ensure a loyal customer base. Noting this trend, John Henry invested in the Walker & Homfray's, John Henry Lees and Manchester breweries. With obvious industry knowledge, more significant roles as a director and chairman soon followed. In his spare time, he and Amy involved themselves in local charities, and some sports, including bowls, cycling and horse racing.

***

The Anglo-Boer War rages on but Harry Stafford no longer nervously awaits his call-up. In leaving the LNWR, his time with the Railway Volunteers has, conveniently, come to an end. Two Newton Heath team-mates are not so lucky. Joe Clark and the in-form Gilbert Godsmark are both conscripted in March. With the Boers' strength now fully understood, the British Empire throws in its lot – 450,000 imperial troops soon face the 60,000 Boer soldiers, and victory will inevitably follow. Mafeking, Pretoria and Johannesburg are occupied, and the jingoistic hysteria of Victoria's jubilee prevails again. By September, the war appears won and Prime Minister Lord Salisbury reacts by calling an election, taking advantage of the euphoric mood. The newly formed Labour Representation Committee wins its first two seats as Salisbury secures a large majority.

But the war is not quite won. The subdued Boers reform into guerrilla groups. In response, the British generals convert refugee camps into enormous concentration camps, enacting a scorched earth policy to prevent the Boers from sustaining themselves. 120,000 Boer women and children are herded in, 26,000 of whom die due to horrendous conditions.[10] Disease spreads rapidly, even to British soldiers such as 25-year-old Gilbert Godsmark, who succumbs to it in Pretoria. He's the first Heathen to die on the battlefield.

Back in Manchester, a different horror is unravelling. An excessively high number of patients are suffering from peripheral neuritis, a type of nerve damage with pain in their feet and hands, pins and needles in fingers and toes, loss of limb power, body rashes, puffy faces and, crucially, skin discolouration. A doctor, Ernest Septimus Reynolds, has discovered the cause. There are, he writes in November 1900, three causes of skin discolouration: beriberi, a vitamin deficiency; alcohol; and arsenic. Visiting pubs his patients frequented, Reynolds noted spirit drinkers were healthy, but beer drinkers were ill. Given, he said, 'the drinking of beer is not by any means a new thing', there had to be a linked cause, and like the apple on Isaac's head, it clicked.

In the ultra-competitive beer industry, many brewers lower costs by supplementing low-quality barley malt with sugar, specifically made by the acid hydrolysis of starch. Arsenic has unintentionally penetrated this process, the consequence being that, since March, the north-west's beer has been poisoned. So now beer really does flow through Manchester's streets: down sewers, into the River Irwell, and poured into drains. And in Wrexham, too, where a grimacing Harry Stafford pours barrels of beer away, his pub's reputation irrevocably damaged.

Brewery investor John Henry Davies suffers some short-term losses but spots the opportunity to capitalise on this tragic situation. He buys up shares in suffering breweries at a low price, aware that Manchester loves its beer and punters will very soon be back.

---

10 News trickles back to England of these horrible statistics but despite the hard-fought efforts of many, including Emily Hobhouse, review of the concentration camps is too late to enact real change and save lives.

This beer crisis will define both men's futures, and quickly. In fact, within three months of the new year, they will be sharing a drink.

9

Newton Heath's bazaar

*'He needs to be a case-hardened blast-furnace
sort of enthusiast who can say he goes to
watch football [at Newton Heath] purely for
pleasure's sake.'*

– *Athletic News*, 7 January 1901.

January 1901 – 'Louis, my friend, what can I do for you?'

Louis Rocca is knocking on doors, strolling through the cobbled streets of Ancoats. Newton Heath are in trouble and the 18-year-old is synonymous with the club in Manchester's 'Little Italy', in no small part thanks to regular, somewhat exaggerated boasting about his role with the Football League team. His day job remains with the family ice cream business.

Rocca explains Newton Heath's perilous financial situation to a sympathetic friend of his recently passed father. 'I'm sorry, Louis, it's a hard time,' he replies. And it is. It always is round these parts. Spare money to prop up a failing football club is nigh on impossible to find, especially just after Christmas.

Harry Stafford adopts a different tactic, with his home towns of Crewe and Wrexham hardly likely to provide much support. He asks Lancashire and Cheshire's most famous sportsmen to invest in the club, but the response is disheartening.

It has been a year of turmoil and change for the Heathens. A fourth-placed finish made it six seasons without promotion

59

and the club's finances are so shaky they are becoming notorious. In April 1900, the directors sold all-time top goalscorer and fan favourite Joe Cassidy to Manchester City, citing financial reasons. A month later, secretary Alf Albut resigned after eight strenuous years of back-against-the-wall, creative book-balancing. His work is the undoubted reason behind Newton Heath's Football League survival, but another season of losses on and off the pitch, debts, and missing out on promotion was wearying for the 50-year-old. An unjustly brief vote of thanks is given at the club's summer meeting, with focus devoted instead to detailing the finances. The club are £2,176 3s in the red.[11] Chairman Fred Palmer bemoans the poor weather for hindering large crowds.

The *Athletic News* deem Newton Heath's 'rightful place' to be the First Division and say the Railwaymen will be 'enthusiastic and energetic' in targeting that. *Sporting Life* offers more pertinent commentary.

'Like several other clubs, Newton Heath are suffering from financial difficulties, and a bazaar is to be held shortly at which it is hoped a goodly sum will be realised.'

A bazaar – a colourful fundraiser – has been discussed for six months, but arrangements have been slow. Bury's February fete successfully raised £1,140, while Bolton Wanderers go a long way to clearing their £2,000 debt in October. Chorley, Barnsley, Woolwich Arsenal and many others commit to the same method of turning red ink into black.

As 1901 comes in and Stafford and Rocca attend the half-annual meeting on Oldham Road, Newton Heath are tenth. 'Bright times ahead,' insists new club secretary James West, previously of Lincoln City, but it hinges entirely on a successful bazaar. To that end, West, Rocca, Stafford and many others work tirelessly to deliver an enticing occasion.

Any sort of festivities are put on hold as Queen Victoria is reported seriously ill 19 days into the year. Three days

---

11 The equivalent to around £300,000 in 2023.

later, she dies and her 63-year reign is over. Her son Albert Edward succeeds her, as King Edward VII. Windsor Castle hosts a state funeral in February, the month in which Winston Churchill makes his maiden House of Commons speech, regarding the increasingly concerning Boer War, and Newton Heath hold their bazaar.

***

Decorations up, Harry Stafford wearily pats Louis Rocca on the back. Major, Harry's St Bernard dog, is lapping at his ankles. Around the trio are colourful stalls, all erected in the hope of raising enough money to propel Newton Heath from a flailing old institution into a First Division club. The bazaar's theme is 'Sunny Lands'. The place is a hotchpotch of foreign inspiration. One area is designed to appear Indian, another Mediterranean, another like the Nile and another Italian, embellished with Rocca's gelato. St James's Hall, on Manchester's Oxford Road, is transformed. Tomorrow morning, they will return for the bazaar's beginning, but for now, they head off for a drink, locking up carefully behind them.

Through their attendance and overwhelmingly positive speeches, senior politicians of all parties demonstrate their support for and the significance of football in Edwardian Manchester. The Edinburgh-born aristocrat Sir James Fergusson, formerly Governor of South Australia, New Zealand and Bombay and now the local MP, declares the bazaar officially open. He declares football to be a 'manly form of sport' and a 'most valuable game'. His words could be those of a schoolmaster on the playing fields of Rugby, which he attended. Over the next three days, several similar sermons are made.

Unfortunately, poor weather discourages attendees. It is clear by the end of the bazaar's fourth day that sufficient success has not been achieved. The expenses of over £400 have thankfully been covered, and a small amount will be added to club coffers, but the large quantity of goods still unsold betrays any idea of success.

After the last day concludes without the grand finish it requires, Louis Rocca acts as nightwatchman at St James's Hall, protecting the merchandise and takings inside. Operating in two-hour shifts with a colleague, Rocca sits and watches the place quietly.

Smashing glass, crashing metal and thudding wood pierce Rocca's peaceful bubble. His colleague stirs, too, and so does the night fireman, who rushes out of his cabin to join the party.

'Sure to God, it's the Devil himself that's up there,' the superstitious fireman mutters. Rocca climbs the staircase to investigate. As the crashing is replaced by the clapping of Rocca's own footsteps on wood, he looks up the staircase and back at him stares a pair of green eyes, visible through the dull light. A moment of silence, and then another crash, this time accompanied by a light panting as a dog hurtles down the stairs, crashes into Rocca's legs and charges out of the side entrance on to the Oxford Road. The confident St Bernard pounds out into the late Manchester night. Rocca, his colleague and the night fireman are bemused as they survey the damage in the building's smaller hall, in which he had been tied up – not tightly enough, it is now clear.

The dog finds his way to Wills' restaurant just off St Ann's Square, a normally bustling area dominated by the shadow of the Royal Exchange building. The restaurant, owned by a John Robert Thomas, is popular with local businessmen who trade in the Exchange and come for oysters and steak. John Henry Davies is a businessman with enough cash to regularly treat himself to long lunches and Wills' is only a couple of doors down from Davies's offices. When he arrives at the restaurant the following day, he's enamoured with the friendly dog that Thomas unintentionally picked up the night before. Thomas is less enthused by the steak-munching hound and when Davies offers to take the assumed stray away, he agrees.

The St Bernard is taken to Davies's Alderley Edge mansion, where John Henry's 11-year-old daughter Elsie reads the following message on his collar:

'My name is Major, of Railway Street Crewe. I am Harry Stafford's dog, whose dog are you?'

* * *

The tag on Major's collar is outdated. He and his owner, Harry Stafford, live in Wrexham now. But when John Henry's wife Amy's eye is caught by the below in the *Manchester Evening News*, Stafford is summoned to Alderley Edge.

'LOST. Lemon and White St Bernard DOG, answers to Major, from St James's Hall, Saturday night, about 11 30. – Apply F.W. Palmer, 38, Gibbon-street, Manchester. Reward.'

When Stafford arrives, Davies is welcoming, charming even, but businesslike. He wants to buy Major for his daughter Elsie.

'I wouldn't sell it to anyone in the world,' Harry replied, 'that dog saved my life at sea.'

Despite the speedy impasse, Stafford and Davies chat freely about exactly how Major happened to go bounding around Manchester given Harry lives in Wrexham. They subsequently discuss Newton Heath's financial struggles, and, after discovering each other's professions, they ponder the difficulties of the pub trade. Davies, the experienced brewery chairman, knows all too well the trouble a newbie publican like Stafford has encountered over these last 18 months. Nevertheless, much to John and Elsie's dismay, Major returns to Wrexham at Harry's side.

After the weather-affected bazaar, itself required to fix Newton Heath's weather-weakened finances, Stafford's well-deserved benefit match proves an even greater failure, it too 'reduced to a farce by the weather'. Harry puts on a typically flamboyant and experimental event, a midweek match illuminated by intense artificial lights. The ball is gilded to help players and supporters follow play more easily and a spectacular sight is indeed achieved for a moment or two, but one by one, the lights puff out into the damp air, a heavy rain accompanied by unhelpful gusts of wind. The game is called off and Stafford rushes around promising spectators that he'll arrange free entry to the rearranged affair. The opposition on both occasions is New Brighton Tower, but this second time, rather than Stafford centring a Newton Heath XI, he leads a combined side of Heathens alongside players from Manchester City, including Billy Meredith. They play under a previously unheard-of name: 'Manchester United'.

The attendance is unfortunately small and so Stafford returns to Wrexham after an exhausting few months with very little to show for himself or his club, who have endured their worst Football League season yet, finishing tenth. A 4-0 Manchester Cup Final thumping to City follows and the directors can only cross their fingers and hope the weather improves next season.

On a personal level, things take a positive turn for Harry when John Henry Davies gets back in touch. The wealthy brewer offers Stafford a pub to manage, the Manchester Brewery Company's Bridge Inn. It's a move to Ancoats where Harry will be near-neighbours with Louis Rocca. Davies is shrewd, hiring a semi-celebrity to run one of his pubs, and it's a fresh start for Stafford after a difficult time in Wrexham. Fans and players alike are soon crossing the Rochdale Canal on the Royle Bridge and settling down in the Ancoats watering hole for a word with Newton Heath's captain marvel.

10

Roberts and iron

'My prince of centre-halves is
Charlie Roberts.'

– Billy Meredith writing in the *Derby Daily*
Telegraph, 6 October 1923.

September 1901 – Every street in Rise Carr, Darlington is adorned by a public house. Ironwork is a thirst-inducing job, and workers here are given beer vouchers to use in their 20-minute breaks. Dashing out of the front gates, they are greeted by the Stag's Head and the Forge Inn, while further up the street is the Rise Carr Hotel – decorated by an eccentric stonemason with grotesque carved heads – the Alexandra, the Prince of Wales, and the Warwick Brewery, the Elm Street, the Globe and the Locomotive. There's plenty of choice, but it's not break time yet.

Charlie Roberts wrestles with his furnace. The heat draws beads of sweat out of his biceps. The incessant clunking noise pounds his ears, only interrupted by the enormous crashes of the scrapyard outside in which his father works. Darlington's 'rolling mills' are blisteringly hot, chaotic places where 200-metre bright orange sausage-shaped lumps of burning iron pass across equally enormous rollers. The heat warps the workers' vision of the outdoors, the nearby railway lines flickering ever so slightly in the haze. It was upon those rails that Britain's first-ever public steam train travelled, handing out free celebratory coal sacks to local residents. More than a half-century on, Rise Carr's workers still churn out puddled iron, used to lay tracks down across England's north-east.

Charlie leaves the industrial scene, wiping his brow and nodding to his father, Jacob, in the scrapyard. He turns left towards the family home just 50 metres away on Low Boyne Street where terraced houses pen you in. The street runs parallel to the railway tracks. Charlie ducks his head in water, rips off his sweat-encrusted grimy outer work clothes and sits down. His mother, Elizabeth, has prepared him an inch-thick sandwich. She's a Staffordshire girl, a potter's daughter who moved to Darlington with work-chasing Jacob long enough ago that the couple are now the eldest on the street. Elizabeth watches her son quickly eat and leave. She wishes him good luck.

Charlie is a young Victorian man following the typical path, that of his father. He passes Ianson and Fry streets, named after the founders of the rolling mills who constructed this part of town to accommodate the workers of their rampantly successful business. Looking through Ianson Street, he can see, smell and hear the Victoria Brewery and, past it, the North Road Recreation Ground, on which Charlie sees young Ralph and William Park, the Roberts's neighbours, kicking a leather-cased brown-bladder ball on the tufty grass. He too had played football there at their age, and now he's on his way to do just that.

Fry Street was where he was born, on 6 April 1883 – nine years after Billy Meredith – as the sixth child of Jacob and Elizabeth, and the youngest by a distance. There, aged five, Charlie put his head in his mother's lap, asking what was wrong. Elder brother Isaac had died, aged 16. Now in his teens himself, Charlie is the only Roberts child still at home. Having left school aged 12, he works as a furnace man's labourer at the rolling mills. A quick glance to his right on the long, winding Wessoe Street and there they are: imposing, dominant, the heartbeat of the area. It's in places like these many football clubs have been formed, companies seeking to provide an alternative pastime to alcoholic indulgences, as exemplified by Newton Heath two decades before. Charlie plays casually with work colleagues but has looked elsewhere for seriously competitive fixtures.

He moves past the endless smattering of pubs and the dominating shed of the rolling mill is sharply cut off, replaced by scrapyards filled with cranes, weighing machines, coal depots and signal posts. He walks past Hammer Street, where family grocer and tea dealer Timothy Thompson sells Wensleydale cheese, and Wessoe Street begins to curve towards the east and one of England's true rail centres. Charlie pauses at tracks which swing across the street and into the locomotive works. Employing 3,000 people, these too are an enormous bustling centre of activity. Charlie finally reaches Wessoe Street's end and turns on to North Road, on the corner of which a few cattle grunt in their pens. Hope Town Station is on the right. It is this set of tracks, now embellished by a further ten alongside them, that turned north Darlington, and then the whole town, from agricultural to industrial. Railways changed Newton Heath, Crewe and the world, but before that, they changed Darlington.

Rail had existed before 1825 but was mainly operated by cart-pulling horses and used privately by mine and quarry owners. The Pease family, prominent local Quakers, had long held an interest in improving local transport. Young Edward Pease wanted to construct canals across Stockton and Darlington, areas with good mining resources but which were unable to compete with those of nearby Tyneside due to transport difficulties. This initial aim, as successfully achieved in Louis Rocca's Ancoats, was eventually superseded by rail thanks to George Stephenson, who walked nearly 40 miles from near Newcastle to Pease's house – a train really would have been helpful – nervously chatting to Nicholas Wood en route. Like Stephenson, Wood was an engineer, but also manager of the Killingworth Colliery. At the Bulmer Stone, a relic from the ice age which marked the northern edge of town, Stephenson and Wood changed their muddy footwear for clean shoes before nervously going into Pease's home. Stephenson was shy, with a strong accent. He brought Wood along to help better explain his thinking. Together, they successfully convinced Pease to build a revolutionary steam railway, not one led by horses and certainly not a canal.

This railway's September 1825 opening heralded the start of the modern world's steam train age. Although a grand ceremony took place, the momentousness – that British society's nucleus would shift from small agricultural communities to big city life – cannot have been known at the time. *Active* became the first steam locomotive to make a public journey. It was basically a shed on wheels which hit bursts of 24mph but took a full two hours to complete the first four kilometres of the journey to Darlington. It then went all over the world on display. Darlington's greatest child yet had been exhibited in Philadelphia and Paris by the time another of its great sons, Charlie Roberts, was born.

The 19-year-old walks past Hopetown Goods Station. Darlington's history probably interests him little but it makes him the man he is. He's been walking for 15 minutes. He moves past a sawmill and into the Darlington St Augustine's football ground. It sits between the River Skerne and a weir which flicks around it as if it were an island. One great stand makes this the north-east's finest football arena, and it's matchday.

Charlie made his start in football, apart from on the North Road playing fields, with Rise Carr Rangers. With a decent height to him, he was first tried out in goal, which interested him little, but he soon settled at centre-half with St Augustine's, a more well-established and reputable outfit. Charlie has become a regular starter for Saints and by Christmas, his performances are pricking the ears of several teams. He'll not stay in Darlington for long.

11

The end for Newton Heath

*'All lovers of Association football will be sorry
to hear that the financial position of the
Newton Heath club is such that there is every
probability of the concern being wound up.'*

– *Manchester Evening News*, 8 January 1902.

December 1901 – Christmas brings no gifts for Newton
Heath. The directors instead slump in their chairs, heads
in hands, another fixture postponed. The weather, again.
Worse still, these festive matches are the season's most popular
with families gleefully coming to celebrate Christ's birth by
watching men kick lumps out of each other. A critical chunk of
ticket income vanishes with postponement. The directors go
home for their turkey or goose dinners with Newton Heath's
finances weighing heavy on their minds.

The new year provides neither respite nor resolutions.
With 'great reluctance', he says, former club president William
Healey has taken Newton Heath to court due to unpaid debts.
'What is a football club?' the judge asks. 'How do they carry on
business? Do they make money?' he continues. It is explained
that, yes, they make money, but only in order to play more
football, not to take dividends. Newton Heath are wound up
as a limited company and so the club now quivers on an ever-
thinning precipice, but club secretary James West remains
blindly positive in the style of a ladder-climbing politician. He
claims the court proceedings have encouraged old supporters

69

who had lost interest to help out again. The reality is West and his club are now entirely reliant on the loyalty of their players, all of whose contracts have been automatically annulled by the club's winding up.

Captain Harry Stafford welcomes his team-mates into the Bridge Inn for an important conference on this matter. He serves up drinks, occasionally jumping out of his seat to respond to a regular at the bar, and the players chat. Harry is the most vocal. He subsequently announces to the local press that the players, a group of working-class lads, have agreed to an enormous sacrifice: none of them will leave on free transfers, and they will play without pay if they must. And they must.

It's a relief for all Heathens, but the club urgently requires money, no longer to pay its players, but simply to travel to games. Stafford duly creates subscription lists for his flailing club. His job title can now hardly be limited to 'footballer'. It's not been a year since he and Louis Rocca traipsed around Manchester asking for donations ahead of the failed bazaar. Now they do so again.

Stafford's renewed pleas are met with a hearty response and while Bank Street's gates remain locked by the Official Receiver, the first team can use public donations to travel to Bristol. One dedicated player tells the *Evening News* he 'never knew the team to train harder than they have done this week' but despite 'a magnificent exhibition' of 'powerful kicking' and 'great marking' from Stafford, Newton Heath suffer a comprehensive beating after the most stressful of weeks.

Perched on a Bristol stone wall, Harry is shovelling down a post-match meal of greasy battered fish and thick chips. He can be pleased with his own performance, on and off the pitch. Newton Heath raised £80 odd during the week, covering their journey to and from Bristol with a little left over for food, but it's Stafford who stumps up when the team is a couple of coppers short to pay the bill. He digs some spare change out of his pocket and hands it to their Bristolian host, who thanks them in a West Country drawl.

***

Metaphorical sun eventually shines on the Heathens. A meeting with the Official Receiver and the stadium's landlord allows Bank Street to open again, while £1,000 has been removed from the shoulders of the directors, seemingly breaking up the dark and heavy clouds overhead. But the Heathens have done something to upset Mother Nature – whether it's Harry's hard tackling or the foul-mouthed fan who cheers him on – for she ensures snow falls once again when sun is needed most. A pitiful crowd show up to watch the visiting Blackpool win by one goal to nil. That won't do it, nor will an even smaller audience for victory over Burnley a fortnight later.

John Henry Davies is heading home from work on one of these Saturday lunchtimes, returning from a late lunch with his wife Amy, when his vehicle knocks down a man fiercely pedalling away on his bicycle. Both men prepare for a verbal confrontation, the cyclist rising from the ground and John Henry stepping out of his cart, but when they come face to face, they pause. George Lawton is a fellow child of Chorlton-upon-Medlock, a couple of years Davies's senior, and an accountant for the Walker & Homfrays Brewery which Davies chairs. 'It's Saturday, I'm going up the Oldham Road to see the football,' Lawton says, when questioned by his confused employer. Lawton is a lover of fine arts – classical music, the theatre and literature – who sometimes sings as a tenor in town. He is not, certainly in Davies's opinion, your typical association football fan, only heightening the brewery man's surprise and intrigue.

The two eventually go their separate ways, Davies impressed by the enthusiasm of Lawton, who himself is simply eager to watch his team play. He's friendly with the captain, Harry Stafford, and when he arrives at Bank Street and discusses the flailing finances post-match with the skipper, he mentions his boss.

The Bank Street crowd swells for a rare weekend victory. They watch another impressive Stafford display and a late penalty earns a deserved win, although Glossop North End's young Herbert Burgess is picked out for praise.[12] The gate receipts head straight into the Official Receiver's hands.

In the following days, a special FA–Football League committee convenes in Manchester to deliberate on Newton Heath's situation. The essential question is this: did the directors contribute to the club's downfall and winding-up order, intending to personally benefit by removing their debt? If the answer is 'yes', Newton Heath will disappear from the Football League. Thankfully, the answer is 'no'. The committee duly permits 'an entirely new club' to form and take over the 'old' club's fixtures. They can use the 'old' club's players, but cannot sell them for any profit.

Stafford's team endure another winless month. It's all well and good being allowed to continue as a club, but there'll be no real future if the team continues to slide towards the table's bottom. An investor is needed and Stafford has found one. After Heathens supporter George Lawton was knocked off his bike by his boss, Stafford has gone again to meet John Henry Davies, whose daughter Elsie's 12th birthday is nearing.

'Which means the most to you, your club or your dog?' Harry is asked, sitting in the morning room at Davies's Cheshire home.

'Well, I love my dog, and I love my team as well. What would you do?'

'I would take it over completely, furnish it with a brand new team, you would still be retained as captain, we'd make the ground decent and everything will be made all right for you. If I do that, will you let me have the dog?'

---

12 This isn't the last you'll hear of Herbie.

'Well,' Harry replies, still with some conflicting emotions, 'under those circumstances, we can make it a bargain.'

* * *

On Tuesday, 18 March, a day after yet another defeat, Newton Heath's supporters gather at the New Islington Hall. Often host to speakers from the Ancoats Brotherhood such as Sylvia Pankhurst and George Bernard Shaw, now shoulder-to-shoulder is the full set of Heathens fans, the old guard who'd seen the club in its cup-winning pre-Football League days, and the fresher-faced, come-to-expect-nothing younger generation.

Speaking to a sea of cloth caps, over which heavy tobacco smoke wafts upwards, chairman Fred Palmer thanks the players for their unerring loyalty in standing by the directors and allowing their wages to go unpaid. He asks the supporters to make sure that those wages are paid as soon as possible by attending matches. It is that debt of £181 10s 6d to the players, and that debt only – the rest has been paid off by recent gate receipts – which the club now has on its shoulders, but to give themselves a chance of anything but a season of lower-table strife, more money will be needed. There is no opportunity to fundraise through player sales anymore.

Stafford, the club captain mingling amongst the supporters, asks the directors what sum would be needed to get the club back on track. 'It was at this point that the surprise was sprung,' lyricises the *Courier*'s attending reporter. Stafford says he has found five men who will give £200 each, and as soon as tomorrow, if need be.

The gathered supporters' attentive listening is replaced by celebrations and excitement equivalent only to a goal being scored. Only when Stafford prepares to offer more information, climbing up on to the platform, does an excitable hush begin to spread. He names the five individuals, including a Mr Davies and himself. Cheers ensue once more. The *Sheffield Daily Telegraph* describes Stafford's act of generosity and determination as 'an emphatic retort to those who have always spoken of professionalism in football as abhorrent, and of professionals as only a little higher than the brute creation'.

Newton Heath's supporters go home abuzz with excitement at what they have witnessed, heard and can now foresee. One old club member even suggests the club be renamed at this important juncture. His suggestion is Manchester United. Little comes of it for now.

***

Supporters endure an agonising week without further updates as discussions progress between the Stafford-led quintet and the current directors, but the reality is that this is no Stafford-led venture.

John Henry Davies, via a St Bernard dog, an oyster restaurant and a knocked-over cycling accountant, is responsible. He wants to take control of the club, rather than simply donate a sum. His opening offer of £110 – a fee covering the stands and stadium equipment – is rejected. The Newton Heath directors have made a mess of things, no doubt, but this group of ordinary men – a tobacconist, a pawnbroker, a publican, a grocer and a clerk – have invested significant amounts of money, time and effort into their club.

April's start comes and goes without the impasse being overcome. 'Put before the supporters the position between them,' an agitated fan tells the *Evening News*. 'After all, the supporters are the best people to judge.' But that isn't necessary. 'An amicable settlement' is announced just in time for it to make the *Evening News*' Friday, 11 April edition. Davies has added £100 to his offer and it's been accepted. Harry Stafford is widely credited as the chief saviour of Newton Heath. 'But for the efforts he has made,' the *Evening News* states, 'the club might very possibly have died a natural death at the end of this month.'

The Heathens finish their season with a draw, two wins and a satisfying Manchester Cup victory over City. Their lowly 15th position, their worst yet, is irrelevant. The ground is to be refurbished and Stafford, who is to be made a director, a rare honour for a player, and West, who retains his role as secretary for now, travel nationwide to find talented players who will join the rejuvenated Newton Heath.

* * *

But there will be no Newton Heath. In a meeting chaired by J.J. Bown – Davies's right-hand man – on 24 April, secretary James West apologises to the proud supporters who live in Newton Heath itself, but, he reluctantly admits, the name has to go. Too many opposition sides have travelled to the wrong place on account of it, and the new name is more directly associated with Manchester, a fact John Henry Davies thinks is of the utmost importance. The matter is put to a vote at the New Islington Hall and it's agreed: the reformed club will be known as **Manchester United.**

Part Two:
Birth of United, 1902–07

1

John Henry's innovation

'As Meredith is concerned, an interesting proposition has been made by one of the leading clubs.'

– *Manchester Evening News*, Saturday 26 April 1902.

May 1902 – When the FA officially accept the name 'Manchester United' in late May, work has long begun to achieve new president John Henry Davies's first aim, to have a ground 'second to none'.

John's impact on United, name aside, is immediate. Business acumen, so long lacked at the club, is ever-present. Davies believes success will be determined by supporters' matchday experience, itself dependent on two things: spectator comfort and on-pitch quality. A careful process is duly in operation in Clayton.

Davies wants an air of sociability about Bank Street for more esteemed guests but sufficient space for the sixpenny ticket holders.

After soil and earth are ripped up and the rails around the pitch removed, a 28-yard embankment to hold 9,000 cheap ticket holders is created. The pitch has even been moved closer to the now-sparkling main stand: fresh white paint, 200 plush covered chairs, stone clippings and hanging plants. 'Every consideration and comfort' is promised to 'lady visitors' too because Davies believes there is an untapped market to be capitalised upon.

Focusing on making similarly marginal on-pitch gains, new dressing rooms are erected comparable only with the Crystal Palace ground, which hosts the English Cup Final. The cherry on a rather expensive cake, including a gymnasium for indoor practice, is an underground passage to allow players and officials to avoid barging through a throng of spectators. Bank Street is expanded, comfortable, plush and ready to host the new Manchester United, who will play in fresh red and white shirts, returning to the club's early 1880s colours. The team looks as smart as their home.

Although £600 worth of season tickets are sold by September, old habits clearly die hard because the ground is rented out for grazing purposes. Such creative cash-generating methods aren't needed with Davies's unrelenting money pump, a fact Harry Stafford and James West appear all too aware of in the transfer market. They act like the Robin Hoods of the Football League as players come in for decent fees at ever-increasing speed.

The other task is to convince the sought-after Walter Cartwright to stay, which Davies achieves by gifting him a place to live. Though in his infancy as a club owner, Davies has quickly understood that, like in his own businesses, what people want beyond cash is what will turn their heads. Cartwright follows his childhood friend Stafford, and United, in benefitting from the John Henry touch, but United's slapdash spending enchants the football press less than another matter: Billy Meredith's future.

Manchester City have been relegated. Division One sides realised that by double- or triple-marking Meredith they could entirely nullify City's threat. An inability to conquer this issue and arrest a poor run of results led to a club reshuffle. Tom Maley is now secretary under the new directorship of Edward Hulton, son of *Athletic News* founder Edward Senior.

Relegation deeply frustrates Meredith, who is no less stubborn than when he refused to turn professional with Manchester City eight years ago. When he had finally taken the plunge, he vowed to approach it with the same consistent dedication as any other job, or more. His life and emotion thus revolve almost entirely around the game. Matchdays mean focus – as well as a diet of port and boiled chicken – and defeats mean sour responses and short-tempered answers, even to his new wife, childhood sweetheart Ellen, a lively Chirk girl with Yorkshire roots who keeps him in line and expertly manoeuvres through his moods. They married a year ago when City gifted Ellen a silver-mounted satchel and a gold bracelet, and Billy a gold watch. They received a marble clock from the players, which sits on their new mantelpiece on Nut Street. They live in a simple two-up-two-down a mile from the City ground where Meredith can go out the back on to a field and train. He does so relentlessly.

Billy's life is stable but, with City now in Division Two, the leading clubs of England are circling; Everton, Bolton Wanderers and Aston Villa most prominently. He deserves better wing partners than those available at City, with the *Lancashire Evening Post* recommending Derby County's great Steve Bloomer.

Meredith has recently been ably assisted by his hero from the Preston 'Invincibles', Jimmy Ross. Together, they'd helped City to promotion, but Ross is a veteran, now primarily coaching the club's youngsters while providing the occasional first-team contribution.

And then, in June, Jimmy Ross is dead. Aged 36, the 'little demon' catches a cold and complains of facial trouble which develops into a fatal skin condition, erysipelas. Without any support structure, his family is left near-destitute. Meredith has lost a personal friend and an idol, and this tragic summer worsens two months later when Di Jones, a fellow son of Chirk, cuts his knee in a mid-August practice match. He plays the brave man, refusing assistance and walking more than 100 yards to an ambulance. The grit remaining after an insufficient on-pitch cleaning penetrates the wound further during his fatal walk. At hospital, it's stitched and dressed, but Jones asks to go home. He leaves in a cab, only after being pleaded with not to travel by tram. He dies from tetanus soon after. Mourners gather around his house in Bolton before his body is taken back to near Chirk, where he and Meredith had played small-sided matches years before. A large crowd greets the train at Trevor Station, with a melancholy Billy in attendance.

Thankfully in this time of grieving, Meredith does not have to leave City. His ideal partner comes to him instead. Sandy Turnbull originally intended to join Bolton Wanderers after coming down from Scotland but changed his mind late on. He won't regret it. He and Billy hit it off.

John Henry's Manchester United, meanwhile – and there is no doubt it is exclusively John Henry's – takes its first, confident steps. On 6 September, the Manchester United era begins, the Reds travelling to Lincolnshire town Gainsborough. Spectators expect a poor game due to high temperatures but an entertaining, even contest follows between a more 'scientific' United side and a gritty, determined Gainsborough Trinity. With five minutes left, Charlie Richards – similarly named but of no relation or similarity to Charlie Roberts – begins a century-long tradition of late United goals to take the two points for victory home.

Summer signing Daniel Hurst maintains the habit a week later, receiving Jack Peddie's ball on the left wing and driving it into the Burton United net. Davies rises from his president's seat to applaud, gazing excitedly around a Bank Street stadium alive with noise, colour and excitement. With each match, John becomes increasingly convinced in his decision, and never more so than on Christmas Day for the first true *Manchester* derby.

United are enjoying a good first season, sitting sixth and enjoying a decent cup run. City are similarly rejuvenated, Meredith flourishing alongside stocky Scotsman Sandy Turnbull. The Blues have scored 40 goals in 16 matches, winning 12 of them. They lead Division Two and promotion will surely be earned with ease.

December it may be, but Bank Street's white main stand still pops out in contrast to the browns, blacks and greys of the 40,000 spectators within them. A strong wind assists City in the first half and helps waft away the smoke of the belching chemical works next door, but the game is scrappy. Bannister nets for City after half-time before Pegg, his magnificent handlebar moustache quivering in the breeze, levels for United. It is a decent result for United and a happy day for Manchester. John Henry carries a beaming smile. Bellowing from his gut so his companion can hear him above the noise of the vast throng, he says: 'What a pity it would have been if all these folks had been deprived of their sport.'

United are a little off the promotion pace, and Stafford seeks further reinforcements in the New Year. One such is Alec Bell, a 20-year-old Cape Town-born left-half recommended to Harry by a former Newton Heath player in Scotland. Bell's mother had been reluctant to let him go, but only until Stafford bids farewell to the family, 'accidentally' dropping a gold sovereign as he did so. When Alec's mam tried to return it, he told her not to worry, and her son duly makes his United debut in a 3-1 win against Glossop in January. The famous long-distance runner Fred Bacon arrives too, not to sprint down the wings, but to train United, who are frustrated by low fitness levels hindering them in the toughest matches. Bacon begins work as United prepare for an English Cup tie against Division One Liverpool by training in Lytham St Anne's.

Despite the old veteran Harry Stafford and his knackered ankle receiving his marching orders in the game, for tripping the quick England international winger Jack Cox one too many times, United beat Liverpool 2-1 to progress. On the same day, Meredith's City are knocked out by Preston North End, conquerors in the previous round of Bishop Auckland, for whom Charlie Roberts has become the key player.

Outstanding performances for Darlington St Augustine's earned Roberts a natural promotion to the north-east's leading amateur side, Bishop Auckland, who are serial finalists and frequent championship challengers. Charlie made an immediate and excellent impression there, too, and word has quickly gone around of this industrious and talented centre-half.

An agent acting on behalf of Aston Villa approaches Roberts soon after his cup performance against Preston but nothing comes of it for now. There is a general sense that Charlie's talents are being overlooked. Newcastle, Sunderland and Middlesbrough, the north-east's three largest clubs, are all made aware of his quality, but none see fit to snap him up. On several occasions, opposition players, including those at Newcastle, have recommended him to their club secretaries as an excellent signing, impressed by his expectation-defying hooked tackles and pinpoint accurate passing.

In late April, recently relegated Grimsby Town take the punt and Roberts becomes a professional footballer on £2 a week. Charlie moves 126 miles south and sets his suitcase down in his small accommodation next to the River Humber. 'He must certainly be reckoned a capture,' decrees the local paper.

Grimsby are relegated to Division Two before Charlie can get a game but he settles in well. Many footballers play cricket in the summer, but Charlie is not one of them. Shortly after arriving, he uses his summer weeks off to earn some extra money. The trawler boats that set off from Grimsby pay well, much better than football clubs. They must because the conditions are severe.

Roberts likes the way the wind whips at his cheeks and how the waves swell – their fury hiding the tranquillity below. His lungs relish the freshest of air and the salt encrusts his lips. The boat's route takes him past Edinburgh far in the distance and then swings around John O'Groats, the very tip of Britain. On his way back, after days spent near Iceland's coast, Roberts passes Edinburgh again where United secretary James West has been enjoying a slightly warmer – and certainly more steady – summer, negotiating for talent.

United were knocked out of the cup in round two by Everton, and the player churn has continued. Harry Stafford made his 200th and final appearance for the club in a home defeat to Lincoln City which left the *Athletic News* labelling United 'the most inconsistent team in the Second Division'. Away victory at Lincoln earlier in the year saw the Reds tipped for promotion, but home defeat left them 21 points adrift of leaders City, who were then promoted as champions having scored 21 more goals than any other team, exactly the number that Meredith netted while playing in all 34 league games.

United finished fifth, leading the rest of the pack while still some distance off the teams above them. James West heads to Scotland to sign yet more players while Stafford deals with a personal matter. He and Mary had a son last year and now Harry's had a second child, a girl called Eva. He'll not see much of her, for she's born to Harriet Sturgess, not his new wife, but his mistress, a 27-year-old greengrocer's daughter. Mary must live with it.

James West returns to Manchester from Scotland with three Robertsons, two called Alex and one called James. He brings in two goalkeepers from the south, Sutcliffe of Millwall and Moger of Southampton. McCartney, Bonthron and Valentine make for three additional incomings as ten players depart. It's some turnover, and the paperwork is hardly made easier when five Clayton kids break into Bank Street and nick bottles of champagne and rum, four United shirts, several balls and other bits and pieces. They mix the drinks together to celebrate but are caught when their mothers tell on them. The United directors say they wish to see no punishment, but they're given a birch striking nonetheless. While Scandinavians use birch twigs tied together to open their pores and increase blood circulation in saunas, they're pretty painful for kids when they come striking down on your arse.

* * *

Louis Rocca, 21 years old and recently married to local lass Mary Emily Wrenshall, is made United's head of the ground committee. He now paints the fences that once held cheeky youngsters like him off the pitch, and he's not the club's only off-pitch addition. United have a new chairman who is one of football's most powerful figures.

It was John James Bentley whom Football League founder William McGregor approached in 1888 because of his influence over Lancashire football and Bentley became league president upon McGregor's retirement six years later. John was Turton FC captain in football's early, disorganised days and even then, he had an inspiring vision for what the sport could become. He rose to prominence as Bolton Wanderers secretary, then editor of the *Athletic News*. The initials 'JJB' are familiar to football fans nationwide. Now in his 40s, Bentley has aged well, his beardless face fattening ever so slightly with each passing year. He has short hair, scraped towards the right and a relatively big nose sits over a long moustache, deliberately thinned at the ends as it comes down below his mouth. Though from a lower-working-class background, he resembles an elder statesman, and in this capacity he will act for United. Bentley's football knowledge and connections are hardly paralleled and his presence has an immediate influence. Next Easter's England–Scotland Inter-League game is arranged to be played at Bank Street, while the FA may even consider the ground for the English Cup Final.

'It is well to have friends at court,' *Sporting Life* pertinently remarks.

2

A new secretary

'Mr Mangnall has done wonders at Burnley, having pulled the club round from bankruptcy to a sound financial position. What is Burnley's loss is Manchester United's gain.'

– *Sporting Life*, 7 October 1903.

September 1903 – Given John Henry Davies's investment, Manchester United's results under secretary James West have been poor. He jumps before being pushed and is given a sweetener upon his exit. Swapping football for beer, West takes over the Davies-owned Union Inn on the corner of Princess and Canal Street. Meanwhile, **Ernest Mangnall** leaves behind a life chasing elephants at miserly Burnley to frolic in the cash storm down the road.

Mangnall arrived at Burnley in 1900 upon the recommendation of his school friend J.J. Bentley, with whom he worked on Bolton Wanderers' committee. More recently, Bentley recommended Mangnall to Everton but, despite Bentley's glowing words, the Merseysiders looked elsewhere.

To understand Mangnall's Burnley success, one must pull back the covers. Like Alf Albut before at Newton Heath, Ernest is well-versed in the language of persuasion and well-practised in the art of the graft. The late-30s Bolton-born man once went four months without pay. Whereas Albut once advertised a Bank Street 'canary', Mangnall arranged for elephants at Turf Moor. Unfortunately, the elephants couldn't fit through the door. The menagerie[13] set up in the town's marketplace instead but, to Ernest, it mattered little that his ground was unused. Armed with his agreement, he sought his fee, and got it.

Results-wise, it has never been the happiest of partnerships. The Clarets' most recent season has been typical: half a dozen home wins accompanied by a bleak 16 defeats from 17 away games which left them begging for mercy from relegation. But Mangnall has done the most important job: keeping Burnley afloat. He has spent almost nothing and sold expertly, and when Bentley is given responsibility for finding United's new secretary, he once again turns to his old pal.

Ernest has turned down offers to leave Burnley before because he was unhappy with the club's position, but not this time. Before his departure, he entertains directors, players and friends to dinner where several speeches detail his excellent work and a vote of thanks is followed by the singing of the national anthem. And so, riding the semibreves and minims of 'God Save the King', Ernest Mangnall arrives at Manchester United.

His role is certainly one of secretary and administrator, not manager and tactician. That much is clear when his United tenure begins with a 4-0 defeat to Woolwich Arsenal and the key issue then clouding Mangnall's first months is that of the goalkeeper. Louis Rocca writes in to the *Evening News* to say the omission of 6ft 3in big-handed Harry Moger is causing 'no little uneasiness among the club's supporters'. His view on the lanky Moger – the average male is eight inches shorter – is echoed by local journalists.

Over at Hyde Road, Meredith's promoted Manchester City are flying in Division One. Billy's Blues top the table at Christmas and go unbeaten from New Year's Day to late March. Their stellar league form is matched in the English Cup where Sandy Turnbull leads the way, scoring in wins

---

13 A travelling collection of animals.

over Sunderland, Woolwich Arsenal, Middlesbrough and The Wednesday.[14] City will play Bolton Wanderers in the final, neither Lancashire side having lifted the petite silver trophy before.

Much of the unrelenting coverage focuses exclusively on Meredith. In the semi-final, the *Daily Telegraph* detailed his every touch. Cigarette cards feature cartoons of him dribbling, special pamphlets bear his image on their fronts, and the newspapers are obsessive. United chairman J.J. Bentley greatly admires Billy, but he grows weary of it all.

'I expect any day now,' he writes, 'to read the headline that Meredith has cut himself shaving this morning and lost two spots of blood.'

Billy enjoys the spotlight, but even he's aware it's not his football skill alone that has launched him to unequalled fame.

'It is wonderful what trifles help to make a man famous,' he writes. 'Long after my fame as a football internationalist has become dim, my name will be remembered as the man who required a toothpick to help him play football.'

It's true, and many young Blues fans are spotted chewing toothpicks in an ode to their hero as thousands of Lancastrians invade London for the cup final. But why does Billy play with a toothpick bobbing up and down at the side of his mouth?

'Welsh miners chew tobacco. I chewed tobacco. When it got worked up I made more steam than I could consume.' The groundsman swore that if Billy Meredith did not stop chewing twist there would not be a single blade of grass on the ground next season. One opponent observed, 'I don't mind a fellow taking the game seriously. Still, there is no reason for him to froth at the mouth.'

'It wasn't nice I quite admit, but habit had made it necessary to chew something while getting coal, and habit is more than second nature. My pals tried to help me. Some suggested thistles and I tried straw. But I ate straw too quickly.

---

14 The Wednesday did not become Sheffield Wednesday until 1929.

By accident, I took a wooden toothpick from the table where I had lunch one Saturday. Putting it between my teeth I discovered that I had it. I could nibble away, and by the time I had got through with it the ref had whistled us off the field.'

Drawn in by the pre-eminence of the Welsh toothpick-chewing wing wizard, celebrities turn out in their droves in London. Club officials from across England are also in the capital for the grand occasion. At a plush Holborn restaurant, Grimsby Town's Joseph Bellows is looking at a thin, round-faced Lancashire lad with a bushy moustache and a hint of autocratic charm. It's J.J. Bentley, Manchester United chairman and president of the Football League. Simultaneously, in Grimsby, on the Humber's shore, Charlie Roberts has been met by an effervescent character wearing a brightly coloured waistcoat named Harry Stafford.

***

Roberts has played just 30-odd games for Grimsby, of which United secretary Mangnall has seen no more than four, but the Reds are fully convinced by his performance in Grimsby's 3-1 league win over United in late March. Stafford has been back and forth from the Humber watching Roberts and what he and Mangnall see is an all-action centre-half who tackles with power, stands tall above his team-mates, passes with first-class ability, wins possession back with ease and creates chances from deep. He is the new mould of centre-half, a master of both destruction and construction, and United are far from the only club in pursuit.

Charlie has enjoyed Grimsby, teaching at Sunday School and fishing regularly, which proved particularly helpful as he dealt with the death of his 59-year-old mother Elizabeth in January, but Stafford convinces him. He has emphasised Manchester United's ambition, offered to double his wages and make him the centre of United's team. In London, Bentley agrees a record £600 fee with Grimsby's chairman and United thus usurp City and other First Division teams by bringing the sought-after 21-year-old Charlie Roberts to Bank Street.

So it is that on English Cup Final day, Charlie makes a composed United debut. He's deemed 'the best half-back in the Second Division' after a 2-0 victory over Burton, at half-time of which, the cup final score is communicated to fans in Clayton, eager to hear how their Manchester brethren are faring in London. They hear that City lead 1-0. Billy Meredith has lived up to the hype. After 23 minutes, he skipped past a defender, moved into the penalty area and scored the only goal of the game. City win the all-Lancashire cup final and Meredith, as captain and match-winner, is the first to get his hands on the trophy.

In City's team photo, Meredith sits centrally with the cup at his feet. He is the main man. A film of the final, Meredith's goal the central focus, is shown across Manchester and Salford and the sport's popularity soars. The scenes of celebration upon return to Manchester are magnificent. In tough times in working-class Manchester, football's unifying nature is evident and this is a moment to truly cherish. Just as the balance of power between rugby and football is shifting, the equilibrium between red and blue will soon tilt, too.

* * *

Mangnall's team is more settled now, with Harry Moger established as first-choice goalkeeper, much to Louis Rocca's satisfaction. Charlie Roberts's quality is clear as he plays United's final three games, but despite a late flourish, Preston are second-tier champions and Woolwich Arsenal beat United to second by a point. They have narrowly missed the promotion boat once again. Had either Mangnall or Roberts arrived earlier, perhaps United would be a top-flight team already.

Ernest's managerial style is pragmatic and old-fashioned. He seeks to concede fewer, rather than score more, than the opposition. He sees good character and hard work as crucial traits and fitness is a fundamental of his own personality and therefore his management too. He limits ball work, believing it'll make his players hungrier on matchday, and he regularly takes United to Lytham St Anne's to train, believing in the therapeutic qualities of salt water and the bracing sea air.

Charlie disagrees with the ball starvation tactic, but he's pleased with the coastal trips. He finds that the United squad take self-ownership of their play, devising set-piece plans or certain patterns of passing to beat the opposition. The players' individual quality means the Reds can produce some scintillating football despite the defence-first policy. Expectations are therefore high for the new 1904/05 season and Mangnall's team start well enough.

In mid-October, they travel to Leicester Fosse and come away 3-0 winners. Starting alongside Roberts are Dick Duckworth and Alec Bell. Duckworth is a Collyhurst-born right-half, brought in by Harry Stafford from Newton Heath Athletic a year ago; Bell is the Cape Town-born Scottish player recently converted to left-half due to an injury crisis. He never looks back, and nor do United. The trio are formidable. United keep seven consecutive clean sheets and Duc-Ro-Bell win 29 of their first 34 games played together. By mid-December, United, Liverpool and Bolton Wanderers are all running at the same pace at the top.

3

Falling short

'Suspension of Manchester United director'

– *Manchester Evening News*, 13 December 1904.

December 1904 – Former Newton Heath secretary Alf Albut's interest is piqued while reading the *Evening News*. There has been a metronomic regularity to their recent reports on his old, now-revived club. 'Another Manchester United victory' has become the season's increasingly familiar four-word motto, but this week is different. United have won again, yes, and for the tenth time this season, but there's more:

'Suspension of Manchester United director'

It's been a few years now since Albut left a then-struggling football club, and what he'd give to oversee things under rich brewery owner John Henry Davies. Albut is back living in the Midlands in his father-in-law's home, but visits Manchester semi-regularly as a travelling sugar agent.

The United director in question is the club's resuscitator and saviour, Harry Stafford. Investigating some exuberant spending since Davies's arrival, the FA's auditor Thomas Hindle has found Stafford and Albut's successor James West to be guilty of making illegal payments to players and failing to keep proper accounts.

These accounts no doubt exist, but would prove the guilt of others at the club. West and Stafford, the effervescent wheeler-dealer, have fallen on their swords by preventing the FA from properly investigating United's

93

affairs. Both men are suspended from all football activities until 1 May 1907.

Albut is dismayed for his friend. He knows Stafford loves his club, even more than he loved his St Bernard dog. The fearless full-back turned enthusiastic administrator and scout receives the sympathy of the entire football public and press. It's an interesting case, for while great emphasis is placed on playing within the rules *on* the pitch, here is a man who has broken them off it and is greeted with tender praise. Unfortunately for Stafford, the FA is unforgiving. He will miss the football at Clayton immensely, but things won't be so bad. He's an excellent publican – the social side of it certainly suits him – and Davies rewards his loyalty by upgrading him from Ancoats' Bridge Inn to the larger Imperial Hotel, a fine city-centre establishment.

***

Soon enough the bars in Shudehill and Ancoats, Stafford's included, are filled with Christmas spirit. Not far away in Exchange Square, children's sweet-sounding, high-pitched carols echo off the cobbles, their diffusion suffocated by a dense street-level fog.

Manchester United's players aren't in town on this winter evening. The Reds are third in Division Two, and could reach the tree's top by winning a game in hand. Ernest Mangnall has taken them to Lytham St Anne's. It's been something of a regularity throughout the season and a rare comfort. On standard away trips, Charlie Roberts takes a nail to knock into the dressing room wall so he has something to hang his clothes on, off the dirt-encrusted floor.

The dense fog's overnight persistence casts doubt upon United's Christmas Eve fixture, but the weather holds out as they seek to leapfrog visitors Liverpool into second with a win. It has been a fantastic run for Mangnall's team. Roberts scored his first United goal with a thumping, match-winning penalty against Glossop North End in late September and the form he is showing is quite something. He scores his second goal of the season against Liverpool, ramming a high shot in just under the bar as United rise to second.

As 1905 begins, United's ever-stretching winning record reaches 13 games when Roberts scores twice in a 7-0 victory against Bradford City. Focus immediately turns to the next day's fixture at the league leaders.

Thousands descend on promotion rivals Bolton Wanderers' Burnden Park, 5,000 leaving on trains from Manchester Victoria Station alone. The weather is dull and grey, but the excitement tangible.

'I gave one of my very best displays,' Charlie Roberts later writes.

'Twice we got the lead, and twice it was taken from us, but at length, we forged ahead, and in the end managed to win by four goals to two.

'That day made my name in the football world; hence I look back on it with no end of pleasure.'

Roberts's match-winning performance earns wide acclaim. Indeed, shortly after, Roberts is selected for the North versus South trial match, arranged to allow FA selectors to determine England's squad for the upcoming international fixtures. 'The clever tackling of the half-backs' is picked out in the North's 3-1 win at Bristol and 21-year-old Charlie is selected for his first cap. A mere 18 months earlier, he had just left the amateur Bishop Auckland team to sign for Grimsby Town. Now he is the first Manchester United player to represent England, and the first Division Two player to be selected for many years.

* * *

Drizzling rain is falling in North Yorkshire. England's international players have just arrived at Saltburn-by-the-Sea, where they will stay in comfortable quarters. Included among them is Charlie Roberts, who's not so far from home. Darlington is a mere 30 miles away, and many childhood friends will come to watch him play against Ireland in

Middlesbrough. As rain falls on a dark February evening, the Ayresome Park groundsman prods away at the turf, trying to even out any particularly bumpy sections, and hoping there will be no pools of water by the time the 22 internationals stride out tomorrow.

He does a good job. The turf is in fine condition by kick-off. Charlie walks out into a fantastic atmosphere wearing the white of England for the first time. Unlike his team-mates, his shorts are pulled up well above his knees. This semi-rebellious appearance irks the more traditional men among the FA officials.

Early on, Roberts plays a good, long ball upfield to Booth, who crosses well, only for M'Cracken to clear. It's typical of his style, summed up in yesterday's papers as 'the half-back of the future'. England dominate the first half, and Roberts plays well. He provides several excellent passes and shaves a lick of paint off the crossbar with a good effort, while his defensive work is as reliable as ever. Both teams score in quick succession shortly after the restart but the big win anticipated for England does not play out. It's a fantastic result for Ireland, only the second time they have avoided defeat in this fixture from 24 attempts. Roberts returns to Manchester as an international footballer, but he's not pleased with his display. 'I don't think I let the side down exactly, but I know I ought to have done better,' he tells his girlfriend, May.

Charlie's many commitments have had a disastrous effect on United's promotion hopes. As well as missing games in January, due to injury, and February, due to England duties, Roberts is again absent in March. He helps United to victory against West Brom but when he's away again – scoring in victory for the English League against the Scottish League in Glasgow – United lose 2-0 to Burnley and the gap to league leaders Bolton stretches to three points.

Charlie is juggling duties like a Shudehill street performer. After helping United to victory at Blackpool, he plays for England in Liverpool two days later, against Billy Meredith's

Wales. The Three Lions need victories against both Wales and Scotland if they are to win the Home Championship.

After the inter-league win against Scotland, *Sporting Life* described England as 'painfully deficient in class halves', doubting 'whether Wolstenholme, Roberts, and Leake' would be able to cope with the 'brilliant and incisive' Welsh attack. Charlie proves those doubters wrong, giving a 'grand exhibition' at centre-half as his country win 3-1. England then defeat Scotland on April Fool's Day to wrap up the Home Championship with victory.

'Nothing could have been much better than the performance of Leake and Roberts,' says one reporter as the rest of United's players finally prove themselves to be no fools too, thrashing Doncaster Rovers 6-0 to seal a first Roberts-less league win since January. Charlie has played all three games in a Championship-winning year for England. He looks sure to have a long and prosperous international career, with his United side's promotion likely, too.

But the Reds fall short. Two defeats over Easter condemn Mangnall's team to another third-place finish, making United's record-breaking 14-game winning streak earlier in the season futile. They finish three points off promotion. While Roberts was away on England or Football League duties, the Reds dropped one point to Barnsley and two to Burnley; three, in total. United are proud of his selection but rueful of the impact it has had. The glumness persists when they lose to Bury in the Manchester Cup Final.

* * *

While United's season fizzles out somewhat, Manchester City's erupts.

Billy Meredith's third-place Blues go to Villa Park on the final day knowing victory will give them the title if results elsewhere go their way. The Welsh winger's status as one of the game's finest forwards is unaltered, unlike City's reputation, which took a hit when an FA investigation concluded in the suspension of four directors, a £250 fine and a two-game ground closure. Like Harry Stafford, City had been caught slipping unauthorised signing-on fees to players. They are no different from any other club, they'd just had the misfortune of being caught.

In good form, City make just one change, restoring Sandy Turnbull to the line-up after injury. It proves a portentous decision.

In a vibrant atmosphere, newly crowned English Cup winners Villa put on an exhibition. They score three before 30 minutes are up, shredding City's already-slim title hopes. Geordie Livingstone's fierce strike for City before half-time stirs thoughts of a comeback, but three second-half goals are needed. Meredith crosses brilliantly for Turnbull to head home nine minutes after the break and they then monopolise the ball, but without finding another goal. What follows instead is Edwardian football's biggest scandal.

4

Meredith and scandal

'FOOTBALL SENSATION'

August 1905 – The announcements at Friday, 4 August's FA Council meeting begin with the ordinary and build up to a stunning peak. Forget the rest, Welsh wing wizard Billy Meredith has been suspended from all football activities until April of next year. The charge? Offering a £10 bribe to Aston Villa captain Alec Leake to throw April's decisive match in Manchester City's favour.

On Friday, Billy returned to his wife's home back in Chirk and was greeted warmly by everyone he passed. The people here adore the miner-boy-made-good. He gets a good night's sleep, for he finds the air cleaner and less noisy than in Manchester, but in the morning, news of his nine-month suspension bowls him over. It says something that he finds out in the press.

Once he's regained his mental footing, he's furious. When reporters turn up mid-morning, Billy needs little invitation to unload.

'I am entirely innocent, and am suffering for others. Such an allegation as that of bribery is preposterous. I could never risk my reputation and future by such an action, and I repeat I never made any such offer. It is totally unjustifiable and grossly unfair.

'This sort of thing will demoralise football. Manchester has not many friends among the Association officials, and I doubt if the decision would be reversed, or the suspension period lessened, if the whole case was re-opened and again inquired into. Had I been anyone but a Welshman I should have been better dealt with.'

By losing at Aston Villa in April, Meredith's City team finished third. Near the game's end, Sandy Turnbull hit Villa captain Alec Leake, who was then restrained by his team-mates as he attempted to respond. In the following days, Britain's football writers were at loggerheads as much as the two offending players. Within the *Athletic News* on the same day, two reporters offered starkly contrasting accounts of events. Birmingham-based journalists insisted Turnbull hit Leake out of the blue; Manchester's hinted at something different.

Worse still than Turnbull and Leake's on-pitch exchange, which went unpunished by the referee, was what occurred after full time. Turnbull was bundled into the Villa dressing room and assaulted. A commission investigated the affair, but things were suspiciously quiet all summer. Now its explosive findings focus only somewhat on the Turnbull versus Leake affair, and much more deeply on Meredith.

Billy insists to journalists he'll speak no further, but he can't help himself. The most grating thing, he continues, is that he has been left out in the cold, receiving no updates on the investigation's progress and, he claims to sympathetic reporters, no opportunity to prove his innocence.

***

In Birmingham, Alec Leake is also talking to reporters. The England centre-back has received no charge for his role. Sandy Turnbull has.

Leake is delighted that he's been exonerated but expresses sympathy for Meredith.

'When Meredith spoke to me I advised him not to be foolish,' he says.

'When I was questioned as to the alleged bribery, while I had to admit that an offer was made, I said I regarded it more as a joke than anything to be taken seriously.'

Leake is anxious it be understood that he did not report the matter. He declares the actual informer to be a gentleman who overheard a conversation on the subject which took place between other members of the team when the match was over.

Sporting reporters and columnists are baffled by these events. There is complete disbelief that Meredith would attempt to bribe Leake, for several reasons: £10 would be insufficient to buy a top-flight match, Meredith wouldn't risk his reputation and future earnings for one match, even if City won it wasn't enough to win the Championship and, finally, no one mentioned a bribe either after the game or over the several following weeks.

'Is a closed court just?' *Athletic News* editor Jimmy Catton questions, criticising the lack of transparency.

'The Commissioners do not even mention names. They do not even say the witnesses who were called. They avoid expressing the opinion that the charge was substantiated or proved. They merely publish the conviction by suspending Meredith for a whole season. Is this official silence justifiable? Is it fair to Meredith, to Manchester City, or to those of us who believe in honest sportsmanship and support association football? I ask these questions because I confess that the method seems un-English, most autocratic and arbitrary. This must necessarily be so when the tribunal is closed.'

Catton accepts that it seems mad to think the FA's trusted, trained and experienced lawyer J.C. Clegg would suspend Meredith unless he was convinced beyond doubt as to his guilt. An ex-player himself, Sheffield-born Clegg complained in his day of an anti-northern bias, such as that floated by Meredith. And yet, Catton says, 'such extraordinary convictions have taken place, even in courts of law, that one may be pardoned for entertaining a doubt upon this matter. There are, to my thinking, so many reasons why Meredith should not have acted in this manner, apart altogether from his natural instincts as a man.'

'In the absence of ALL evidence we have a right to consider the improbability of the act imputed to Meredith and the absence of any direct motive, while we cannot shut our eyes to "his previous good conduct". I am not convinced he is guilty.'

Letters flood into Monday's *Athletic News* with ex-footballers and fans alike dismayed by the lack of published evidence but also the injustice in the sentencing. Why, one asks, is five-cap England man Alec Leake omitted completely from the report and its punishments when his team assaulted Sandy Turnbull? Even the newspaper's Birmingham correspondent doubts Meredith's guilt and concedes Leake 'must regard himself a lucky man'. Is it luck, or is it a process prejudiced against the Welsh Meredith of northern *nouveau riche* Manchester City, in favour of the long-time elite Aston Villa, and the English Leake?

'I suppose I must have twelve months' rest,' an Eeyore-like Meredith sadly concludes.

5

Roberts, the captain

*'The half-back line should form the
foundation in the building of a team. They
are essentially its backbone.'*

'Peter The Great', Newcastle United left-half,
1902–11.

August 1905 – While Manchester City captain Billy Meredith
is banned, his career hanging in the balance, Manchester
United appoint a new leader in Charlie Roberts.

His centre-half position is football's most important,
determining a team's style and success through the intimate
involvement in attack and defence. 'Show me your centre-
half, and I will tell you what sort of a team you have,' is a
common dictum.

Six feet tall and 14 stone, Roberts is robust and broad-
shouldered, but hardly bulky. He uses his weight well and
his long legs allow him to cover ground quickly, and to make
expectation-defying scissor tackles in recovery. His play is
marked by coolness and skill, his distribution is precise, the
passes he provides to his forwards are unerringly excellent,
and when he wins possession back, he traps the ball, carefully
considers the best route into attack and speeds a pass in that
direction, almost always across the ground. His kicks are
rarely airborne, and never aimless. When United's attack is
too narrow, his passes force the wingers out. When there is no
passing opportunity, his dribbling draws defenders in, opening
up the pitch. This is his philosophy: draw the opponent in,

and attack. Attack, attack, attack. In this sense, he differs greatly from the men responsible for managing United and England's national team. They do not think that attack is the best form of defence.

Much of Roberts's work goes unnoticed by the average punter. He's the players' player. His length of stride makes it appear easy sometimes, as opposed to smaller centre-halves such as Bristol City's Billy 'Fatty' Wedlock, a podgy 5ft 3in man with immense energy, and a future international.

United take on Wedlock's Bristol on the season's opening day. They have prepared for the season, at John Henry Davies's enthusiastic urging, with practice matches dedicated to charitable causes. A bed is duly named after the club at Ancoats Hospital and hundreds more are raised for the Clayton Nurses' Institution. Then, in a rivalry just beginning to brew, Roberts takes a lead over Wedlock, conducting his team to a 5-1 victory on his captaincy debut.

Exciting new signing Charlie Sagar – a double cup winner with Bury – scores four in his first three games, but when the Reds travel to Glossop, their new scoring sensation is absent along with goalkeeper Harry Moger. It's a bright autumn day and Louis Rocca, the second-generation Italian immigrant, teaboy, groundsman, kitman, scout and all-round helper, carries a large red-and-white-striped umbrella. 'The Rocca Brigade' is an enthusiastic supporters' group, recognisable and ever-present, and these travelling Reds have overtaken and made more colourful than ever the small Derbyshire market town of Glossop.

Mancunians in red, carrying bugles and rattles, shout 'Are we downhearted?' – the refrain of a popular music hall song.

At full-time, with United's winning record maintained, an ear-splitting cacophony of rattles, cheers and bugles' parps arises from the 10,000 in attendance. A few fans spill on to the pitch, one climbing the goalposts to sit atop the crossbar, waving his umbrella.

'United would be considered very unlucky indeed if they are left out in the cold again,' comments one newspaper. 'The club possesses a class of supporters who will stick to them through thick and thin. With such an enthusiastic spirit as this prevailing, it should not be long before the Manchester United star is found in the ascendant.'

As that star ascends, those wishing to catch a glimpse increase in number. Huge crowds follow the team that *Sporting Life* calls 'the famous Manchester United' across the north. Famous how, is not clear, for the Reds have won neither the league nor the cup in their 25-year existence, but they are playing some fine football now as they march towards promotion.

There are, however, some minor slip-ups in a season as unaccepting of stutters as a playground bully. Dropped points at West Brom, Gainsborough and Chesterfield allow Wedlock's Bristol City to lead the table.

The arrival of 1906 heralds a General Election in Britain after a tumultuous month in Westminster. Campaigning has begun and Manchester East's MP Arthur Balfour, who resigned as Prime Minister in December, needs every vote he can muster. Down he heads to Clayton, then, to woo the fans of Manchester United. A tall man with an almost snarling resting expression, Balfour's unflattering, slicked-back, middle-parting hair is hidden by a Homburg hat. He towers somewhat over the players, his smart shoes not entirely appropriate for the flat, muddy surface at Bank Street which resembles the smooth swathes of wet sand left by an outward-heading tide. He makes a 'sickly effort at setting the ball rolling', and loses his seat and the election, emphatically. United do the opposite, putting five past Grimsby Town without reply. Their campaign is progressing better than Balfour's.

Winston Churchill visits a week later as United easily advance in the FA Cup. Churchill's kick isn't much better than Balfour's, but the crowd afford him a warmer reception.

Two days later, spirits are significantly dampened, however, by United's first home defeat, against the newly formed Leeds City of Elland Road. The sides met in December but play was paused when Charlie Roberts collided with the goalpost. Dense fog worsened while the dazed captain's condition was assessed, and play never resumed in a forgettable but controversial start to this Lancashire–Yorkshire rivalry. Having led the fixture at its abandonment, United lose the replayed match 3-0. It's a sickening loss.

Two wins restore United's confidence before, on 8 February, Arthur Balfour's humiliating election defeat is confirmed. Two days later, HMS *Dreadnought* is launched at Portsmouth, part of Britain and Germany's escalating naval race. The dreadnought is a new class of battleship designed around the firepower of heavy guns, and fighting steals the headlines in the football world too.

6

United and riots

'Manchester United Attacked'
– Sheffield Evening Telegraph

'Regrettable scenes'
– Lancashire Evening Post

'Football riots in Yorkshire'
– Daily Mirror

February 1906 – Manchester United's players escape unharmed to the dressing rooms, but further trouble is clearly brewing. As the hard-tackling full-back Bob Bonthron changes out of his bespattered uniform, an ominous crowd loiters outside. United have humbled Bradford, five goals to one, and the local Yorkshire public's principal enemy is Bonthron, who has engaged in consistent battle with Bradford's winger, a feisty enough player himself. The Valley Parade atmosphere corrodes as regular clashes throughout the game are part of a vicious cycle of constant revenge left uncontrolled by the referee, who, upon exit, has his pipe knocked out of his mouth, taking a fair splattering of mud.

The United players receive a partial police escort which can do little to protect them. Bonthron is slapped by one supporter and emerges muddy brown from head to toe. As stones join the raining debris, he is dragged into the Belle Vue Hotel for safety. He boards United's cabs, which Bradford's secretary sits himself at the front of in an attempt to avoid further trouble, but stones are still thrown, including one hurled through J.J. Bentley and Ernest Mangnall's window. United, with some haste, head for their training quarters at Norbreck in Blackpool.

The affair is reported nationwide. While the country's jingoistic columnists demand more and more massive battleships, they condemn the 'disgraceful' scenes at the football, which can only be caused, says the *Mirror*'s writer, by 'the gambling spirit'.

It is four decades since churches, communities and factories turned to football to keep their men out of trouble, replacing cock fighting, gambling and drinking with a healthy sporting interest. Football has indeed proved itself in that regard year after year, but the envisaged ideal is far from a constant reality; 'hooliganism' is rearing its head semi-regularly.

A week later, bittersweet thanks are given when England overlook Charlie Roberts in favour of top-flight talent. Unlike last year, the Reds thus retain the services of their best player and captain, who instead deals with the fall-out of events at Bradford, appearing in front of an FA commission along with directors and players of both clubs. Valley Parade is closed for a fortnight and the directors are told to promptly clear the public from the ground at full time. This is the FA's regular response to 'hooligan' incidents.

All this proves something of a distraction to United's upcoming FA Cup match against the holders Aston Villa, a fixture arousing understandable excitement at Clayton. John Henry Davies and Ernest Mangnall are thrilled for the renovated Bank Street's capacity to be tested, Roberts is eager to prove himself against the country's best, and hopefully in front of an England selector, while Louis Rocca's band of supporters eagerly await a tantalising tie, though they are perturbed when a new ticket pricing scheme is introduced exclusively for the match. United's directors are criticised for partaking in what the *Mirror* calls football's 'growing evil': 'sordid commercialism'. Every ticket in the ground is to be priced at one shilling, a discount for some but a doubling in price for the regular 6d-paying patrons.

'No club in the kingdom has been better supported by the real working class than Manchester United and it is nothing less than a scandal that the very men who have made the club what it is should be practically fined for seeing their own club figure at home in an important Cup-tie!'

The crowd is enormous, nevertheless. Exact numbers are hard to estimate, but the ground has exceeded its capacity an hour before kick-off and crushes develop outside with would-be spectators desperate to get in. Cash flows more healthily than people, and Davies's accountant George Lawton will count up £1,460 from gate receipts post-match. That number could be doubled if Bank Street was bigger. Perhaps United need a new home.

Having established a 2-1 half-time lead in an even game, Roberts's lads purr after the break. The Reds swoop down with unrelenting force on Villa's goal to earn second-tier United a stupefying 5-1 victory over the cup holders. 'The day's football made out Manchester United to be quite a wonderful side,' comments the *Morning Post*. 'Five goals to one was a remarkable score, but it in no degree exaggerated the run of the game. Manchester United's inside-forwards were well served by the half-back line. They always looked like easy winners.'

Woolwich Arsenal, a bottom-half top-flight club, are United's next cup opponents and a fourth consecutive home draw proves Lady Luck is on Mangnall's side. Billy Meredith counts himself less fortune. It has been almost a year since the Villa Park affair and Billy is restless, still furious about his ban which he fails to adhere to. He regularly visits Hyde Road, demanding his wages be paid. Meredith feels City's officials have offered him no support, so his fury multiplies.

***

Bank Street is overflowing for another hair-raising cup tie when Arsenal visit. Fans unable to enter via the turnstiles take to the roofs. They perch precariously, silhouetted alongside the chemical works' belching chimneys. An enormous, expectant crowd surrounds this mud bath. United play in blue change strips and Arsenal in red, despite the location.

The cheers have hardly dissipated from Charlie Sagar's early opener when Arsenal's Coleman breaks through at the other end. Harry Moger bats his shot away but Freeman equalises from the rebound. By the break, both sides have scored another and then Freeman finds a winner for the visitors, whose goalkeeper is lifted towards the dressing room such are his late heroics. United are out, despite proving themselves a fine side.

Focus returns to the league, and Mangnall and Davies discuss how to avoid falling short again this season. The players will travel to long-distance away matches two days beforehand to allow them to rest and acclimatise, and a new signing is made.

Barnsley come to east Manchester in March and leave with no points and one fewer player. The scorer of their only goal in a 5-1 defeat is to become a Red. Louis Rocca has watched George Wall play several times before for Barnsley and been impressed. He has recommended Wall to Mangnall, but the latter has been a little doubtful of his size and strength. Going up against the fearsome Bob Bonthron is a good litmus test, Rocca and Mangnall both think, and Wall excels. He makes Bonthron look small. United have been convinced.

Rocca heads into the dressing room at half-time and sees big Bonthron making all kinds of promises to hack Wall down in the second half. He won't be doing that. With Davies having agreed to sign Wall, Rocca tells Bonthron to go easy on him. Bonthron does and, sure enough, Wall joins United. It's a show of faith from Davies and a crucial end-of-season boost. Wall's quality is unmistakable. He scores on his debut, a 1-0 win at Clapton Orient in London, where United play again a couple of days later on Good Friday, drawing 1-1 with promotion rivals Chelsea in front of a record-breaking

60,000 crowd. Many have travelled down from Manchester to watch during the holidays, and many Londoners leave with an affection for the quality United side they have seen. A draw means Mangnall's team are almost certain to go up, barring any major mistakes.

Promotion promises

*'At last! Manchester United, after striving
for three years, have won their way into the
First Division.'*

– *Empire News & The Umpire*, 22 April 1906.

April 1906 – There are no mistakes. In a victorious homecoming, Manchester United overwhelm Burton United 6-0 in late April. At full-time, the fans rush on to the field and carry the players off. Like baying wolves, the supporters stay put, celebrating in front of the directors' box for an hour. The cheers won't cease and, eventually, they are happily pacified by an address from John Henry Davies and Ernest Mangnall. As hundreds of souvenirs are thrown from the magnificently decorated red-and-white box, the club president and secretary are greeted like Roman emperors. And so they should be. A mere four years ago, Newton Heath FC was on the brink of extinction. Now the reformed Manchester United are in Division One.

A fantastic back end to the season, eight wins from nine, has earned United's rise. They've scored 90 goals in 38 games and conceded 28, and the statement cup thrashing of Aston Villa has, as much as anything, proved they are top-flight ready.

John Henry is delighted. He revels in the supporters' enthusiasm and takes pride in every congratulatory handshake he receives. Mangnall and the players have lived up to his expectations and Davies has thus requested a local medal maker to replicate the gold medals given to champions Bristol, which are 15-carat gold and busily decorated, with 'M.U.F.C' at the top of one side.

Twenty-three-year-old Charlie Roberts sits contently in the dressing room. He has waited a long time; he was scouted but not signed by Division One clubs six years ago, he joined Grimsby Town only for them to drop down before he could play, and he has twice come close with United, too. Now he will finally have the opportunity to prove himself at the top.

Roberts's girlfriend Mary Elizabeth Cammiss is just as pleased. A sailmaker's daughter, May met Charlie working as a waitress in Grimsby. She moved to Manchester with him and was promised marriage once United secured promotion as part of a pact Charlie made with his manager, 36-year-old Ernest Mangnall, who commits his future to Eliza Hobson, a girl from Lytham St Anne's, where United – conveniently – train regularly. Charlie and Ernest both make good on their promises. Wedding bells ring.

* * *

Billy Meredith's wife Ellen might have one or two warnings about becoming a footballer's other half. Her Welshman has been sulking for some months, his once fast-paced celebrity life pedestrianised to the extreme. His continued presence at City's Hyde Road ground has proven a thorn in the side of a club attempting to restore its reputation but, sufficiently frustrated, Billy's new tactic is disruption.

'I found them shilly-shallying and putting me off until I got tired,' the 31-year-old says.

He now admits he did offer Villa captain Alec Leake a £10 bribe, but only at the behest of City secretary, Tom Maley, and the rest of the team. Maley denies such claims and the truth is hard to establish. Perhaps Billy is owning up, or he's deliberately, and falsely, casting a conveniently large shadow over the whole City club.

His next claim is even more inflammatory.

'What was the secret of the success of the Manchester City team?' this maverick footballer asks in the newspaper, before revealing that the players were paid more than the FA-stipulated £4 maximum wage, introduced in 1901.

The *Athletic News*, owned by City backer Edward Hulton, cries that Meredith has 'dragged everyone else into the same mess' with 'no sense of gratitude' having been 'most lavishly and generously paid by the club'.

While the FA – equally furious, but at Hulton and City – opens a fresh investigation, the frustrated Meredith organises a transfer away. Never a fan of anywhere more than Chirk but content in Manchester – he now part-owns a sports shop in St Peter's Square, has many friends in the area and is adored by the public – Meredith would like to stay here. He has kept himself fit, dribbling between bottles behind his house and landing crosses on a handkerchief laid in the penalty area.

If he wants advice from a fellow maverick and member of football's exiled community, he can step into the Harry Stafford-run Imperial Hotel. United's and City's players have long held good relations and Meredith played in Stafford's 1901 testimonial, under the moniker 'Manchester United'. If there's one man who'll always advocate a move to the club that has since assumed that name, it's Harry Stafford.

After an explosive meeting with City's most senior directors, Meredith is transfer-listed. It's exactly what he wants, but there's still more.

'The City club put a transfer fee of £600 on my head, but I refused to let them pay a half-penny. I had cost no fee and I was determined that I would have no fee placed on my head. I was prepared to fight the matter. The City club were not.'

Meredith helpfully points out that City owe him a benefit match, in which he'd be guaranteed to raise roughly the same as his transfer fee. He agrees to 'forget' about the promised benefit match if he can leave for free. And to Manchester

United and John Henry Davies, he explains they need not pay City, but they can pay him the equivalent instead.

'I was given a free transfer and, as a result, I got £500 from a gentleman to sign for Manchester United.'

And so it is that, in mid-May, to surprisingly little fanfare, Billy Meredith crosses the red–blue divide.

* * *

The investigation sparked by Meredith's comments results in an FA pillage of Manchester City. Undeterred by the protests of northern newspapers, City fans, fellow northern football clubs and players, the FA march through Hyde Road, ripping out the art, shipping the statues home, pulling away the copper and leaving with anything of any value, including every player of quality.

The secretary, directors and 17 players, Meredith included, are suspended. The club receives a £250 fine, and the players together £900 because the commission finds Billy was right. City have consistently paid players above the £4 maximum weekly wage. The FA have long suspected such wrongdoing but were unable to find sufficient evidence. With Meredith's testimony, they've proved City have funnelled ticket money straight into club directors' bank accounts and, from there, paid the players extra, keeping things off the books. Furthermore, Meredith's regular presence at Hyde Road has been explained. City had promised him a full salary for the duration of his suspension.

For those truly in the know, none of this is so remarkable, for although City are clearly major breakers of the rules – perhaps the most flagrant – there are few successful English teams not finding a way past the FA's maximum wage. One could only look close by in Clayton and find John Henry Davies helping players out with side jobs, houses and investments into private ventures.

Meredith is not delighted at City's demise but is darkly humoured by the FA's hypocrisy. While the association passes their 'pious resolution', he says, other clubs are canvassing the 'villains' to sign for them for even more money than they'd been 'illegally' paid by City. 'Clubs are not punished for breaking the law,' he says. 'They are punished for being found out.'

Billy himself has received a £100 fine from the FA, the most of any player, but he won't pay it. That cost is covered by his new club, Manchester United. A 'pious resolution', indeed.

8

Blue to Red

*'When Meredith comes into the
attack next January, he will make an
enormous difference, for he has no equal at
outside-right.'*

– *Sporting Life*, 28 August 1906.

August 1906 – Given United's own illicit payments, John
Henry Davies could be forgiven for needing a stiff drink after
reading about City's severe punishment. And another drink,
for more celebratory reasons. Davies has struck gold in the
form of salt on his 160-acre Holford Hall estate, 193 feet
of it, and he will take little notice of the FA's regulations in
spending the proceeds.

Contrastingly, Manchester United's supporters are
dismayed to learn that Davies and the directors have put up
season ticket prices upon promotion. 'We have paid first-class
prices for second-class football for a long time and should be
rewarded, rather than punished for that loyalty,' they argue.
Business is business, the directors think, having made further
improvements to Bank Street. Furthermore, they insist, they
don't want to undercut their friendly rivals at City.

On the Football League's blisteringly hot opening day, the
Blues have three players carried off through heat exhaustion
while Charlie Roberts makes his long-awaited top-flight debut
with chalk-lined boots – Ernest Mangnall's instructions, to
soak up the sweat. The massive-handed goalkeeper Harry

Moger – praised for 'catching the ball like it's a cricket ball' – dons a huge sun hat. Charlie and Jack Picken's goals have United leading 2-1 at half time before an exciting game at Bristol peters out in the humidity, United thus securing the full two points in their first top-flight match for a decade.

Inconsistent form follows with Moger and Roberts United's stand-out players, a fact indicating where the team's weakness lies; in its attack. Charlie's creative endeavours are often in vain, though United do score enough to be a comfortable seventh by November, allowing them to focus on their other competitions: the English, Lancashire and Manchester cups.

A rainstorm interrupts November's midweek Lancashire Cup tie at Liverpool, and United's players duly return to their dressing room, where, believing the match is postponed, they get into the baths. When the referee orders play's resumption to a group of six or seven naked men in murky water, the misunderstanding remains distinctly unresolved. United are fined, kicked out of the tournament and Liverpool's supporters are so upset they put on a little demonstration outside Anfield.[15] Just the two cups to compete in, then.

Back in the league, United mark December's start by visiting Hyde Road for Division One's first-ever Manchester derby. The stadium is pushed to its limits and several spectators are injured when crushes develop. The match showcases United's problems. Defender Bob Bonthron works tirelessly but finds himself doing two men's work and scores an own goal. The half-back line provides chances aplenty to the forwards, but for all Duc-Ro-Bell's untiring work, United cannot finish. Division One standard firepower is missing and here, at their rivals' home in a 3-0 defeat, it will be found, because Saturday, 1 December 1906 is the first date on which clubs can legally approach Manchester City regarding the 17

---

15 This is, perhaps, the first sign of trouble in a United versus Liverpool fixture.

players suspended after the Billy Meredith scandal. While Meredith is a United player already, though he cannot yet play, and his old striking partner Billy Gillespie has headed to the United States, there's plenty of gold remaining and, with the warm glow of derby victory descending over Hyde Road, City's directors hold a fire sale at the Queen's Hotel.

Football League founder William McGregor aptly describes a 'frantic scramble to secure the spoil'. Ex-Glossop full-back Herbert Burgess is most sought after. Celtic and Everton both believe a deal is done, but the knowledgeable McGregor dismisses this. 'Evidently on Saturday's form, the United require him,' he explains.

He's right, and although Everton vehemently insist they've signed Burgess as part of a deal that saw their player already join City, Herbie becomes a Red. The Football League, under United employee J.J. Bentley's presidency, will reject any appeals.

United get Sandy Turnbull too, perhaps the pick of the bunch, the meaty kind-faced 5ft 7in Scottish forward with an almost unmatched heading ability whose slap of Alec Leake began this farce. Aberdeen are left wistfully wanting. Jimmy Bannister, another of Meredith's favourites, is the final signing. He'll play next to Meredith at inside-right, as they did together at City. And together, these four boys in blue, soon to don red, will propel United upwards. Their bans expire in a month, on the first day of 1907.

* * *

After so long out of the game, Meredith is agitated with excitement at the prospect of representing United, despite his dozen-year acquaintance with City. Charlie Roberts walks the short distance from his home to Bank Street thrilled to have Meredith, Turnbull and Bannister running on to his passes, and Burgess behind him. There's been little time to train together due to the festive schedule, but they've had plenty of conversations, and the City boys easily settle in.

The full quartet debut together on New Year's Day. Charlie Roberts leads his new team-mates out to a 40,000 crowd and an amazing tumult of waving arms and handkerchiefs. 'A greater roar of cheering has probably never sounded over a football ground,' the *Manchester Guardian*'s over-excited reporter writes.

Sandy Turnbull's left boot turns home a low Meredith cross as United beat Aston Villa, the club who contributed to their bans. It's a sweet day, and several more follow. United win 11 of the next 17 games, a far superior record to their pre-Christmas form. Turnbull scores six in 15 while it's five in 18 for Meredith.

Crowds at United's home increase in size each week, but United's home is problematic. Thirteen chimneys belch out fumes across the grandstand and the pitch is a bed of grit and mud. United have finished eighth, a mere nine points behind champions Newcastle, but while the playing squad now resembles something quite special, even expanded embankments and decorated stands can't disguise Bank Street's inadequacy. John Henry Davies wants more. And that salt he found, well, that might just fund it. Manchester United aim to build a new ground, Old Trafford the most likely home.

Part Three:
Success, 1907–11

1

Charlie's league leaders

*'It is evident that the captain Charlie Roberts
is a man of thought as well as of action.'*

– Athletic News.

November 1907 – 'Our run of luck,' Charlie Roberts reflects modestly, 'has been due to our combination.'

En route to Sheffield, Manchester United's captain has been cornered by the *Athletic News* reporter who accompanies the team.

'Our players blend in style, and that unity is strengthened by the fact that my team-mates are speedy. Our games are very fast, and this pace, and the cooperation of the half-backs with the vanguard, often gives us the advantage of eight forwards.

'I also think the youth of our team is a powerful factor in our success. The average age of our team must be no greater than 24. We are fresh, also, because we are not overtrained. We undergo official preparation two days in each week, on Tuesday and on Thursday. Given the nature of the season – eight months long – this is all that is required. Nevertheless, what has been crucial is our fortune with regard to injuries. We have had great immunity from accident so far, and so we have a powerful eleven.'

United are runaway league leaders with 13 wins and 48 goals in 14 matches. They thrashed Aston Villa away from home on the opening day and never looked back, hitting Liverpool, Chelsea, Nottingham Forest, Birmingham and Everton for four, Blackburn for five and Newcastle for six.

Last week, leading goalscorer Sandy Turnbull added to his 15 goals in 13 games with a remarkable quartet to down Arsenal, after which United celebrated raucously at Harry Stafford's Imperial Hotel. Drinks were knocked back with sufficient haste to see Harry charged with allowing drunkenness on his property. The old Newton Heath captain relishes the distraction of a rambunctious night because he is grieving once more. His second wife, Mary, has died aged 32. In football terms, though, Stafford's long FA suspension has expired and he revels in his restored freedom even if he's not resumed an official role at United, who today travel to Sheffield on a ten-match, free-scoring winning run.

For Charlie Roberts, too, United's successes have offered much-needed occasional interruptions to grief. In January, he and May had their first child, Charles. At the end of October, their little boy died, just nine months old.

English infant mortality remains heart-wrenchingly high despite a recent decline in the overall death rate. Around a quarter of all children die before their fifth birthday but knowledge of this does little to ease the numb pain felt by May, who is heavily pregnant with a second child, and 24-year-old Charlie. United's young fixer Louis Rocca, a year Charlie's senior, felt the same pain 18 months ago. Louis Jr, bearing the same anglicised name as Louis and his father Luigi Snr, died three months short of his second birthday. Louis offers Charlie his understanding and sympathies and, as a devout Catholic, encourages the club captain to lean on his own faith to get him through it. 'He's safe in the arms of Jesus,' Rocca insists.

* * *

The Wednesday end United's long winning run, narrowing the gap to four points. Two days later, Billy Meredith and Charlie Roberts return to the Imperial Hotel, the site of those boisterous post-Arsenal celebrations. Two months ago, in the midst of United's outstanding autumn form, Billy wrote an impassioned plea to English football's foremost players.

2

Meredith's union

'It is one of the rudiments of political economy that an article is worth what it will fetch, and this surely applies to the services of a football player.'

– *Sporting Life*, 18 December 1907.

December 1907 – In the Victorian age of the free market, meritocracy and the self-made man, football has missed out. Billy Meredith is out to change that by founding a new footballers' trade union.

The sporting media offer their wholehearted support for his campaign but do so alongside another conflicting, majority-held opinion: the idea is doomed to fail. Journalists remember the last attempt of this sort, but so does Billy.

Although far from a figurehead, Meredith himself was part of the Association Footballers' Union (1898–1901) which sought to reform the transfer system and oppose the introduction of a maximum wage, the arrival of which caused the union's dissolution. Football's regulations were and are anti-free market, anti-Victorian and undoubtedly anti-footballer.

That is not to say, though, these regulations were originally mean-spirited – not consciously, at least. The FA desperately desired a level playing field unaffected by imbalanced financial resources. This reflected the era's dominant philosophy: the 'play the game' ideal taught in public schools nationwide.

To 'play the game', to these men, was, and is, to partake in sport not with the intention of victory or financial gain, but of self-improvement, of cultivating 'pluck and nerve' , gentleness, restraint, selflessness, fairness, humility and discipline. These were seen as distinctly masculine traits which created the good English soldier. So dominant was this philosophy that by the 19th century's end, it was dubbed the public school 'games cult'.

Its consequence is a militaristic hyper-masculinity present in the minds of several generations of middle- and upper-class men. The problem, it has become clear, is in how these men adjusted to the rise of *professional* football. Some find it easy enough, re-emphasising the benefits of team sports. Others, not so much. Scouts founder Robert Baden-Powell believes that professional football is 'a vicious game' when it prevents 'lads playing the game themselves' by making them 'mere onlookers.' Local *Manchester Evening News* columnist A.C.C. even blames the city's poor recruitment figures during the Boer War on its penchant for watching elite football. A recent investigation into these complaints has shown Manchester's working class are in fact deprived of any significant exercise space and the city's air is dense with pollution. Anyone looking at the Town Hall could have determined that. Its velvet-like exterior may appear luxurious, but it's simply soot settled oppressively on its roof.

Those in senior FA positions justify their involvement in the professional game by imposing strict restrictions on its management. The public school masculine ideals are ever so restrictive, and its graduates never seem able to break free of its grasp. On the pitch, this means severe punishments for bad language, aggressive conduct and 'excessive' emotional interactions between players, referees and supporters. Off it, this means restricting the influence of money. With this in mind, the retain-and-transfer system began, effectively making footballers owned property by ensuring they can only move teams if their current club permits them, even if their contract – and thus payment – has ended.

The maximum wage arrived in 1901, the year of Queen Victoria's death. It is fundamentally un-Victorian. And un-Edwardian, for that matter. While there is no single set of values dominant in 1907 English society – one must only look to the suffragette movement, to debates over Irish Home Rule or the role of the House of Lords or the new Liberal government's welfare schemes to see that – two key ideas are relatively uncontested: the free market and support for the self-made man. These concepts have a century of support behind them, but were alien to the football world in 1901, and remain so now. Football's administrators are preoccupied with the 'play the game' ideal.

The original union failed because it was unable to captivate the average footballer, who, rarely receiving anything close to the maximum wage, had less compulsion to remove it. It's these memories of 1898–1901 that inspire newspapers' scepticism at Meredith's new venture, but he has it well thought through.

Thirty-three-year-old Billy's personal experience and motivation make him uniquely placed to drive this forward. Two decades ago, his intolerance for unwanted authority began down the pits as a teenage miner. His years in the grub exposed him to regular workplace strikes during which his mother, Jane, would receive bread and potato deliveries from the union. Billy's recent FA suspension has only intensified his hostility to those above him, but not quite as much as his dismay at the demise of those close to him.

First, lads who Billy idolised died, and then lads who idolised him died. All left little behind. In June 1902, it was Jimmy Ross, Meredith's hero from Preston's 'Invincibles'. Di Jones, a mentor and team-mate, followed two months later. More recently, only in April, poor Tommy Blackstock, a young Scot playing for United's reserves, collapsed after heading a heavy wet ball. The coroner declared this sequence of events inconsequential to his death, meaning United paid his family no compensation. These are the cases close to Billy, but there are others. Plenty of others. Not all of these men died due to poor player welfare, but such was the shackled system in which they operated that these stars of the day left their families financially destitute. Billy is inspired by their plight.

His own experience motivates him, too. He had plenty of thinking time during his long FA suspension and, although he's happily settled in at the in-form, table-topping Manchester United, he remains resentful. Fortunately, similar feelings are present in United's squad, debated over hotpot suppers at Meredith's house because hands-off secretary Ernest Mangnall leaves much of the team's tactical decisions and plans to the players themselves. Once the on-pitch logistics are coordinated, there's time to debate other issues.

Billy's crucial ally is United captain Charlie Roberts, who grew up in railway town Darlington and, like Billy, began working as a young teen in a traditional unionised industry. The pair are bright and determined. Learning from the failed union, they believe success will be dependent on establishing a permanent office with a full-time, non-playing secretary and achieving large numbers in members and funds. As for objectives, well, little has changed. The new union will contest what the old one opposed: restrictions on a footballer's right to earn what he's worth.

***

Two days after United's defeat at The Wednesday, the *Association Football Players' and Trainers' Union* is formally founded at Harry Stafford's Imperial Hotel. Billy Meredith chairs a stimulating three-hour meeting, attended by the full squads of Manchester United and Manchester City and representatives from clubs across the north, from Aston Villa to Newcastle.

Billy is vitalised by it all. He plays at Bank Street at the weekend – United beat Bristol City – before travelling to London to host the Players' Union's second meeting. Membership swells so quickly that the union is geographically divided. Meredith will sit on Lancashire's committee.

Public reaction to all this is generally positive but with an undercurrent of mistrust reflecting the 'play the game' ideal. Trevor Burleigh from Ealing, for example, writes in to his local paper to call Billy 'the best outside-right in the world'. Trevor wishes the union success. The important 'but' follows: 'Success to it, but please do not strike.'

3

Meredith in excelsis

*'Over and over again I have bemoaned
modern players trying aerial football. The
United delighted me by passing all along
the ground. This is the puzzle of scientific
football. The United provide an object lesson
to every team.'*

– Jimmy Catton, *Athletic News.*

December 1907 – Manchester United's Bank Street ground is a deplorable bog with sawdust liberally sprinkled in the goalmouths and centre circle to dry out the surface. Captain Charlie Roberts competes for the coin toss in drizzling rain, but twice the referee tries and twice the coin gets stuck upright in the mud. The thwarted trio, Charlie cracking a smile, move almost into the stands, where United win the toss, electing to kick with the wind at their backs.

A frantic game immediately ensues in front of 30,000. Today's visitors are Manchester City and Christmastime derbies are always special. Harry Moger's shins deny City's James Conlin, George Wall whistles a shot over the crossbar and soon puts United in front with a deflected shot from Billy Meredith's cross. Charlie Roberts's ball-winning and passing abilities from deep prevent City from regularly escaping their own third, but Moger is thrice called into action in quick succession and charges out of his goal nearly to the corner flag to tackle, and foul, the lively Conlin. This first pause in a breathless fixture allows a City player's eyes to be cleared of mud. And then it begins again, and soon Meredith's crossed free kick is satisfyingly headed in off the upright by Sandy Turnbull.

At half-time, City's blue shirts are almost indistinguishable from United's red so they don fresh ones. So does United goalkeeper Moger, but Roberts and his outfield team-mates re-emerge in their mud-spattered uniforms. They resemble fighters and fight they will in this half. Turnbull's high shot extends United's advantage but City soon get one back. Former Blue Herbert Burgess is then forced off injured, and at Charlie's orders, United adapt to a 2-3-4 formation. Inside-right Jimmy Bannister abandons Meredith to join the half-back line, replacing Dick Duckworth who shifts backwards into defence. With 20 minutes remaining, double-goalscorer Turnbull is sent off for a succession of fouls and despite the protestations of a confused and angry crowd, United must play with nine men. Billy Meredith looks behind him and sees Charlie Roberts rolling up his now brown sleeves. In an inspired captain's performance that Billy will remember for life, Charlie orchestrates the shut-out and a United victory.

* * *

Meredith is fully cleaned up and smartly dressed two days later as he chairs the Players' Union's third meeting. At Nottingham's Maypole Hotel, United's reserve goalkeeper Herbert Broomfield is named permanent secretary. He must combine both these roles with his day job as a master painter and decorator in Northwich.

Another two days on and Bank Street hosts 45,000 for the Christmas Day fixture against Bury. Emphasising their unparalleled supremacy thus far, a 2-1 victory establishes a nine-point lead for United at the table's top. Praise is forthcoming from all quarters. If Billy picks up a newspaper, he'll read the headline:

'MEREDITH IN EXCELSIS'

His goal against Bury was delightful, a lashed strike in off the left post. Aged 33, he leads off the pitch and inspires on it in one of his finest seasons. Some label him 'the greatest forward of all time', others 'the star artist', 'the side's greatest factor' or 'the mastermind'.

With Billy's starring skill, Manchester United are a drawing power equivalent to the Preston North End side of his youth. Football enthusiasts travel from afar to see the club dominating headlines each week and, in falling in love with Meredith's skill, Englishmen nationwide develop a soft spot for United.

A draw with North End concludes United's schedule for 1907, a year which began with the debuts of four ex-City players and ends with that same quartet having catapulted the Reds to the top of the table. As the new year begins, Herbert Broomfield occupies the Players' Union's new offices, conveniently only metres away from Billy's successful sports shop in St Peter's Square.

The Union makes positive progress under Broomfield and Meredith's direction. United president John Henry Davies has now proudly accepted the position of union president and a support fund is created for the family of Frank Levick, whose recent death was linked to a broken collarbone suffered while playing for Sheffield United. Without insurance, no compensation was delivered, and so Broomfield asks the FA for permission to host a fundraising match. They agree, and the FA Council wish the union every success, thereby offering them official recognition.

On the pitch, such were United's dizzying pre-Christmas heights, a minor January/February hiccup represents a major thud back down to earth. Their free-scoring run is over. From December's 0-0 draw with Preston until 14 March, United do not score more than one goal in a league game and they win only three of six matches. Injuries are the likely cause. Even Broomfield has to step in as reserve goalkeeper once when Moger is out and the ever-dependable Charlie Roberts picks up a couple of knocks, too. To miss a match infuriates Roberts – though he still attends the games as a spectator when injured – but it hurts him less this time around. He and his wife May have had a second son, called William, and after losing their firstborn in November, they cherish these precious first months.

* * *

United's first-half-of-the-season excellence makes March defeats to Arsenal and Liverpool inconsequential. Nine games remain and the question is no longer whether United will be champions, but whether they will achieve a record points total.

As in United's promotion year, Mangnall and Davies have made a late-season signing to ensure success. While in London to take on Arsenal, Mangnall negotiated with Southend for the transfer of Harold Halse, a 21-year-old centre-forward with an outrageous record of 82 goals already this season. Such wild scoring statistics are made more credible when he nets a minute into his debut. United beat The Wednesday and Bank Street's crowd is infatuated with their new striker.

A breathless April begins at Bristol City, one-time title challengers whose form has nosedived since the new year. They nevertheless take a point off United with a 1-1 draw, even without their centre-half talisman 'Fatty' Wedlock, who has taken Charlie's place in the England team. It is a decision which causes some agitation. Roberts is widely viewed as the Football League's foremost centre-half. Yes, his three performances for England in 1905 had, by his own admission, been decent rather than outstanding, but he helped the side to the Home Championship and he has almost led United to the title. Many critics think ignorance is to blame. When Charlie was once called before an FA commission to discuss a spectator misconduct incident, a committee member had to ask who he was. The same man was part of the FA selection committee. Public examples such as this ensure the clamour for Roberts's inclusion, especially from the northern public and press, never dies down.

United follow the draw at Bristol by beating Everton at Goodison Park meaning, on return to Clayton, they need only one point to secure the championship. The sense of occasion for Mangnall and Davies is heightened by the opportunity to finally unveil the fruits of their hard behind-the-scenes labour. In the club's offices, reporters instinctively lean forwards to get a better view of the impressive model on display. Manchester United's new stadium is laid out before them. Old Trafford remains the likely home.

The on-pitch display fails to match the excitement this generates. United's mediocre form is evidenced in all its ugliness. Meredith is away with Wales, and Roberts and Halse are injured, but there's no excuse for defeat. George Wall misses a second-half penalty, some claim deliberately due to unrest in the squad – who aren't happy with the Bank Street conditions – and Notts County score late on. United's coronation is delayed.

But then all of a sudden, it's not. Defeats for The Wednesday and Manchester City mean neither club can match United's current points total of 48. The Reds are champions. They truly have walked backwards into their crown. Before New Year's Day, Mangnall's team had won over 80 per cent of their games. That figure has halved since. United fail to score in their three games over Easter, earning just one point. It's a peculiarly painful time for supporters. Their team, which only recently touched the extreme of brilliance, has now reached the other extreme of ineffectiveness. 'We don't seem to be able to do right now; at one time we could not do wrong,' one remarks.

The team do finally play up for the season's conclusion, though tellingly Roberts, Burgess, both Turnbulls and Duckworth are all absent. United's poor form is injury-inflicted. Mangnall used 15 players before New Year but 25 after. Billy Meredith, though, is present, having missed only one game, while playing for Wales. He may be 33, but he may also be the league's fittest player. Sandy Turnbull has scored 25 goals in 30 games, Harold Halse has made a key impact since March, and Charlie Roberts has led the team fantastically. He is described as 'the star among stars'.

Despite three wins from their last 11 games – this torrid form meaning only 8,000 watch Bank Street's title celebrations – victory over Preston North End gives United a record-breaking points total. The few thousand hardcore in attendance savour the occasion. A red-and-white 'Rocca Brigade' umbrella juts out as thousands gather in front of the grandstand to celebrate the first Mancunian club bringing the title to Cottonopolis. John Henry Davies is beaming, throwing down souvenirs from his seat to the supporters waiting below.

Even after eight league games, United's busy April is far from over. Billy Meredith scores a stunning long shot in the first-ever Charity Shield. A 1-1 draw against Southern League champions Queens Park Rangers means a replay will follow, but there's no time for it now. United instead race to Newcastle, where they win 4-1 in a Players' Union fundraiser.

On the same day, the FA's Rules Revision Committee recommends that the maximum wage, transfer fee, and signing-on fee are all abolished. The FA Council approves these recommendations, doing so before the Players' Union has seriously brought the issue forward. The union's strength and its businesslike capabilities have no doubt encouraged the speedy action. However, two-thirds of clubs will need to vote for abolition to change the rules, and turkeys don't vote for Christmas.

Rounding April off after eight league games, the title won, Charity Shield drawn and a successful fundraising match, United win the Manchester Cup for the first time since their 1902 reformation. Jimmy Bannister scores the only goal in a 1-0 win against Bury. There has been no time for a title-winning parade, and there won't be because the hectic schedule does not stop here. Far from it.

4

United enter Europe

'If you come from Paris to Budapest, you
think you are in Moscow. But if you go
from Moscow to Budapest, you think you
are in Paris.'

– Gyorgy Ligeti, Hungarian composer.

May 1908 – Manchester United's title-winning squad is relishing the beautiful, unhurried 12-hour journey out of bustling Vienna and towards the Hungarian capital, Budapest. As they travel with the current down one of Europe's great rivers, the Danube, they watch the busy Austrian city fade away, replaced on the riverbanks by old castles and magnificent stately homes. These are soon supplanted by hundreds of water mills, not so far removed from those of Lancashire. The Danube's current turns the corn-grinding mills and customers arrive in small boats to take the resulting flour away.

On their first European tour, Mangnall's Reds are following British teams big and small. Britons playing football on the continent began with sailors, port workers and school students, but it is now a path well-trodden by Britain's elite clubs; it's about time United took it. The English champions are ever so glad they have.

As United's ferry passes an idyllic mountain stretching down to the river's edge and then a ruined castle, the noise of approaching Budapest gradually begins to overcome the churn of the steam-powered vessel. Mangnall stirs from his relaxed state – the journey has taken several hours – and enters into full secretarial mode.

Ernest has come a long way from wheeling and dealing at Turf Moor, chasing elephants and the like, and his keenness to make the most of United's wealth is unwavering. His boss J.H. Davies is equally as ambitious and rich enough to fund a trip such as this one. Together, they have brought United level with the country's most forward-thinking clubs, and perhaps they are the foremost now. They are the champions, after all, and with pure financial bonuses limited by strict FA regulations, a holiday like this – albeit a busman's – is an excellent reward for the players' championship-winning season.

A faded, pale blue evening sky greets United in Budapest and the river reflects a soft moon. The Hungarian capital looks extraordinary in such circumstances. Magnificent bridges hang over the Danube and it is still early enough to see the stunning parliament building, completed just four years ago, stretch across the riverbank in all its symmetrical, gothic glory.

In Budapest, United are at a long trip's end. They first headed from Calais to Paris, where they saw the sights, and then by train to Zurich, and Lucerne, Innsbruck and Munich. They have played in several cities and been greeted and hosted by British consuls and other significant immigrant figures. The games have been straightforward enough, against physical but unchallenging continental opposition. United have been able to play around a bit. After scoring a fourth goal against a combined Zurich XI, goalkeeper Harry Moger ventured out to play at inside-right, Billy Meredith dropped into defence with Sandy Turnbull and George Wall took up the position between the sticks.

Meredith was mainly seeking some space to play in back in defence. His continental stardom means he's often found himself marked by three or four men. 'They would have followed me right through the town!' he joked, the first time.

Despite the excessive attention, Billy has enjoyed the games for what they are: a bit of fun. They've socialised with their opponents after, too. Many are English-speaking, having lived in England before, hence their football ability, but it's the others who entertain Billy most.

'The players are a cheery, sporting set, and they do their best to make us at home and to help us enjoy ourselves,' Billy writes home.

'If you tell the players you are speaking to that you like his necktie, he will at once pull it off and hand it to you with a smile. How different the Britisher!'

The only stain on this experience came in Prague. It had started off fine enough, Jack Picken and Jimmy Bannister scoring one each in victory over the SK Slavia side, but when the scoreline repeated itself the following day, the atmosphere deteriorated suddenly. Slavia's dismayed fans reacted furiously and launched a semi-riot, greeted by mounted police who drew swords to protect United's players from what the players later called 'a wild, uncivilised mob who made no secret of carrying revolvers and daggers'.

Billy reflected without surprise, highlighting the 'bitter racial feeling' present in Prague, the biggest city in the Kingdom of Bohemia, which is developing its own national identity within the massive Austro-Hungarian Empire. The point he alludes to is correct. United are gaining first-hand evidence of Europe's rising nationalistic tensions.

Arrived in Budapest, Meredith listens as Mangnall, acting the schoolteacher, gather his players around. He hands out room keys and explains their commitments for the next few days. United have a couple of games, but plenty of time to relax, including this evening. Billy's room-mate is Sandy Turnbull. The pair are the squad's main pranksters, but their efforts on this trip have been a little limited. By the time they settle into the luxurious Grand Hotel Hungaria, they have realised that their regular japes of taking laces out of boots, tying them together or leaving precious items in their mate's pockets don't go down well with the frowning hotel workers.

Heading for their rooms after the relaxed but lengthy journey, Meredith says he'd pay a pound for a pot of good English tea. 'I'd give five pounds for a real British steak and chips,' claims Herbert Burgess. And he's probably telling the truth. The boys know the food is meant to be good, but they just can't enjoy it themselves. They head out into Budapest, not expecting to find tea or steak and chips, and they'd be right. Coffee and goulash, more likely.

The squad did get some home comforts back in Vienna when a group of Oldham immigrants employed in the city paid the dear fee to gain entry, seeking to secure a taste of home, and belted out the familiar English chant: 'Are we downhearted?' United's players were at first shocked, and then greatly cheered by the familiar refrain. Their good mood was maintained by the referee, who Meredith called 'the feature of the match' and 'in a class by himself'. Roberts described him as 'easily worth a pound a minute'. Rather than standing in the centre of the field and following the play, he slightly misunderstood and instead dashed up and down the touchline in a 'tremendous state of excitement'. His display left Meredith, Roberts and their team-mates in fits of laughter.

Despite the erratic officiating, football has really begun to blossom in Budapest and Vienna, the two cities linked at the centre of the Austro-Hungarian Empire. Vienna is the empire's largest city and capital, home to an explosive fusion of culture and thinking. In this first decade of the 20th century, Sigmund Freud develops his ideas of psychoanalysis, Adolf Hitler his thoughts around Nazism and Theodor Herzl considers Zionism. All in Vienna.

Football here, meanwhile, was developed by British immigrants. An invitation from a Prague club, named Regatta, brought football to the area, and it proliferated at speed. In 1902, Austria and Hungary faced off in the first international match between two non-British European teams. Austria won 5-0. United achieve a similarly emphatic scoreline in their games against Viennese opposition, two 4-0s and a 5-0, but they are impressed by the opposition, and tell them as much. These compliments are ecstatically received.

Now in Budapest, the Reds take on a combined team of MTK, Ferencváros and BTC. On a strange-shaped pitch, 130 yards long but only 65 yards wide, United concede a shock goal within five minutes.[16] The Hungarian crowd go berserk, their roar comparable to the loudest heard at Bank Street, but their enthusiasm settles rather than shakes United's men, who consequently play up a gear. After goals from Jack Picken and Dick Duckworth, the team go hard but with some enjoyment. Meredith takes advantage, toying with the opposition when given space. They are not so used to wingers who go this way and that rather than heading straight down the line. United eventually win 6-2. As the team leave the ground, Meredith is approached by a Budapest local, who proves particularly keen on the Welsh star. He wants to buy his boots. After some to and fro, Meredith passes over his footwear for a small fee. His team-mates are greatly amused.

The Hungarians are a powerful team but lack a slice of serious quality on the wings. That said, long gone are the days when these European sides were nothing but a collection of English immigrants. Local talent has flourished in the last two decades. In Budapest, youngsters grow up playing in *grunds*, empty space left unbuilt on between houses as Budapest rapidly expands. It's not so different from Manchester. The ground is sticky sand, reducing the ball's bounce. As a result, fast, technical players develop, like Ferencváros's goalscoring superstar, 19-year-old Imre Schlosser.

Budapest is a relatively new city whose culture revolves around its many coffee shops, in which everything and anything is discussed, from simple gossip to politics, the arts

---

16 For context, a standard football pitch in the modern era is 115 x 74 yards.

and sport, including football.[17] The eager-to-learn Hungarian players greatly admire United's quality. They review post-match Duc-Ro-Bell's skill as individuals and a collective, Meredith's individualistic style and the inside-forward's clever support.

Meanwhile, when Manchester United's players settle down for a coffee in their hotel, they're told progress has been made on a new ground. The team will definitely be moving in the next season or so.

'We are more than glad of it,' Meredith comments. 'Apart from the nature of its surroundings, Clayton is the worst playing piece in the country. At Old Trafford there will be purer air, a better ground, and larger "gates". So by all means let us go to Old Trafford as quickly as we can.'

Back home, newspapers explain to supporters that United intended to move to Old Trafford in readiness for the new season, but the aim is now for Christmas. Even that seems a little optimistic given the breathtaking targeted capacity of 100,000.

On Sunday 24 May, United play the tour's final game and make global news in the process, and not because goalkeeper Harry Moger scores from the penalty spot, nor due to the 7-0 scoreline.

The Reds escape from the ground under police cover and a flurry of jagged stones. They dominated the second game just as they did the first, and the complications came not in the result but with the referee, who at one point sought to send two or three United players off. His limited English made for a tricky conversation. The United players instead

---

17 A fact which proves significant, Jonathan Wilson says. 'In Britain, football tended to be discussed in pubs by men standing up with a pint in their hand. In the coffee houses, the tendency was for customers to sit down at a table, and so it became possible to illustrate tactical arguments using the simple props of a cup, a spoon or a sugar bowl. Once that level of abstraction was reached, it was a short step to begin drawing diagrams, something that would have seemed preposterous to most in Britain at the time.'

physically guided him over and worked things out after some time, explaining they were following the rules as they are played in England. Watching from afar, and believing the physical contact with the referee to be some kind of assault, the furious crowd responded. The game was paused for some time, eventually restarting with the 'three unscrupulous players', as a Hungarian newspaper describes them, still on the pitch.

'The audience of ten thousand on Sunday left the arena with very mixed emotions,' said Budapest's *Sport-Világ*.

'On the one hand, with admiration, for the brilliant technique we have never seen before, and on the other hand, with the ingrained awareness that the champions of England are selected from a rough population that is not at the most basic level of education.

'No wonder, after so much rudeness, the agitated audience wanted to beat the English, who left under police cover, but also the referee, whose weakness was one of the reasons for the incident. He did not escape the stones when he left.'

Mounted police protected United from the barrage of stones. One player was struck in the head but it left nothing but a bruise.

***

United arrive home in Manchester shortly before four o'clock, five days after the Budapest drama. A medium-sized crowd of friends, family and some supporters give them a hearty welcome. The boys have been gone for more than three weeks. Mangnall steps off the train, his cheeks tinted from the continental sun, and declares the tour an 'unqualified success', with the exception of the engagements with Budapest and the Slavia Club. Not entirely 'unqualified', then.

While Mangnall delivers his thoughts to the eager, waiting reporters, the United players catch up with their families. Billy's Ellen and their daughters are there, and Charlie is met by May and their young son William.

'You say the Buda Pesth team dined with us after the match,' Mangnall says. 'That was not true. We have not seen the Buda Pesth team since the match, and, of course, we did not dine with them. We will not meet with either them or Slavia again.'[18]

The stones were unpleasant, but the tour, costing the club £1,183, was successful. The players have been justly rewarded for an excellent season, United have shown their quality on the continent, and the club are now global news. In July, a report on the Budapest match reaches the New Zealand newspapers. This little Clayton club have gone global.

---

18 United will not go on another European tour until 1927, and do not return to Budapest for some 57 years. Herbert Burgess goes back sooner than the team. He plays for MTK Budapest from 1914-18 and, three years later, answers an advert in the *Athletic News* in 1921 asking for a British manager to take charge of MTK.

John Henry's day in the sun

'Meredith's twisted legs and pinched face
caricature one's idea of what figure of a
man the athlete should present. He is fleet
of foot – he is something more than a mere
sprinter – makes the ball completely sensitive
to his touch, and in these times, when our
footballers seem to be no sort of individualist
at all, he proves the efficacy of dribbling,
the most fascinating of all the arts of
forward play.'

– *London Evening Standard*, 31 August 1908.

August 1908 – Two men did not return with Manchester United from Europe. Chairman J.J. Bentley developed gout while in Vienna and stayed there to recover, accompanied by a rather bulky nurse in centre-forward Jimmy Turnbull. They remained in Vienna long enough to be joined by England's national team, undertaking their own first full continental tour. Neither George Wall nor Charlie Roberts were involved, with Bristol's 'Fatty' Wedlock preferred at centre-half again.

When well enough to return home, Bentley gifts Turnbull a gold watch in gratitude. Both men are present as United's squad and staff assemble at Davies's Moseley Hall in Cheadle, finally afforded the opportunity to properly celebrate their title victory after playing another charity fundraiser match from which £105 is donated to build Manchester's new infirmary.

Ernest Mangnall presents the championship winners' medals to the players, trainers and officials. There's an additional medal, too, specially reserved for the club's saviour-in-chief. Harry Stafford appreciates the gesture, and the chance to catch up with his old pal, Major the St Bernard, who otherwise runs around with Elsie.

J.J. Bentley soon brings out the league trophy. John Henry receives it ecstatically and the portly, bespectacled mid-40s man beams beneath his walrus moustache. There are few better days than this. He's surrounded by his family and people whose lives he is fascinated by and whose sporting prowess evokes passion in him that he simply didn't know he had.

Fresh off the back of their long-awaited celebrations, United travel to London for a second stab at the Charity Shield. Jimmy Turnbull's hat-trick, including two headers from Meredith crosses, helps United to a convincing victory over QPR.

'Perhaps the feature of the match was the finished display given by Willie Meredith,' reports the *Daily Mirror*.

'At times, his display was positively dazzling. He is still the best outside-right playing, despite the fact that Father Time is inexorably drawing his active career to a close.

'Charles Roberts at centre-half, the United captain, was as good as a sixth forward. As an intelligent half-back display his work would be hard to beat.'

Davies receives the Shield, United's players add another medal to their burgeoning collections and £1,304 is raised for charity.[19]

A smaller but admirable amount is raised back in Manchester as a Harry Stafford-captained Newton Heath old boys side faces United's reserves. Donations are made to the families of 76 men tragically killed in a recent colliery

---

19 Equivalent to £200,000 in 2023.

disaster. The old boys win 4-3 in a game punctuated by roars of laughter as the veterans find their limbs stiffening up late on. Harry's Imperial Hotel hosts a series of knocked-back drinks as the Heathens catch up and reminisce. United return from London with sights set on besting last season's achievements.

6

One lucky horseshoe

*'Clayton is not by any means an ideal
place to say farewell to the English Cup
competition. There's nothing romantic about
it. At Manchester on Saturday, I found that
the locals were inclined to be apologetic over
United's enclosure, and such remarks as "wait
till we go to our new ground, though!" were
frequently heard.'*

– *Liverpool Echo*, 8 February 1909.

January 1909 – Manchester United's English Cup campaign
is to begin with a home match against Brighton. The
players undergo preparations in Sandiway, Cheshire, where
considerable excitement prevails amongst the reigning league
champions, not only for cup kick-off, but because progress has
been made on a new ground.

Manchester United's Old Trafford move was officially
confirmed back in November and plans were duly deposited
with the Stretford Urban Council for review and approval.
Ever since, John Henry Davies has had labourers ready with
some hope that the stadium might open for the 1909/10 season.

The design's grandness is punctuated by its advertised
capacity of a breathtaking 100,000 people. Players and
pressmen are enamoured by what they hear, but excitable
anticipation is not felt by everyone involved with the club.
The supporters have backed United in all its incarnations,

red and white, blue and white, green and gold, in Newton Heath, Bradford and Clayton. They have stood by it through significant strife and now their club will be moved five miles away to the exact opposite side of Manchester. In fact, Manchester United will no longer play in Manchester itself, but in Trafford. It will be the furthest any Football League club has moved.

As the players pound the soft Cheshire ground three days before United's match against Brighton, it's announced that the Stretford District Council has 'to all intents and purposes' approved the Old Trafford plans. The pitch will be sunk by nine feet to allow for a larger capacity, the club's offices will have an electric lift and the players will have billiard, reading, recreation and massage rooms, a gymnasium and potentially even a restaurant. Captain Charlie Roberts will be able to hold his well-deserved forthcoming benefit at the magnificent new ground, which has been designed by the pre-eminent Scottish architect Archibald Leitch. He's also designing Tottenham Hotspur's new ground at White Hart Lane and the race is on for which club's stadium will open first.

United are currently fourth in Division One with a good record of 13 wins from 22 games. Mangnall's men very much have their sights on repeating last year's triumph and looked likely to do so with five successive wins to open the season before injuries to key players, most crucially captain Charlie Roberts, interrupted their flow. A couple of heavy defeats followed, including 6-1 at Sunderland. They have rebounded now but are all too willing to take the distraction of the English Cup.

Training is light in Cheshire, with nothing more than a 'long walk' on Thursday. Due to some knocks, the side won't be selected until they reach Manchester on Saturday lunchtime, with 15 men to pick from. Southern League team Brighton are the opposition.

Billy Meredith assists a woeful game's only goal, scored by Harold Halse, but then watches the final minutes on the touchline having received his first-ever dismissal for kicking out at Brighton's left-back after receiving one heavy tackle too many.

'It is a thousand pities that so great a player did not conquer his wrath,' comments the *Athletic News*. It says a great deal about expectations of masculinity within football that Meredith receives more widespread criticism for this incident than for his alleged bribery of Alec Leake four years earlier. He has broken a key tenet of the athletic masculinity espoused by those running the game: emotional stoicism, the ability to reign in one's anger. He receives a harsh month-long suspension, but at least United are through.

Meredith dedicates his freer schedule to the Players' Union, whose once comfortable, fast-growing status is being deliberately challenged by the FA. There are now more than 1,000 members and at the union's recent AGM, its objectives were publicly re-stated: an end to restrictions on earnings, allow players to negotiate their own contracts and transfer agreements and take a cut of any transfer fee. These intentions were criticised over Christmas as 'the dreams of visionaries'. An FA councillor complains, 'There is not one word of loyalty to the FA.' Burnley's chairman, who was best man at Mangnall's wedding, describes the players as having 'inward greed', declaring, 'We were running football years before they knew anything about it!' The applecart is teetering on upset.

Billy is suspended for United's next cup match, a home draw against Everton. While training in Cheshire again, Sandy Turnbull's house is broken into and thieves make off with his 1904 English Cup medal, won with City. He's devastated, and his team-mates are on his behalf. Sandy asks Billy for assistance but the union can do little but offer their sympathies in this instance.

On matchday, several thousand stand outside Bank Street listening to the cheering, painting a picture in their head of the action. The ground was packed a full 90 minutes before kick-off and crushes have regularly developed, one causing a substantial brick wall to fall down, leaving several injured and some trampled. Down at Portsmouth on the same day, three fans are hospitalised with broken legs after similar incidents. Only the crowd's community-like nature and good fortune prevents fatalities. Harold Halse does the job for United again in another one-goal win.

Blackburn Rovers are next. They are in good form and it's expected that this tie will go to a replay.

Back in Cheshire, the Reds enjoy a team stroll through the Delamere Forest, during which they stumble upon a whole horseshoe. Trainer Fred Bacon is superstitious enough to count it lucky and he places it in the kit basket. Its effect appears immediate, for Charlie Roberts and Dick Duckworth regain fitness during midweek training at Sandiway.

Another bumper Bank Street crowd greets United, a strong sun beating down through the chemical smog. Louis Rocca grins as that wonderful Saturday noise of clicking turnstiles begins just after one o'clock. From then on, a constant, sometimes unmanageable, stream of people proceed into the ground. The police and St John Ambulance Brigade are kept busy, pulling fainting supporters out of the huge mass.

Twelve minutes in, Roberts passes wide to George Wall, whose steady pass is received by Sandy Turnbull and struck home low. It's a tight game and Bacon's lucky horseshoe now does the trick. Harry Moger comes up with several big saves to retain a somewhat fortunate advantage up to half-time, after which United find that unmatchable level they have so often played at in these last 18 months. Roberts wins the ball back in his own half and feeds Jimmy Turnbull, who lofts the ball over the out-rushing Ashcroft's head. He scores two more, and so does Sandy to make it a hat-trick apiece for United's unrelated pair of Turnbulls. Bacon's horseshoe is mounted upon a wood panel, inscribed with 'Manchester United Football Club' and decorated in red and white. It's hung in the training quarters and guarded closely. Footballers are a superstitious bunch.

While United thrash Blackburn, Players' Union secretary Herbert Broomfield is down the road in St Peter's Square.

Letters between Broomfield and his FA counterpart Frederick Wall are no longer courteous, instead littered with petty, sassy remarks amidst the football world's simmering tensions. The union still seeks the maximum wage's abolition, but this battle regards another issue.

The union believe footballers have the right to take action in a court of law when a club fails to meet their obligations as an employer. As Broomfield writes to Wall in February 1909: 'We are not convinced that we are expected to regard seriously an opinion that a football player forfeits a common legal right on entering into a professional engagement with a football club.'

The FA disagree. They believe any player–club disagreement must come before them first. That the union has initiated legal proceedings against several clubs angers them greatly and they set about reducing the union's power base. While Broomfield can occasionally be overzealous, FA officials are long-used to the tactics of the English establishment. They do their dirty work privately and patiently. Last summer they offered an amnesty on financial misconduct to all Football League clubs, a move removing the threat of players snitching on clubs' wrongdoing to the FA, as Meredith did in 1905. The clubs have now accepted this amnesty, a decision league founder William McGregor says proves 'Association Football today is nothing less than an organised hypocrisy.'

As February ends and the FA/union dispute escalates, London's Palace Theatre hosts the first colour film in the United Kingdom. Audiences leave shocked, amazed and enamoured. Manchester talks of something equally grand as Old Trafford finally receives full council approval. Work on what is described as a 'glorious amphitheatre' commences immediately.

Billy Meredith marks his return from suspension with a stand-out performance for Wales in a 3-2 victory over Scotland. He joins up with United in Cheshire immediately after, preparing for the FA Cup quarter-final at Burnley.

Pennine snow has somewhat dampened numbers, but

a bubbling Turf Moor atmosphere develops regardless, particularly when the home side, Burnley, start strong and gain the lead. United struggle to claw things back in the tough conditions but Fred Bacon's lucky horseshoe does its job. With just 18 minutes remaining and Burnley set to secure a semi-final berth, referee Herbert Bamlett declares the blizzard conditions unplayable. In fact, Bamlett's hands are so cold he asks Charlie Roberts to blow for time instead. Roberts uses the referee's whistle to end the game, much to the home supporters' horror. The atrocious conditions justify the decision, but Burnley's fans have every right to be enraged by the process and outcome: the match will have to be replayed in full.

When the players walk out into more favourable weather on Wednesday, boos swell around Turf Moor. 'Stop the game, it's snowing,' is soon the chant, partly in jest, partly in frustration, which turns to fury by full-time when United have won by three goals to two. Fred Bacon's lucky horseshoe remains hung on the wall.

Victory is particularly impressive given the disruption United's more prominent union members have endured between the two games. On Monday morning, the FA's well-orchestrated behind-the-scenes manoeuvring caused a double hammer blow to the effectiveness and reputation of the Players' Union. First, the FA confirmed the amnesty to clubs in return for 'the promise of loyalty to the FA and honourable observance to the rules' going forward. Later in the same meeting, the FA Council withdrew their recognition of the Players' Union because they 'not only deliberately failed to observe the rules of the FA, but intend to pursue such conduct in future'.

English clubs are now not only aligned with the FA but, due to the second statement, also against their own players. For much of the football-attending public, who implicitly trust the FA, the withdrawal of recognition means the union must be in the wrong. Public and private support of the union is diminished greatly. The union's management committee, Meredith and Roberts included, convene to work out next steps.

*　*　*

Back in January, Meredith wrote a light-hearted article about a dream he'd had, tilted 'If the Pros Struck'. The reaction at the time was bad. Now, it's worse. The press is convinced that plans are afoot to disrupt the upcoming England versus Scotland match. In fact, the FA's selection committee are sufficiently concerned to delay their squad announcement.

As a result, the talk prior to a mouth-watering English Cup semi-final clash between league leaders and three-time cup finalists Newcastle and title-holders and semi-final debutants Manchester United is almost entirely about off-pitch matters. It's a remarkable situation whereby, ahead of his team's most important game of the season, United chairman J.J. Bentley speaks in direct opposition to his own players, representing the majority-held view. 'This cannot be too strongly condemned,' he writes. 'The Union are making the pace too hot to last. They will have their knuckles rapped.'

United and Newcastle are the best teams remaining in the competition. This match feels like the final itself and Charlie Roberts is thankful to receive some additional fortune-bringing items. In addition to Fred Bacon's horseshoe, Charlie is gifted a battered old American coin by one supporter, while another sends a ragged, faded half of an old red and white scarf, explaining he wore it at every cup tie played by Sheffield United when they last won the cup.

The sun bursts through shortly before kick-off and a 50,000-strong crowd sees United attack with more method than Newcastle, supported by an in-form half-back line. Duckworth expertly checks the talents of Stewart and Anderson, and Roberts' pale face bobs up all over the pitch with metronomic regularity. The natural sequel to United's dominance is a goal, and Halse is, yet again, the scorer.

Light cloud dampens the light, rain begins to fall and the pitch gradually begins to churn up during a tense final 15 minutes. Roberts's influence does not diminish in another fine performance that takes Manchester United to their first English Cup Final.

Praise for Charlie and his team is significant but undermined by the continued furore around the union which he helped birth.

When the union receives messages of support from club captains nationwide, the FA are somewhat taken by surprise and turn to more drastic measures, adding a new line to the registration forms footballers must sign at the start of each season: 'I undertake to observe the rules, regulations and by-laws of the Football Association.' This, they think, will prevent union members from taking clubs to court. But elsewhere in London, union secretary Herbert Broomfield is meeting with the General Federation of Trade Unions (GFTU), a national body representing 700,000 workmen across several industries. Membership of this body would provide the players with the necessary financial and tactical support to take on the FA. But when Broomfield and the GFTU explain that any strike action will be postponed until after the England versus Scotland match, this admission of a potential strike relights the fire of press disgust and any public support lent to the players and to Broomfield is withdrawn in the most immediate sense.

The international match goes ahead. United winger George Wall scores two fine goals in victory over Scotland on the Crystal Palace ground, where in just a fortnight he will represent his club in the English Cup Final. Now, the press is certain fresh plans are afoot. They think the cup final itself might not be played. The union wants to strike.

7

Red and white rosettes

*'We do not want to provoke a quarrel, but we
are not slaves – though we are sold like prime
cattle through the columns of the sporting
papers.'*

– Walter Bull (Tottenham Hotspur), writing in
The Modern Man.

April 1909 – In reality, plans to strike for the English Cup
Final appear non-existent. It's possible the union is leaking
false plans to intimidate the FA, but given the subsequent loss
of public support, this seems unlikely. A cynic would suggest
the FA are falsely briefing reporters to diminish the Players'
Union's public support.

The union's keenness to join the Grand Federation of
Trade Unions (GFTU) and be backed by a major force is
clear and understandable, but it first needs to make some
administrative changes. For now, the GFTU's secretary Mr
Appleton advises 'the most cautious procedure' to maintain
public sympathy. Union meetings are held in Birmingham and
Manchester and, upon counsel, it's determined that the FA's
new player registration clause will prove ineffective in court.
The players remain bullish, and they should. They are backed
by the law of the land and if they stay loyal to one another and
stick to their guns, they are likely to win this fight, hence the
FA's panic. Clearly concerned by union members' continued
confidence, the FA propose another rule change to limit its

influence. 'Every professional,' they say, '*APPROVED BY THE COUNCIL*, shall be registered on a form to be supplied by the secretary of this Association.' This could, in theory, see all union members barred from playing.

And yet, when journalists visit union founders Billy Meredith and Charlie Roberts at their hotel ahead of the English Cup Final, this is not what's on the agenda. Some matches, it seems, are simply too momentous to be derailed by off-pitch matters.

'Yes, we ought to win on Saturday at the Palace,' Billy confidently tells a reporter at Chingford's Royal Forest Hotel where Manchester United have been 'training' for some days. A brief excursion away to Leicester for a 3-2 league defeat aside, it's actually been a relaxing few days. They endure an hour's morning run followed by sprint training and a light gym workout. After lunch, they play cricket, golf or croquet. Billy's attempts at golf are laughable. He is built to play football and football only. Alec Downie, on the other hand, is a talented, competition-winning golfer while Halse and Vince Hayes stand out with the cricket bat. In the evenings, the team plays cards, billiards or enjoys a sing-song. Sandy Turnbull's smooth tenor voice is missing for some days as the stocky Scotsman is tucked up in bed with flu. Sandy is also recovering from strained thigh muscles. This is of particular concern for fans who recall that Sandy's 1904 winners' medal was nicked only a few months ago. He'll need to play to get another medal. Mangnall thus brings a well-known specialist to Chingford to treat Sandy.

United's final opposition Bristol City also have injury concerns and send their free-scoring centre-forward Rippon to London to see a surgeon. The two clubs were promoted together in 1906 and have the country's finest centre-halves in Roberts and 'Fatty' Wedlock, who could hardly be more different in style and stature.

Charlie has missed much of United's Chingford stay looking after his daughter in Clayton after she contracted bronchitis. With memories of young Charles' death two years ago heavy on his mind, thankfully Margaret recovers sufficiently to allow Roberts to relax. He joins up with United on Monday, six days before matchday.

Charlie is less assertive in his confidence than Billy Meredith.

'It will be hard luck for us if Sandy Turnbull cannot play,' he admits, while bouncing a tennis ball up and down, 'but Picken is a good lad, and as we are all fit and as happy as we can be with the hotel and golf, I fancy we will do it.'

The newspapers carry endless match previews with an overwhelming focus on United, the reigning English champions deemed the favourites primarily because in Turnbull and Meredith they have the only two previous finalists in either squad. As in 1904, the Welsh winger's face is plastered everywhere, on posters, cartoons in newspapers, cigarette boxes and cards. His name appears in almost every sporting column for a week.

The other storyline centres around the dual rise of United and Bristol, promoted together in 1906, and their centre-halves, Roberts and Wedlock. The pair have competed for England caps for the past few years, Roberts going first aged 21 and then the 26-year-old Wedlock taking over in 1907. The latter has proved himself to be the FA's clear favourite.

Wedlock is a short, fat, stubborn human hurricane. His ability to wreck attacks is hardly paralleled. Of his rival, Charlie says: 'I admire him, because he is a never-give-in kind of chap. He is always on the go and never beaten.' But most agree that Roberts is the better player. Seven inches taller with broad shoulders, he looks and acts the part. He is strong, quick and his leadership is renowned. The pivot of United's team, opposition attacks end at his feet and United's start at his command. If there is one criticism of his game, it is an inability to score more often. Dick Duckworth, Roberts's brilliant half-back partner, is a better striker of the ball.

* * *

Back in Manchester, Mancunians have spent the last few weeks scrambling enough cash together for the London excursion. Some head into town to subscribe to Thomas Cook & Sons' package trip. The travel company have party bookings from practically every industrial town in Lancashire and the north. For six shillings, they offer travel to London, a hot meat breakfast, a three-hour driving tour around London, a hot dinner and then a taxicab to the Crystal Palace ground, which will host the final.

Other fans busy themselves collecting and sending off coupons to Oxo, the stock cube company who have put on a competition for cup final travel and tickets. Oxo is well experienced in sports marketing, having sponsored London's Olympic Games only last year. It is a growing industry and one which United benefit from. They are sponsored by Andrews Liver Salts and Wincarnis tonic wine. 'Manchester United have found it very useful in their training for the final tie,' the Wincarnis advert says. It's hardly the catchiest tagline.

Cup fever has coloured Manchester red and white. Rosettes are sold on every street in town, along with similarly coloured umbrellas, scarves and, for a dearer price, miniature metal cup models. Shops are decked out in United colours, including, of course, Charlie Roberts's tobacconists and newsagents, while Harry Stafford's Imperial Hotel hands out souvenirs to all those making the trip.

8

Cockney Reds

'There is a magnetism about the Final of the
Association Cup which is irresistible.'

– *Globe*, 24 April 1909.

April 1909 – It's dark, but Manchester London Road Station's
two windowed upper floors are lit, as is the roof's clock. It's
late, but a couple of horse and carts wait outside, given away
by the occasional snort. A worker pushes a heavy two-wheeled
suitcase trolley up the long ramp in an urgent fashion.

It's gone past 10pm on the eve of the English Cup Final.
A permanent awning stretches out from the station building.
'London' is written on one section. A group of Manchester
United fans walk under the word for luck, as if headed on a
pilgrimage. It's dark inside. Several trains awaiting departure
softly belch steam which rises high, acting as a supportive
cushion to London Road's huge metal roof.[20] There is a
sense of early anticipation. Trains from across the north are
preparing to leave for London's Euston, St Pancras, King's
Cross, and Marylebone stations. There will be 150 special
excursion trains arriving in England's capital in Saturday's
early hours, with nearly every rail company offering services,
including, appropriately, the Lancashire & Yorkshire Railway,
whose workers began kicking a ball in Newton Heath some
30 years ago.

---

20 The station is later renamed Piccadilly.

This group of United fans leave London Road at 11:25pm. More join at Stockport ten minutes later and from there, it's straight to Euston, where they pull in at 4:20am on cup final day. As the train slows and the passengers stir from their slumber, the platform's gas lights illuminate busy workers. It's still mainly dark, the spring sky only just beginning to turn from black to dark blue. With weary eyes, these Reds head instinctively towards the nearest information board. One lights a pipe, another yanks his coat more snuggly around his shoulders. The board is faintly lit, and it volunteers nothing useful.

London's famous 'UNDERGROUND' is not yet open for the day, so these Reds walk out on to Drummond Street, weaving without precise direction through Euston and Russell Squares, past the British Museum and Royal Opera House. They stumble into Covent Garden and encounter a sudden cacophony of commotion, startling them out of any lingering sleepiness. There is an endless bustle of be-capped men scampering between fruit and flower stalls with great purpose. Manchester has its own markets, of course, but this is grander in size and even faster-paced. With no shortage of time to kill, they watch on, fleeing only when a heavy storm mercilessly unloads on them. By the time they find proper cover, they are drenched from head to toe, making the offer of a two-pence 'wash and brush up' service particularly tempting. A couple of them take it and freshen up while the others wait to dry in the spring morning chill.

As the hours tick by, it becomes hard to look down a street without seeing United's red and white or blue and white, the colours Bristolians adopt for the day, as another team normally in red. Like in Manchester, street sellers abound, and they're doing good business. A wonderful medley of Bristolian, Lancastrian and London accents sings on the banks of the River Thames. All around have two things in common: a cup final dream, and a smile.

United fans cheer as they walk past each other, down Fleet Street, the Strand, Holborn and Oxford Street. Many have brought packed lunches, much to the amusement of London's roving reporters.

> 'Another notable point is the attention paid by the Northern continent to the matter of the commissariat. They bring stone jars of strong ale and sandwiches an inch thick packed in the little wicker baskets which are also used for conveying carrier-pigeons.'

There are fans who support neither United nor Bristol, but they have inevitably chosen one for today. Neutral southerners put their weight behind Bristol, and the northerners back United. Londoners are the anomaly. The delights of Billy Meredith's wing play in last year's Charity Shield and many a London match for United, City and Wales have created many Edwardian Cockney Reds.

After lunching, fans head towards St Paul's to finish sightseeing. From there, they travel to Palace (High Level Station), where packed trains disgorge their human loads into colour-filled roads humming with excitement.

Fans drop their shilling into a small box at the turnstiles. It's some several hours until kick-off but the sloping sides of the Crystal Palace ground are littered with picnics. It resembles a massive garden party more than a football match. In that regard, the Palace is well-prepared with 60,000 slices of bread and butter, 14,000 sandwiches, 3,500 pork pies, 75 beef rumps, 100 mutton loins, 50,000 pieces of cake, 100 beer barrels, 2,000 bottles of whisky and spirits and 1,200 pounds of tea and coffee.

Flowers border the pitch with an equal split between red and white and blue and white. The morning's rain has been replaced by the coming and going of sun and shadow and the green grass is smooth. The scale of the place is magnificent. As the mass of humanity gets denser, picnics are gathered up hurriedly and places with good views assumed. Some climb up trees and sit in branches. The red-and-white decked set of United fans who arrived at Euston at 4:20am once stood out on the sides; now they are nothing but dots in a sea of heads. Flying above them are a notable number of kites. Attached to these are flags which read not 'Rocca Brigade', nor 'Play Up United', but 'Votes For Women'. The suffragettes are in town, too.

The mood is excellent, exhilarating even. It's a spectacle many have never experienced. It is enthusiasm, excitement and enjoyment in a ground brimming with life from across England and Britain. It's the English Cup Final – Manchester United's first.

9

United's cup final

*'Oh I wish I was you Billy Meredith / I wish
I was you / I envy you / Indeed I do!'*

– Manchester United supporters' song.

April 1909 – Excitement abounds outside, but busy match preparations continue inside the main stand. FA secretary Frederick Wall, Players' Union antagoniser, works away to accommodate his many celebrity guests, cricketer W.G. Grace among them. Reporters begin to find their press box seats while others send early reports back inside the telegraph office.

Manchester United have endured a restless morning in their Chingford Hotel, with two exceptions: the poised Billy Meredith and Sandy Turnbull, who have been here before. The squad takes breakfast before travelling to the Great Eastern Hotel, next to Liverpool Street Station, for lunch and taxicabs to the Crystal Palace.

There, Louis Rocca lays United's English Cup Final kit out. Heavy white cotton is bedecked with a red chevron, below which is stitched the red rose of Lancashire. The smart-looking outfit with its lace-up neck has been donated by famous stage performer and friend of the club, George Robey. He and United have organised several charity matches together in the past. Being the two stars of the day in their respective fields, Meredith and Robey are particularly close.

United's players are deliberate in their movements upon arrival while secretary Ernest Mangnall still deliberates on his team selection because Sandy Turnbull might be calm, but he's not fully fit. Ultimately, Charlie Roberts convinces Mangnall: 'He might get a goal, and if he does, we can afford to carry a passenger.' Ernest agrees. Sandy is delighted.

Frederick Wall, upstairs duties complete, sweeps in and lurks in the dressing room as proceedings continue. Roberts, his shorts still worn rebelliously above his knee, rises from the bench with purpose and tells Wall to be gone, he's about to deliver his team talk. Wall is miffed but he departs.

Charlie soon leads his players out, following the Billy Wedlock-led Bristol. They make a most dissimilar pair, Wedlock's little form in rich blue overshadowed by the tall, athletic United captain, whose rare bright white outfit exaggerates his eye-filling appearance.

United pass the ball around between themselves as Charlie wins the coin toss against his England rival. United will play with the wind and sun on their backs; the semibreves of the national anthem and 'Rule Britannia' fade away and Bristol start the cup final, greeted by that familiar half-involuntary roar of the crowd.

Twenty-two minutes in, after a succession of headers, Roberts traps the ball and drives forward. He beats Wedlock and releases possession to Harold Halse, the insatiable cup goalscorer. Halse's shot is a stinger, but too high by an inch. It rattles off the crossbar and into the path of half-fit Sandy Turnbull, who pounces and thrashes it home. The pent-up anticipation and enthusiasm of a fortnight's build-up is released in one enormous shout, which shifts the air upwards. Travelling Lancastrians jump in ecstasy, wave their colours in delight, and embrace one another in instinctual elation, Harry Stafford and Louis Rocca included. In Manchester, the same scene is replicated outside newspaper offices which receive updates via telegram and report to the waiting masses.

It's a deserved goal. United have dominated, pinning Bristol back with ease. 'There is an expressive football colloquialism,' a reporter notes. 'It is "making rings" round opponents. Manchester United accomplished a great deal of this kind of thing.'

A half-time lead extends into an hour's lead and then Vince Hayes temporarily retires with a broken rib. Roberts conducts; Duckworth replaces Hayes at full-back and Halse becomes a half-back. When Hayes returns, Roberts maintains the now-settled system, leaving the full-back forward. United continue to dominate. The second half is likened to the 'expert swordsmanship of a great fencer toying with mediocrity'.

' 'Meredith played beautiful football; his clever footwork, rare control of the ball, sure passes and long shots into goal gave the deadliness to his side's attack,' *The Times* reports. 'And Roberts proved himself to be better than Wedlock.'

News of the final whistle in Lancashire is greeted by scenes of uncontrollable enthusiasm. One enterprising newspaper sends out a small fleet of motor cars to display the score in the suburbs and the central streets, selling their copies as they do. Brass bands pick up their instruments and fill the air with celebratory notes. Young Mancunians parade up and down singing their favourite music-hall songs, shouting the name of Sandy Turnbull and Manchester United.

Back in London, Charlie Roberts is presented with the English Cup, the very pinnacle of the national game. Lord Charles Beresford, a famous and popular naval captain, hands the dainty silver trophy over. He insists he has not seen 'finer specimens of British humanity' than those who have finished victors in south London. Charlie becomes the first United captain to take the prize and lifts it to an immense cheer.

10

To Sandy

'Mr George Robey, the well-known
comedian, who is a member of the Manchester
United Club, and was present at the match,
extended an invitation to the players and
directors to take lunch with him on Sunday.
But as fifty people instead of the expected
fifteen turned up the resources of his Finchley
establishment were rather overtaxed.'

– Cork Weekly News, 1 May 1909.

April 1909 – Celebrating Manchester United fans invade London's theatreland. Managers of bars, hotels and restaurants are soon slapping up 'house full' signs.

The team themselves head first to the Alhambra Theatre alongside their opponents and club officials. Jury's Imperial Pictures screen the game back, which Man of the Match Billy Meredith enjoys, sat next to his wife Ellen in box seats. He's stubbornly wearing a 'rather dowdy-looking fit having apparently refused to wear a wing-collar and starched front'. The team head after to the Trocadero Restaurant.

'To Sandy,' Charlie toasts, 'and to United,' his normally pale cheeks flushed by celebratory drinks. After a brief speech paying tribute to United's saviour, Harry Stafford; resuscitator, John Henry Davies; leader, Ernest Mangnall; and many volunteers, Louis Rocca included, they dine. The Trocadero is a suitably grand setting, a little different from the hotpot dinners at the Meredith household in north Manchester where United's players normally muse over tactical plans.

As the night runs away with itself, Charlie is reminded that United have promised George Robey they will be at his nine o'clock performance back at the Alhambra. Rushing off with Sandy Turnbull, Charlie sticks a head back into the Trocadero and yanks a few of his fellow diners out. J.J. Bentley sees the rosy-cheeked, merry group heading off with the English Cup in their possession and stops them.

'I think I'd better come along or I can see the cup being lost in London,' he says.

A delighted Robey directs the group behind the curtains on stage and regally introduces England's finest football team. An enormous cheer greets his announcement but as the curtains rise, Charlie can barely breathe through laughter. He winks at George. The motley crew Roberts has assembled does include some English Cup winners, him and Sandy standing on each side, Jimmy Turnbull, and it also includes Harry Stafford and J.J. Bentley, but the majority of those on display are nothing more than Charlie's old mates. They include a sheepish-looking poultry dealer, bookmaker, builder and greengrocer. The cheers keep coming. Charlie keeps laughing.

The next morning, the English Cup's lid is missing. It's found in Sandy Turnbull's jacket pocket where Meredith, ever the prankster, has placed it the night before. The United team are taken by bus to Hampstead Heath before joining George Robey at his magnificent Finchley home. He has invited them for lunch.

On Monday, sore heads all round, the players and their wives – who are less than eager to leave the capital – do some sightseeing and shopping on Oxford Street. On Tuesday, they head home.

11

See the Conquering Heroes Come

'Charlie Roberts and Dick Duckworth
walked to St Pancras, but the bulk of the
party travelled to the station in omnibuses.
On the platform there was a scene of bustle.
The crowd which had gathered round the
carriage gave voice to their feelings, and
cheers and cries of "Good old Manchester"
were heard all round.'

– Manchester Evening News, 27 April 1909.

April 1909 – Manchester United's train steams into Central Station and wild enthusiasm greets Ernest Mangnall when he steps on to the platform, bearing aloft the English Cup. A local school band plays 'See the conquering hero comes' and the crowd scrambles forwards, hoping to catch a glimpse of their heroes. Some players are lifted shoulder-high towards the waiting coach, red-and-white cardboard representations of the English Cup sell like hot cakes and Louis Rocca, accompanied by his enormous red-and-white umbrella, offers Rocca's Ices for a celebratory bargain price.

All work is suspended in Manchester today. It is a truly unforgettable scene and occasion. Charlie Roberts, club captain, sits at the front of the charabanc, holding the cup. They meander through the crowds to the Town Hall where a civic reception is held while the masses outside remain. Charlie eventually strides back out towards them with the cup in hand, flanked by John Henry Davies. The cheering continues. United board their carriage again and, led by four white horses, head down John Dalton Street, Deansgate, St Mary's Gate and Market Street. On Oldham Street, shop girls hang from upstairs windows and throw red roses down upon the team. Even Manchester's poorest residents find the means to get some form of red and white souvenir.

In a symbol of local unity, United's carriage is driven by Manchester City director Albert Alexander, who fulfilled the same role back in 1904 for the Blues. Charlie is joined at the front by Mangnall and George Wall. He lifts the cup again and again, thrilled by the exuberant roar that propels upwards each time he does. He wears a permanent grin.

The players arrive at Clayton just in time for their last home match of the season against Woolwich Arsenal. They don their cup final colours again, which are much admired, and run out to take more plaudits. The directors' box is beautifully decorated with red and white flowers and the appearance of the cup itself gives way to another outburst of glee.

United are beaten 4-1 by Arsenal. Nobody cares.

The procession re-forms post-match. Those coming out of work now have their opportunity to pay tribute to Manchester's heroes. Such is the size and enthusiasm of the support that it takes until 10:30pm for the team to arrive at the Midland Hotel, where another dinner is held for the players and their families. After a while, Charlie politely slips away from the proceedings with May. It has been a thrill, but he's had enough of the crowd and seeks the quiet, warm glow of home and family. Billy does the same and soon enough he'll take his family and the English Cup itself back to his true home in Chirk.

* * *

A month on, Players' Union secretary Herbert Broomfield looks out of his office at St Peter's Square. The red and white confetti left by United's euphoric supporters in April's parade has long since been cleaned up. Instead, the cobbles outside are damp and their colour dull. The clouded sky above them is the same.

On cup final day itself, Broomfield was focused on George Parsonage's lifetime suspension. The half-back's club, Fulham, accepted an offer for him from Chesterfield, but he didn't want to move north. When Chesterfield offered him the maximum wage and maximum £10 bonus, he laughed and said, 'Make it £50.' The FA have banned him for life. 'It was a pure joke,' Parsonage insists, but they won't relent, despite the union's petitions.

The FA then threatens the union's management Committee with suspension, Billy Meredith included, so all but Broomfield step down, believing they can resume their roles at summer's end. Retaining his, Broomfield is banned, his professional playing career thus coming to an abrupt end.

Relative peace has followed since because many FA officials are absent throughout May on England's tour of Vienna and Budapest. United's George Wall and Harold Halse are involved, with J.J. Bentley among the travelling party. The time provides a much-needed rest for Broomfield, the breath before the plunge.

But a more severe ultimatum has arrived: all union members will be suspended. So now Broomfield's desk is covered by pale yellow papers: a messy collection of telegrams. Their message is simple: 'What to do?' Broomfield's replies are consistent. The FA say they have until 1 July to resign, so he tells his members to ignore their demand to resign for now. The players oblige, for now.

The FA Council's recommendation to abolish the maximum wage is rejected by club directors yet again. Despite a majority, they are ten vote shorts of the two-thirds required. Between this and the threatened suspension of union members, the calm is over. Broomfield takes his breath, sighs, and starts to write.

12

Outcasts

'Nothing less than a complete surrender of
the players' claim to legal rights enjoyed by
all sections of the community will apparently
satisfy the FA. In the words of one councillor,
the players will be "forced to obey the rules,
whether right or wrong"; in the words of
another, 'the Football Association will insist
on governing puppets, not men".

– Herbert Broomfield.

June 1909 – Players' Union secretary Broomfield writes to his members with assertive confidence. The FA have 'overstepped the mark', he says, providing the union with a 'glorious opportunity'.

'The facts are that we are quite prepared to play for our clubs, but the FA won't let us.

'We have waited our chance. It has arrived, and we must decide once and forever whether the professional player is to be a man or a puppet in the hands of the FA.'

And yet, despite his persuasive language, many footballers resign their union membership before the end of June, to avoid FA suspension. They cannot, or do not want to, cope without their summer wages.

A more significant fight against the establishment also grips hold of Manchester and London over summer. Those suffragettes who flew the 'Votes for Women' flags at the cup final are fighting hard. Marion Wallace Dunlop's 91-hour hunger strike attracts publicity sufficient to force the government into discussions. Such determination and commitment are rare amongst most footballers, to Broomfield's great frustration, but he is emboldened by the persistence of Manchester United's star players, Billy Meredith and Charlie Roberts, who have continued to provide their unerring vocal support.

**

July 1909

Charlie hears the papers thud down on the doorstep of his newsagents' shop, opened two years ago near United's Bank Street stadium. He opens the door, igniting the bell's tinkle, and brings them inside. When he flicks through the headlines, he discovers in the inner pages that he and his team-mates, the English Cup winners, have been suspended indefinitely. They have not resigned their union membership.

When United's players, Charlie amongst them, visit the club's offices a few days later to collect their summer wages, secretary Ernest Mangnall is absent. All they can get out of the office boy is 'there are no wages for you, as the FA have suspended you all'.

'Well, something will have to be done,' says Sandy Turnbull, while removing a picture from the wall. He walks out of the office with it under his arm, and the rest of the boys follow suit, picking up and carrying looking glasses, hairbrushes, and whatever else they can find. The office boy is in a terrible panicked state, completely out of his depth and desperate to have the club's items returned. 'Come along with me and I will get them back for you,' says Charlie, with a grin despite the dire situation, 'it's only one of their little jokes.' The belongings are returned, but normality is not. There really are no wages for the boys. They will have to make do without. This is the financial sacrifice they have made for the union.

Roberts is suffering more than most. He is due to be given a benefit match in three months' time, worth roughly £500. As things stand, it won't happen. But like union secretary Broomfield, Charlie is bullish in conversation with the media. 'We will not take this drastic action on the part of the FA lying down,' he says.

*   *   *

Broomfield has not. In St Peter's Square, he has the ear of a journalist and is pleased the next day when he sits in his dark office – the dull sky of June persisting – and reads the *Manchester Guardian* parroting his words.

'The highly-skilled football player is to be denied the right of appeal to the law which is possessed by errand boy or scavenger,' the newspaper comments.

On regular visits to London in the following days, Broomfield feels well-supported, particularly by the Amateur Football Association (AFA), formed in 1907 after a schism grew between FA officials and amateur footballers. The latter do not oppose professionalism in the sport but felt that the FA were making football too businesslike; now the professionals object to the FA treating the game too little as a business. The FA have been caught between two thorns and remain in bitter dispute with them both.

As with the union, the FA's response to the AFA was not to alleviate their concerns but to thrash out like a paranoid dictator. Amateur players were banned from all professional teams, who themselves were forbidden from providing the crucial assistance of facilities and support they once had to amateur clubs. With a shared enemy, the AFA invite the Players' Union to send a team to play the famous Corinthians. Further fixtures are soon arranged against the university sides of Oxford and Cambridge, and Broomfield hears that the players' concerns are to be raised in the House of Commons.

He returns to Manchester confident and meets with United's players. Broomfield then makes a statement to the waiting press. 'The Manchester United players have refused to surrender their legal rights at the bidding of a body of men who do not contribute a penny-piece to the upkeep of football but who, in many instances, are making considerably more money out of their association with the game than is the highest-paid professional.'

They 'put on record their loyalty to their club and their esteemed president, J.H. Davies, and to a loyal public that has frequently and generously appreciated their efforts'. They outline their eagerness to play and their dissatisfaction at being prevented from doing so.

'They leave it to the public,' Broomfield says finally, 'whether they prefer to be entertained by men of their own stamp, or by individuals who have to obey the changing moods of a body which refuses to argue points in dispute, and which demands blind obedience to orders, however unjust or however contradictory.'

Manchester's public responds warmly.

Hoping to rid themselves of the nuisance that is Broomfield, the FA make overtures to other key union figures. They'll accept a footballers' union if Broomfield is excluded and there is a strong suggestion that huge financial incentives are offered to Charlie Roberts.

'Are we going to do it?' Meredith writes. 'I think not. If we did do it, what would we be?'

Charlie agrees.

Broomfield remains and he sends thousands of circulars detailing the footballers' struggle to trade unions, councils and cooperative societies across the country. Support is beginning to come in from the wider trade union movement, particularly in Cheshire, Lancashire and Yorkshire. The *Sheffield Guardian*, a mouthpiece for the local Labour Party, encourages its readers to support the footballers by explaining 'the FA are like the employer who is favourable to Trade Unionism so long as it does not do anything he does not want'.

The union's position appears exceedingly strong. The English Cup winners, United, are standing firm with significant public support behind them and a court has just ruled that West Bromwich Albion are a commercial concern, not a sporting one, as an ex-player is paid compensation in a union 'test case'. In London, the Grand Federation of Trades Unions (GFTU) talks directly with the FA for the first time, the meeting's very existence acknowledgement of a failure to break the Players' Union up.

'This can only mean one thing,' Billy Meredith predicts. 'That if the FA are prepared to adopt a reasonable attitude, and I hope and believe they are, the whole dispute will be speedily settled.'

Billy's writings entirely give away his long-held resentment towards English authority.

'The FA have been ruling us just as the bad barons of old ruled their people, and it is only just being brought home to them that it won't do any longer.'

Soon after the GFTU–FA conference in London, the same FA officials enjoy a luxurious dinner and banquet to celebrate the 21st year of the Football League, funded by income that players like Billy's talent has allowed.

***

August 1909

Manchester United should be at Old Trafford by now, but significant delays have continued, which is fortunate because the club has no team. Roberts, Meredith and co. are all suspended. The Reds are ready to play if the FA will allow them to and to prove this point, union secretary Broomfield finds a ground where they can train. He heads down Oxford Road past the St James's Hall, where Newton Heath held their 1901 bazaar, and towards Fallowfield.

A few days later, Sandy Turnbull is the first to arrive at the Fallowfield Athletic Ground, his leather boots scuffing the ground as he hops off a neat road bike and props it up against the sidings. The short, stocky Scotsman jumps on to a ride-on mower and whiles the time away trimming the grass. Captain Charlie Roberts soon joins him. He has left his wife May managing their newsagents' shop, while their kids kick one of Billy Meredith's footballs around in the concrete backyard. Charlie wears his shorts high up on his waist, falling rebelliously above the knee, just as the FA dislike them.

United trainer Fred Bacon has thrown his lot in with the suspended boys. Goalkeeper Harry Moger strides in, straw hat casting a shadow over his face. He's kept himself fit by playing a full cricket season, the highlight a century and six wickets for West Didsbury. Soon, Burgess, Duckworth, Meredith, Picken and Wall are there, and then the rest. It has been a tricky summer without summer pay for some of them, especially those without businesses on the side like Charlie and Billy, but they are convinced it is worth it.

'We are fighting for our bread and butter, and we shall win too if the Newcastle and other players will only stand by us,' one comments, buoyed by the presence of local journalists and particularly by the supportive Fallowfield locals, who shout, 'Good luck to you, boys!' and 'May you beat the FA!' from the sidelines.

Their training is good. Charlie thanks them all for coming and proudly states they'd be ready for a league match on Saturday if needed. Jimmy Turnbull will join tomorrow. The Scotsman wants to leave United to head back nearer home and play for Falkirk, but the FA claim he has no good reason to leave and so he must stay. And therein lies much of the problem.

The press presence at Fallowfield increases after a couple of days, by which point Everton's Tim Coleman – known as 'the football field comedian' – has joined as well as Jimmy Turnbull. The camaraderie is strong and the mood optimistic. It is quite the story. The English Cup winners of a mere four months ago are suspended from football and are paying £5 a day to train.

The players are happy to oblige for a team photograph. Charlie Roberts picks up a blackboard lying nearby – there to demonstrate tactics on – and writes a name that will stick forever more:

THE OUTCASTS F.C.

* * *

While the Outcasts train in Fallowfield, Herbert Broomfield travels north to Newcastle, Sunderland and Middlesbrough. In the press, FA officials claim there have been mass resignations; Broomfield insists there have not. He's weary of it, and he thinks rumours of resignations are designed to encourage others to follow suit, so he visits clubs personally to prevent that. He gives a speech in Newcastle and the Geordies vote unanimously to stand by United, according the Reds 'a hearty vote of the thanks for the stand they have made on behalf of all professional football players'.

Broomfield enjoys similar success in Sunderland and Middlesbrough and his good mood is bolstered greatly because another court case has gone in the union's favour, a Crystal Palace lad receiving compensation this time. Better still, the country's finest football team are splashed across the newspapers, posing behind a sign that reads 'THE OUTCASTS F.C.'

* * *

When FA and GFTU representatives convene again, they decide another conference should take place, but this time with union representatives in attendance. It's progress, and Birmingham's Grand Hotel will host.

Representing United and the union is Charlie Roberts, not Billy Meredith. To add to this taxing summer, Billy is answering questions in Manchester's Bankruptcy Court about his sports shop business. A late-night fire has torn apart the shop, into which Billy has invested most of his earnings, with John Henry Davies contributing a little on his behalf, too

– a sweetener to top up his wage. It's all gone up in flames. Insurance is set to pay out £2,750 to restore the business on a solid footing, but as things stand, Billy's lost huge amounts. Proceedings are adjourned until September.

Roberts heads to Birmingham for what is deemed the most important conference in association football since the sport's rules were first codified in 1863.

It is not successful.

Talks break up over the union's request for United's players to be given backpay for the summer. They're owed £28 in wages and £20 in an English Cup bonus. One FA official rejected this without thinking.

'I happen to know that that decision was not relished by more than one member of the FA,' Charlie says, 'because several FA colleagues were left a little bemused by the decision, but such is their focus on being seen to be "united" themselves, none of them spoke up.

'More than once lately the FA have thrown it out that the Players' Union is a "one-man show". If ever there was a one-man show in this world that one-man show is the FA. You have only to get among the members to find that out.'

It's a great shame because while certain wordings were causing disagreement, the FA had conceded to allowing a union and some other key points.

And yet, conference adjourned, they double down on their refusal to pay back owed wages by attempting to circumvent and undermine the union, in the form of a conference with all Football and Southern League clubs, but also through the whispered offers to senior union men like Charlie Roberts, who is told his £500 benefit will be doubled to £1,000 if he resigns.

'I would sooner live on bread and water for the rest of my life than submit to the terms of the FA,' he says. Such a message is greeted with a hearty cheer at Fallowfield where United's message is getting across loud and clear: we are ready and keen to play.

Public sympathy is split on the unresolved dispute. Undeniable, though, is that football is suffering. Fewer season tickets than ever have been bought for the new campaign. Fans are waiting to see whether the country's best players will be involved in the Football League or part of some breakaway system instead.

While Broomfield travels to secure support, Roberts and Newcastle United captain Colin Veitch take on the role of spokespersons.

'Our position has been accurately described by the *Daily Mirror* as "white slavery", and if the players do not win this time they will never again have such a magnificent chance.'

But as the FA's underhand tactics secure the crucial support of club directors, including United's, players' confidence – the United boys aside – declines. Broomfield, Meredith and Roberts would happily strike, but most players, the FA, the Football League, the clubs and supporters are terrified of delaying the new season's start.

The press continues to operate in a manic state. One idea is to keep Australia's touring cricketers over for the winter and use them to play 30 Test football matches. The only problem, one reporter concedes, is 'the players would certainly insist on having a tea interval in the middle of each forty-five, and this might create trouble with football spectators who have not the patience that characterises devotees of the summer game'.

A rumour goes round that Sheffield United's directors intend to choose a team from the ranks of the local unemployed if their players are suspended. Thousands of men assemble outside Bramall Lane expressing their willingness to play for £4 a week.

Charlie takes his suspended team to Manchester's Douglas Hotel for an amicable meeting with the directors, where the situation is laid out and the footballers outline their views. They explain to the directors that they mean no harm to them and respect them, but they are fighting for what they believe to be a just principle.

It's now 31 August, one day before the scheduled start of the football season. In Birmingham's Grand Hotel, the FA sits down for a second attempt at negotiations. Discussions begin.

13

Will there be football?

'Are we to have any football at all next week?
That is the question that the man in the street
is asking.'

– *Leeds Mercury*, 28 August 1909.

August 1909 – Charlie stands outside Birmingham's Grand Hotel. He's banned from this conference. He must remain outside and outcast. The FA have gone for divide-and-conquer. They've got the clubs' support, now they seek to get those wavering players to side with them, too.

Between this meeting and the last, the FA has offered to assist – financially and logistically – in forming a new players' organisation. That offer has not yet been taken, but Charlie stands outside the hotel, warning his comrades against sacrificing the power they have earned for themselves over the summer.

Seventy players in total navigate past Roberts and into the Grand Hotel, where long-time opponent to professionalism J.C. Clegg opens proceedings with a long speech, both uninterrupted and unchallenged. Charlie might have had something to say, for Clegg declares the FA to have never objected to what he calls 'the persistently hostile' union, who, he insists, have never properly outlined their demands.

This messaging is eventually challenged when questions come from the floor. The players speak not of high-minded sporting philosophies as Clegg has done but of specifics. What rule have the Manchester United players broken to justify their suspensions? Why was George Parsonage so harshly treated? Why did I not have the opportunity to defend myself when banned? Why have you asked me a question but not listened to the response? The players appear to have the upper hand.

And yet.

Colin Veitch, Newcastle United captain, flat cap at his brown-suited side, no longer covering his smooth face and dark hair, outlines his thoughts: the union should continue, as forming a new one would be too difficult, and the United players must have their back-wages paid. He states this is the key sticking point.

The conference pauses to allow Veitch to telephone Herbert Broomfield back in Manchester. Broomfield is told the FA will acknowledge the union and give them the right to take cases under the Workmen's Compensation Act into court. And, finally, that they are prepared to allow the back-wages of the United players. Broomfield asks for more details, but detail has been rather light in Clegg and Veitch's exchange.

At 5:20pm, 24 hours before the season's start, an amicable peace settlement is achieved. Amid profound silence, Clegg announces: 'We have come to the following resolution …'

The FA have dramatically climbed down in regard to the back-wages and the newspapers thus speak of a grand union success, but the true victory is that the football season will not be delayed and in allowing it to begin, the union has thrown away its key bargaining chip without great reward. The back-wages are good, and the acknowledgement of the union's existence is good, but Veitch has pledged on behalf of the players to abide by the rules and practice of the FA. As Billy Meredith remarks the next day, 'What's the good of belonging to a union if one fetters one's hands like that?'

Broomfield feels similarly. He's praised as 'wonderfully zealous and self-sacrificing' and he espouses victory in the press, but he tells a friend in private: 'I am not overjoyed.'

'There is something sad about the whole business; to think that athletes should be so devoid of moral courage is not a pleasing thought and if you knew my experience the afternoon of the conference you would feel as I do.'

Charlie, Billy and Herbert, like their predecessors in 1898, are left feeling that more could have been done had the country's footballers truly stood by their fellow players. But there is barely time to breathe. The season begins.

14

A legacy in Stretford brick

'UNITED'S NEW GROUND – FINEST
IN THE COUNTRY'

– Manchester Courier.

January 1910 – A cutting wind whips off the leather of John
Henry Davies's gloves. He and the pressmen who accompany
him are well wrapped up. Trench coats. Homburgs. Gloves.
John's voice sometimes carries off into the wind, but the
pressmen are attentive. These lifelong sporting fans affect
professionalism, but they are secretly giddy and in awe of the
orchestra of workers around them providing the final touches
to Britain's newest and finest football arena: Old Trafford.

More than 400 men are busily engaged. Painters, plumbers
and carpenters work on the 12,000-seater grandstand, the
pitch is billiard-table smooth green; England's largest. Eagerly
encouraging progress, Davies has visited on many occasions,
and sometimes a little impatiently. A visit just after Christmas
in piercing weather led to him spending several days in bed
with a severe cold.

The targeted January opening date has not quite been met.
It is now 16 February. A period of bitterly aggressive, numbing
weather has delayed construction. Bricks simply cannot be laid
by unmovable fingers with frozen cement.

***

The delay means Tottenham Hotspur's players suffered
the misfortune of being Bank Street's last visiting team.

Tottenham's players wore kneecaps to protect them from the pitch, which, having been rolled while in a very soft state, featured hard-as-iron frozen ridges, ice patches and holes. The bruised Londoners' studs offered no help, whereas United's 17-year experience here saw them wear corrugated rubber soles and win 5-0. Charlie Roberts scored a brace and Billy Meredith his first goal since Christmas Day 1908.

The next game was a humdinger. Eighth-placed United fell to a three-goal deficit at Newcastle before providing one of their finest-ever performances, a stunning four-goal comeback. Even the home crowd applauded their magnificent effort. After these two fantastic victories, Old Trafford is abuzz with excitement.

Davies guides the pressmen towards the grandstand and their gaze lingers on the pitch's seductively smooth surface. They enter the imposing stand with its zigzag roof – resembling a collection of beach huts – and survey the boardroom, secretary's offices, player's recreation rooms, gymnasium, dressing rooms and an elaborate series of baths. They are left convinced of the stadium's greatness.

Over lunch with the intrigued reporters, Davies is sometimes bullish, but generally relaxed. An FA commission is currently reviewing the club's business and United's president admits that, yes, as charged, the club is a one-man show at times, but that this is a deliberate policy whereby the main directors take on all the risk until a time when United is on sounder financial ground, at which point they will feel justified in asking others to come and join them. He details the financial position since his 1902 arrival. He had initially been told £1,000 would save the club. One thousand after another had been 'evanesced into thin air' and his contribution had reached five figures some time ago. It was only after five seasons that anything near a profit began to be made. The pressmen call in their gushing reports on Davies and Britain's finest football ground.

Back in Clayton, it becomes clear that United have made a timely removal to Old Trafford. The grandstand is destroyed by gusts of wind, with the roof now sitting inconspicuously against nearby houses. With one day to go, a reporter declares: 'Manchester United is dead. Long live Manchester United!'

* * *

The players are given a private viewing of Old Trafford a few days before the big kick-off. Charlie and Billy are shown the match programme. Adorning the cover are photos of their faces, which have developed an additional frown line or two over these tough last few months.

After last summer's controversial affairs, the FA spent many months refusing Charlie's benefit match. A snide punishment, and not the only one. His summer back-wages took just as long to be paid, too, and the FA have been back-tracking like a thief from the police.

United played Bradford just a day after the Birmingham conference. In the morning, Roberts convened with key union men in St Peter's Square to discuss tactics. First up was for United to run out at Bank Street that evening wearing union armbands. They did so, and to an emphatic cheer from the supportive home crowd, but within a month, the FA had forbidden the armbands, contributing to Roberts and Meredith's dismay at the lack of progress since late August. The United pair renewed plans to strike on several occasions and Broomfield and Newcastle captain Veitch, whose role has increased greatly, talked them out of it.

The FA soon demanded, as they suggested they would not in August, that the union disassociate itself from the GFTU, the body that would act as an essential arbitrator and secure the union's power. And the FA's propaganda won. They told the players that football was different, that the sport could manage itself without outside intervention from business. In late October, union members voted. The resolute answer, 470–172, disgusted Roberts.

'I would have seen the FA in Jericho before I would have resigned membership of the GFTU. It was our strength and right arm. To the shame of the majority they voted the only power they had away from themselves and the FA knew it.'

Billy and Charlie realised the significance: the union's cause had been set back many years. Broomfield resigned as secretary in December, feeling his hard work had been wasted.

Charlie's benefit match did eventually come, the FA all too willing to sanction it once the GFTU vote had passed. Roberts took home a healthy four-figure sum from a 25,000 crowd at Bank Street on Christmas Day – a positive day tinged with sadness and anger. Furthermore, that figure would have been significantly larger had, as planned, it been held at Old Trafford's opening. That time has, at least, finally come around.

***

Old Trafford truly is something to wonder at. A little over a decade ago, Newton Heath's players dressed in a hotel and afterwards walked a near-half-hour to reach the ground. Post-match they'd gone to Father Samuel Bird's for a hotpot supper. One cannot but marvel at the progress made since John Henry Davies came to rescue Newton Heath and created Manchester United, perhaps now the world's leading football club: the English Cup holders and recent title-winners whose home is simply unrivalled.

The magnificent 12,000-seater brick grandstand is imposing – larger than any in the country. White-bricked embankments sweep around the luscious pitch, their size breathtaking. When 50,000 in giddy attendance, and several thousand more who have jibbed in, boisterously greet the teams of United and Liverpool for this first game, the sea of humanity is spine-tingling. Only the Crystal Palace ground has greater space, but here at Old Trafford, everyone feels near the pitch. It's compact, yet handsome and enormous.

At first, the game's pace is a little slow. The men struggle to judge their passes, such is the difference in the pitch's surface. Meredith enjoys storming down the wing, uninterrupted by ridges, and United lead by two at half-time. Sandy Turnbull scores the stadium's first goal, Tom Homer the second. Liverpool capitalise on a lapse of concentration to get one back for the visitors, but then Roberts sets up George Wall to make it 3-1. Liverpool come back again, and, remarkably, notch three further goals. A dramatic afternoon is nearly capped off in suitable fashion when Wall shoots well late on, but the goalkeeper is equal to it and turns it around the post. Liverpool are the victors on Old Trafford's first day which, despite defeat, is one of immense pride for Davies and Mangnall, who know they have lain down a legacy for generations to come.

15

One-man show

*'It is really very sad that a gentleman who
has done so much for football and footballers
as Mr Davies has done should not be allowed
to exercise a controlling influence. But for Mr
Davies there would have been no Manchester
United with absolutely the best ground in the
country.'*

– *Manchester Evening News.*

August 1910 – The FA have ordered that John Henry Davies's
'controlling influence' at Manchester United be curtailed.

An investigation into the club's finances has 'revealed'
what everyone already knew: United are a one-man show.
That John Henry's influence has been undoubtedly positive
matters little to the FA, who, in fairness, are seeking a level
playing field. However, their tactics in pursuing this cause
grounds for complaint once again.

Unlike every other club in the country that took part in
last year's amnesty for financial misconduct, the FA exposes
the exact extent to which 'Moneybags United' used illegal
wages and bonuses. Davies paid a total of £5,743 between 1903
and 1909, including £300 a season to chairman J.J. Bentley,
which creates an understandably heated conversation inside
the FA chambers. Bentley is Football League president and
FA vice-president. He has, in effect, personally guaranteed
the club's accounts. In 1904, United insisted they were kept

in the dark about dodgy payments, allowing Harry Stafford and James West to take the blame, but Bentley cannot claim he was unaware of £1,800 he received himself. He duly resigns as FA vice-president. That he has received a larger wage than United's players will no doubt irk Meredith and Roberts, too.

Manchester's football supporters and journalists alike are at odds with the FA's rule-making. They cannot see the downsides to Davies's financial backing. But the clubs represented on the FA and Football League's committees include less-well-off outfits, such as Burnley, who greatly resent United's free spending and the imbalance it causes.

Even the fans' trust in Davies is threatened at one point because the FA claim that John's Manchester Brewery Company, from whom United rent the Old Trafford land, are charging the club excessively. An independent valuation proves them wrong, showing that United are in fact underpaying the brewers by some £200 annually. It is a satisfying conclusion for Davies and his directors, who believe they have been unjustly attacked after delivering something overwhelmingly positive for the club and the city alike. Many commentators agree.

* * *

Ernest Mangnall and Louis Rocca, whose scouting role is increasing year on year, have signed Nottingham Forest forward Enoch 'Knocker' West, who's a real handful, while Charlie Roberts brings in a greyhound. It's a new club mascot, gifted by a Glossop man.

'We hope that its existence on this earthly sphere will be a trifle longer than that enjoyed by the poor little goat we had last season,' Charlie comments.

Billy Meredith is convinced United's last mascot, a nanny goat, was bad luck. A travelling Shakespearean company gifted her to Charlie Roberts, their favourite player. Upon presentation at an Ardwick theatre, she charged Charlie down and while he evaded her horns, bringing the house down with laughter, it proved portentous. Old Trafford's construction and

Charlie's benefit match were delayed, United scored several own goals, suffered major injuries and were knocked out of the English Cup in round one.

The goat was named Union after last summer's discontent, and despite being bad luck, was much-loved. She followed United's players affectionally through the streets of Clayton, one regular stopping point being Charlie's newsagents shop a couple of hundred metres down the road from Bank Street. But, like Bank Street, Union is no more. Charlie has her head preserved for his home.

With the FA's findings hanging over him, United chairman J.J. Bentley has resigned as Football League president, due to 'doctor's advice'. Davies, meanwhile, continues to be a man with great duality. He spends some of his summer demonstrating utter ruthlessness in the brewery trade while demanding United play an additional pre-season match when the funds raised for charity from the first are deemed insufficient. Is it that he seeks popularity from the masses rather than the boardroom few? Or is it a genuine deep-seated desire to do good?

Regardless, Davies hosts a merry and jovial press luncheon in the new Old Trafford boardroom, at which he states that he has 'never been so confident in the team as at present'.

'I am looking forward to one of the best seasons the club has ever had, for the players are now more settled than at this time last year, and good enough to win the highest honours.'

16

United's finesse

*'Sandy Turnbull has been keeping himself in
condition by playing bowls, whilst Meredith,
who is a stickler for training, acted as
linesman in a match between old players of
Chirk and the Oswestry club. Roberts and
Bell have been taking long walks in the
Manchester district.'*

– *Manchester Evening News*, 3 August 1910.

September 1910 – United indeed open their season in
fine form. Free of last year's distractions and aided by Old
Trafford's smooth, wide pitch, Roberts and his half-back line
are playing beautiful football. Their footwork is superb and
the placing and precision of their passes is game-changing.
Duckworth's shooting is excellent, and Bell is neat and
meticulous, but Roberts dominates. He has two involvements
to anyone else's one.

Billy Meredith, 36, remains an insatiable force on the
wing. He twists and turns, making his doubters squirm as
much as his opponents. As with every season's start, critics
insist his age has caught up with him. As with every season's
start, they are quickly silenced. Meredith is an evergreen
entertainer.

J.H. Davies watches with a fulfilled smile as 50,000 watch
another Duc-Ro-Bell masterclass at Old Trafford in a third
consecutive derby win since the December 1906 fire sale. An

away win at Everton wraps up an excellent September, with four wins from five.

Behind the scenes, in the wake of the FA's investigation, United's board floats the need to sell several players to reduce the debt owed to John Henry. Just as the FA's 1905 pillage of Manchester City paved the way for Meredith to cross Manchester, their findings five years on will soon pave the way for another titan of Mancunian football to navigate the red–blue divide.

Victories over The Wednesday, Bristol City and Newcastle United alleviate any short-term concerns. In victory and defeat, Roberts is United's best player as autumn progresses and when injuries afflict Duckworth, Bell, Wall, Turnbull and Holden, Charlie coaches their younger replacements by both example and in-game instruction.

By December's start, with the international matches two months away, the newspapers agree Roberts is playing well enough for a renewed England call-up. Three members of the FA's selection committee watch a virtuosic performance in victory against Aston Villa. He distributes the ball with composure and judgement and nullifies the Villa forwards to absolute impotence. It must leave a mark on the FA's watching men.

It thus appears unjust when the selection committee omit Roberts from the squads chosen for January's trial match. Aston Villa's uncapped Chris Buckley and Billy Wedlock of Bristol City are the preferred central half-backs. They play well in an unexciting affair, and the latter will be England's centre-half once again.

United beat Bradford and Nottingham Forest in the league and Blackpool in the cup, then draw against City and Everton before Charlie welcomes a Wedlock-less Bristol to Old Trafford. United defeat the West Country side by three goals to one and go top of Division One. On the same day, 30-year-old Wedlock receives his 20th cap as England name their oldest-ever line-up. Wedlock's defensive work is good but his contributions to the attack are limited in a poor team performance.

Charlie's 'case' is picked up in the national press. Even in cup defeat at West Ham, he's picked out as 'the finest on the field, and on form [he] should not be passed over for honours'. He is selected by the English Football League, whose selectors are distinct from those of the FA, and at Ibrox, Roberts distinguishes himself against the cream of Scottish football.

The FA still exclude Charlie for England's next match, against Meredith's Wales. Billy has 36 caps for his country now. The *Sports Argus* criticises the FA selection committee for choosing 'their' best team rather than England's best team. 'Wedlock is the team-selectors' favourite, and that has got to suffice. The team-builders chuckle and laugh ha! ha! at the supposed brilliance of Manchester United and Sunderland.'

'It is worthy of note,' the *Daily Telegraph* say in concurrence, 'that the team does not include a single man from Manchester United, Aston Villa, Sunderland, Everton or Newcastle United – the leading clubs in the first league.'

'What is wrong with our national football?' asks another newspaper. 'STRONG PLEA FOR RECOGNITION OF CHARLIE ROBERTS. PRIVATE PREJUDICE TO BLAME.'

'It has been perfectly clear to all who carefully follow football that Roberts is by no means a "persona grata" to the powers that be. The continued freezing-out of one of the greatest players in the country must have something behind it.'

England defeat Wales 3-0 at The Den in London. Wedlock performs well; energetic and committed as ever. The *Telegraph* concedes he 'is not quite as finished in his methods as the Manchester United captain, but he has wonderful energy', but a columnist in the *Star Green 'Un* is left resolutely unconvinced by such an argument.

'Whoever is the best centre-half in the country it is emphatically not William Wedlock of Bristol City.'

Roberts is once again overlooked for the season's third and final international match. England draw with Scotland at Goodison Park on the same day that United beat Liverpool at Old Trafford. Charlie is unperturbed by all this debate. He has a title challenge to focus on.

Main championship rivals Aston Villa are on United's tails, helped by victory over Sheffield United, who the very next day hold Charlie's side to a draw during the punishing Easter schedule. Roberts himself suffers a twisted knee and, though he twice attempts to come back on, is eventually forced off in the second half. United draw, and do the same against The Wednesday two days later. Chairman J.J. Bentley admits 'these two drawn games will probably cost Manchester United the much-coveted championship'.

With two games remaining, injury-afflicted United travel to Aston Villa for 'The Battle for the English Championship'. Down in London on the same day, Bradford and Newcastle play in the English Cup Final at Crystal Palace.

With Roberts unavailable, Villa appear favourites for the match and thus the title. They win the toss and pen United back into their own half, United struggling without Charlie's out-ball quality. A thrilling game sees Harold Halse score two to Villa's four. Meredith is rumoured to have swallowed his customary toothpick but is in fact just bruised in the larynx, and the home team run out 4-2 winners to go top with a game in hand. They draw that game at Blackburn Rovers, leaving them a point in front ahead of the season's final day.

***

Amidst the closest title race in decades, United secretary Mangnall has his work cut out to organise an English Cup Final. When Old Trafford opened, it was predicted it wouldn't be long before it hosted a cup final. One year on, that's become the reality. The match at Crystal Palace was drawn and a replay is scheduled for four days later. All ticket applications, press requests and police arrangements must be handled as part of Mangnall's wide-ranging role.

Helped by Louis Rocca and a team of volunteers, he works through the night. Both the work and the setting are a far cry from the days of Alf Albut evading bankruptcy in a battered old wooden hut at the end of the Bank Street pitch.

Bradford City win their first cup in front of Old Trafford's 66,000-strong crowd, bolstered by hundreds of non-paying supporters. Every window on the popular side has been smashed. It's one of the less inventive methods of gaining entry. More impressive is the tale of a man who leapt on to the back of a police horse and, before its rider could turn around, jumped from its back over the stadium wall in a flash.

United earn ten per cent of the gate receipts, about £4,000. Mangnall has done a good job and it's vindication for John Henry Davies, who faced criticism during the season for some smaller Old Trafford crowds. There is far more empty space than filled for most games and, as for reserve games, Davies has decided that all boys aged 9–14 should be admitted for free to boost attendances and encourage a lifetime of United support. That was a given back when the club were in Clayton, but must now be worked for because United's time-served supporters on the other side of the city often struggle to make kick-off in Stretford. A miner, and there are many in the Clayton district United abandoned, would never have time to catch the two trams necessary after his work finishes at 2pm.

* * *

Attention turns back to the championship, where Aston Villa head to Anfield knowing final-day victory will secure them the title. Manchester United must simply do their best against Sunderland at Old Trafford.

Manchester's winter has refused to give way to spring and pitiful weather reduces the crowd to no more than 10,000. With Roberts, Hofton, Bell and Wall out injured, Sunderland quickly lead, but Charlie proudly watches his team-mates come from behind to run away to a 5-1 victory.

There are still 15 minutes remaining at Anfield when United's match finishes. As Charlie retires to the dressing rooms with the United boys, he is told that Villa trail by two goals to one. The players nervously get into their baths awaiting the final score. Every few minutes, the strains of a cheer sneaks through the floorboards, but none have the true ring of success that the players long for. They have begun to give up hope when a thunderous roar shakes the air and Old Trafford's foundations. It is the celebration of the championship. Charlie and his rejoicing team-mates are joined by a fan drunk equally on beer and excitement who shouts and yells in the dressing room in delight. He jumps on the side of the bath, frenetically attempting to shake the hands of every player inside at once, the result being a dramatic loss of balance. Fully clothed, he plops gracelessly into the water. The players grin as they pull him out. They give him a playing uniform to wear and send him off home to the cheers of the jealous crowd. Manchester United are champions again.

Mangnall has signed well – supported by Louis Rocca's blossoming eye for a player – and managed an injury-stricken squad. Roberts has dragged his side through it all and Meredith has missed only three league games, aged 36, and scored five goals while assisting many more.

It has been nine years since John Henry Davies took a liking to Harry Stafford's St Bernard dog and knocked accountant George Lawton off his bicycle. First Newton Heath had become Manchester United, the boys in red and white. Promotion followed, then the formation of the Players' Union, a league title, a European tour, the English Cup, the finest stadium in the country and now a second league title, perhaps the most impressive of them all. With high-quality challengers and injuries, United have played football worthy of the championship. They have played scientifically, with finesse and entertainment. They are one of the teams of the age.

Part Four:
A Slow Demise,
1911–32

1

Stafford's exit

'Germany is rightly proud of her strength.
Surely it is natural and obvious that the
growth of that fleet must raise apprehensions.'

– Sir Edward Grey, Secretary of State for
Foreign Affairs, 27 November 1911.

June 1911 – King Edward VII is dead. He has been for more
than a year actually, but now his son and successor King
George V will finally be coronated. Great Britain is enduring
its hottest summer on record, in temperature and perhaps in
tension, too. Not a day goes by without a significant strike.
Ordinary people are demanding a greater share of the country's
enormous wealth because Britain is almost its greatest in
size. As government figures proclaim, it's always tea time
somewhere in the empire, on which the sun never sets.

Several strikers are killed in Liverpool and Llanelli as
erratic Home Secretary Winston Churchill clamps down,
fearing the country could fall into an 'abyss of horror'. There
is Parliamentary unrest, too. Frustrated by the House of Lords'
opposition to its 'People's Budget', the Commons removes
the Lords' right to veto financial bills. Establishing the
Commons' dominance allows some, though very far from all,
of the strikers' demands to be met. By December, a National
Insurance scheme will be established.

In this hot, revolutionary summer, the Players' Union
and the Football Association are no longer in direct battle.
The union's activities quietly tick on, except for a headline-

grabbing fundraising Athletics Festival at Old Trafford which demonstrates their ability to provide, promote and control sport.

League champions Manchester United are expected to thrive again in the new season, hopes sparked by a stunning second Charity Shield victory. Wearing blue strips in the capital[21], Harold Halse scores a double hat-trick in a remarkable 8-4 win over Southern League winners Swindon Town. Frustrated journalists debate a term for Halse's feat: 'The double hat-trick is clumsy, so what is the special term to be applied to such an achievement?' They expect it will become more common than it does.[22]

Notable is the reaction to captain Charlie Roberts's display. 'I have never seen him play so well,' says an FA vice-president, which is peculiar because every United fan has seen Roberts play at a much higher level. It appears those selecting England's international side are, though well-meaning, oblivious to some of their finest talent. Roberts is not thinking of this, as he lifts a third trophy in as many years in London. United have developed something of a routine in the Big Smoke now, celebrating once again at the Alhambra. Football League founder William McGregor tips them to be 'somewhere about the honours'.

Four days after United's Charity Shield, Italy and the Ottoman Empire begin hostilities. Within hours, an Italian squadron has attacked and pursued six Turkish torpedo boats off the Greek coast. Trade unions continue to do battle with the government at home while war begins to rumble across Europe.

On another shoreline, England's west, Harry Stafford is departing with an Ancoats girl named Alice Oldham, a former barmaid at his Bridge Inn and then the Imperial Hotel. They are ready to build a new life together.

---

21 As they will in 1948 and 1968.
22 Only George Best has scored a double hat-trick for MUFC since.

John Henry Davies has awarded Stafford, at his own request, £50 for his contributions to United. Stafford claims he's ill and emigrating to a warmer climate – Australia, he says – to set up a new life. Davies is happy to oblige. He and his long-time employee are different characters and the FA's beady eye remains fixed on United, so the once-suspended Stafford's removal is timely. He and Alice board the *Devonian* at Liverpool, paying £19 and ten shillings each for a five-day journey.

While the *Devonian* sways to the Atlantic's pulse, the FA offer a final conclusion to their investigation. Secretary Frederick Wall announces that 'after an exhaustive inquiry', United are now run on a 'satisfactory basis'. Davies sighs with relief. Meanwhile, Stafford has not travelled to Australia. Instead, he and his new girlfriend are met in Boston, Massachusetts, USA by Alice's younger brother Tom, who works on the New York Central railroad.

Strikes have been just as common in the US as in the UK, and Stafford benefits. This tale-twisting entertainer claims to the *Athletic News* he has become a football coach at Harvard, but the reality is less glamorous. The name 'Manchester United' means a great deal less in New York State. Stafford instead joins Alice's brother Tom on the New York Central railroad, openings having arisen after striking workers were sacked.

Stafford thus enjoys an American Christmas. Back in Manchester, John Henry Davies savours a typically lavish affair at the beautiful Moseley Hall. Elsie, owner of Major the St Bernard, is in her twenties now. Charlie Roberts eats well with his wife May, three-year-old son William and the younger Margaret and Charlie in their six-room Clayton home. Just down the road are Ernest and Eliza Mangnall with their four-year-old Ernest and two-year-old Doreen. The Merediths – Billy, Ellen, and daughters Lily and Winnie – are in Stretford, while Louis and Mary Emily Rocca celebrate on Oldham Road with their four kids. Old club secretary Alf

Albut is living with his father-in-law, his wife Selina having sadly died.

Stafford and Albut aside, these men all converge on Old Trafford for the Christmas Day fixture. Alf and Harry's era is truly over now, as the death of William McGregor, father of the Football League, demonstrates. Alf attends his funeral two days before Christmas.

Bradford end United's month-long unbeaten run on Christmas Day, initiating woeful form with only five wins from 21 games until the season's end. In March, they are knocked out of the English Cup at Blackburn. Tempers flare and the squad's harmony is shot to pieces. The effects will be long-lasting.

Defending champions United have finished 13th. An era's end beckons.

The Reds' second-highest goalscorer, Harold Halse, plays cricket back home in London all summer. Much to the supporters' dismay, he does not return to Manchester. The directors sanction a £1,200 deal with Aston Villa. Halse is 26 and at his peak. He has won two titles and an English Cup with the club, and they won't be *his* last trophies.

'Moneybags United' are no more. Mangnall's summer work is tiresome, with spending limited and the directors urging sales. Harry Moger is next to go, and then Charlie Roberts is linked with Manchester City. The Blues have offered £1,000. United ask for £1,500 but no agreement is reached. It's likely Charlie would have gone. He only lives around the corner from City's ground and, if he is to leave United, it would be for a nearby club if possible because his family is well-settled.

Blackburn then offer £1,200 for top goalscorer 'Knocker' West and United reject it, perhaps in an attempt to convince unsettled secretary Ernest Mangnall that they retain the ambition of the last decade. If so, it's an attempt in vain.

2

Red to Blue

*'This is a more prosaic age and we sit silent
and watch with enthusiasm the weaver of
football spells, this wizard whose feet are
as fleet and whose heart is as buoyant as in
that way back day in 1894 when he flashed
into English football, destined to successfully
challenge comparison with the greatest of
outside-rights has gone before.'*

– Manchester United programme.

June 1912 – While Mangnall eyes pastures new, Billy
Meredith anticipates his long-awaited benefit match. Living
in Stretford, he trains over the summer and goes back to Chirk
for prolonged visits to his home countryside. He fishes. He
sees old friends. He prepares for his big day.

In 1904, Manchester City promised him a benefit
which never came to fruition because of the scandal that
followed. He received an equivalent sum when signing for
United, but the occasion itself was sacrificed. Now nearing
his 40th birthday, two decades into an incredible career,
Meredith's savings are small. He and his family live well,
and have done since he started at City in the 1890s, but not
extravagantly. Billy invested much of his money into the
sports shop in St Peter's Square which declared bankruptcy
in 1909 due to fire. Since, the mining boy has pestered
United's directors and, even under financial pressure after

Old Trafford's construction and an FA investigation, they give in to him.

Manchester responds in excess. Dinners and smoking concerts are held in Billy's honour – he does like a pipe – and communication pours in from those touched by his talent in the last 20 years, from Chirk to Manchester, and even Brazil. In attendance will be celebrities alongside Chirk's plentiful supply of footballing sons, including brother Sam, the player, and Elias, the railwayman who took Billy to watch those inspirational Preston Invincibles long ago. And, of course, and to Billy's great pride, Thomas E. Thomas, the brilliant coach and schoolmaster who inspired a generation of north Welsh lads to go into the professional game.

The great peculiarity of Meredith's crowning day, though, is in the status of his manager. Ernest Mangnall has reversed Billy's own move by swapping United for City. The secretaryship was vacant, Ernest applied, and he beat 106 other candidates to the position. The Hyde Road directors are as surprised as everyone else, but they are elated, for obvious reasons. City's future suddenly looks brighter, helmed by this highly experienced, ambitious figure, while United's is suddenly uncertain.

What is so particularly odd is that Mangnall remains United boss until his contract expires in September. It's clear he has little interest left, choosing instead to focus on watching his new team, City, at Hyde Road, but his final match will not present such a problem because Ernest can watch his old and new club simultaneously. In the most remarkable Manchester derby, Mangnall will be secretary for United and cross the divide almost immediately after full time. More fascinating still is that this is the afternoon to celebrate one Billy Meredith, the most famous man to cross that internal Cottonopolis border.

City win the match 1-0, and some claim to spot a wry smile from Mangnall at full time. Nevertheless, J.H. Davies presents the Lancastrian with a handsome silver table ornament and a gold wristlet watch is given to his wife Eliza. John Henry is dismayed at Mangnall's departure but wishes Ernest all the best across the city. The pair share many characteristics and have got on well.

Also leaving wreathed in smiles is Billy Meredith. United have lost, but he is delighted with the day itself. Cheers of 'good old Bill' could be heard from all around, players on both sides joined in huge applause and the band played 'For He's a Jolly Good Fellow' as he went to do the toss for ends. The 39,911 crowd raises a record amount for a benefit: £1,400.

Billy leaves satisfied, comfortable that he has a bit of financial certainty for the future and that his contributions to football have, at long last, been properly recognised. And for the first time, perhaps, this maverick now knows he has more friends in football than enemies.

3

Pastures new

'Manchester United have not yet signed either of their famous trio of half-backs, Duckworth, Roberts and Bell.'

– *Burnley News*, 24 May 1913.

June 1913 – Life with Manchester's Blues began swimmingly for Ernest Mangnall. Several entertaining September victories marked City out as championship contenders for the first time in nearly a decade and while such form didn't persist throughout the campaign, fourth-placed United finish just two points ahead of Mangnall's new side, in sixth. It is a narrowing of the red–blue gap rather than an abolition, but City are undoubtedly headed in an upwards direction. United's trajectory is less certain.

Mangnall's replacement is former chairman J.J. Bentley, who endured a shaky start until a winter uplift saw the Reds considered title challengers again. Like City, United failed to muster that extra push to truly compete for the honours. Bentley's United might have come closer had Charlie Roberts and Billy Meredith, 24 appearances each, been more regularly available, and Alec Bell and Dick Duckworth, too, with only 26 to their name.[23] It has been a decent, but unremarkable season. To mark the campaign's end, Charlie takes his squad to play bowls in Heaton Chapel, where they enjoy tea and

---

23 From a possible 43.

evening drinks. It's a rather more sedate season's end than back in 1908, when the team toured Europe, or 1909, when they lifted the cup, built Old Trafford and went to war with the FA. And that's not so surprising. Manchester United are not operating at an unstoppable pace any more, on or off the pitch.

For the second successive summer, Charlie Roberts is linked with a move away. He has had a request for a second benefit match rejected by United's once extravagant but now frugal board. Still, he eventually re-signs despite their disagreement and all seems well. He settles down for the summer, working at his Clayton tobacco shop and playing with his children in the box backyard. And yet, by September, Manchester United have lost their greatest captain and the team's heartbeat. He signs for Oldham Athletic.

It has been a stop-and-start whirlwind for Charlie. He gave the move serious thought after hearing the first bid but then prepared to settle down at United again. Then one August Saturday afternoon, he played in United's pre-season practice match at Old Trafford, travelled home across town to Clayton and when he arrived in the late evening found several Oldham officials waiting for him to sign documents and complete a transfer.

Oldham are a fairly new club who have risen quickly and craved Charlie's experience and leadership. A Latics director began making discreet enquiries after United's financial difficulties were publicly acknowledged. A £1,000 offer was rejected and United deemed an extra £250 insufficient, too. Charlie assumed the deal to be off, but over several days, Oldham eventually conceded to a £1,500 fee, convincing United's directors, if not the club's fans, who are so devastated by the news that J.J. Bentley is forced to provide an official explanation.

'There is no personal grievance between the directors and Roberts,' he says.

'Needing money, we felt bound to accept the big offer made to us. Roberts has our best wishes for the future.

United officials can never forget all that he has done for the club.'

With United unwilling to guarantee a benefit and Charlie receiving £225 from a deal, he's happy to sign. Oldham are a good club only a half-mile further from Charlie's home than United. He can stay put with his family and his business.

'For many things, I should be sorry to go,' he says, 'but there has been a little trouble at the United, and I thought it best for all concerned that I should leave. I shall be sorry to leave a lot of my old friends, but as I am still going to live in Manchester I shall not be absolutely separated from them.'

Charlie's Oldham boss is Herbert Bamlett, who, you may remember, was the man who refereed that infamous 'snowy' match at Burnley in the 1909 English Cup, when Roberts blew the full-time whistle for him because he was so chilly. Within weeks of Charlie's arrival in Oldham, his new team-mates elect him as captain and he returns to Old Trafford aged 30 and demonstrates his quality. United win, putting on a 'dazzling display', but on an individual level, Roberts plays very well indeed.

So do his old club, actually. United start excellently without their long-serving talisman. They win nine games out of ten, but the fall in the team's quality is made suddenly and abundantly clear by three consecutive losses which begins a major decline. By February, the team is hard to recognise, and by the season's end, they have avoided relegation by just a single point.

Billy Meredith, in particular, misses Charlie's consistently well-weighted distribution and the natural synergy he enjoys with his captain. He's regularly seen scratching his head or twisting his toothpick between his teeth in frustration as a team-mate fails to notice a run or a clever backheel. Meanwhile, Charlie captains Oldham to their best-ever finish: fourth. With 17 wins from 38 games, they are one point off second and eight off easy champions Newcastle, against whom the Latics win 3-0 at home and draw 0-0 away, demonstrating their quality.

Ernest Mangnall's City have now abolished the points gap with United entirely, but rather than fourth and sixth, the Mancunian sides are now 13th and 14th. Billy Meredith is playing well as he nears his 40th birthday, but not quite as well as in his early thirties, and he is enduring the same issues Roberts faced: consistent arguments with United's directors. The warm smiles of autumn 1912 have long since faded. Meredith claims he is yet to receive the money from his benefit match in full, and he's telling the truth. Billy would like the money to invest in a new venture: the Church Hotel in Longsight. This teetotaller is becoming a publican.

* * *

Further north in Manchester, past Newton Heath, a young lad called **Raymond Walter Crickmer** is helping his father out in a tobacco shop similar to that of Charlie Roberts. Born in the 19th century's final fortnight, Ray is now 14. His father Walter is a tobacconist salesman from East Anglia and his Dublin-born mum Alice Kelly has followed her mother in becoming a dressmaker. The Crickmers had four children die during pregnancy, at birth or in their infant years before Ray survived – God's long-awaited blessing – and was joined by Percy six years later.

They live in Blackley on Moston Lane, just down from Boggart Hole Brook, by the public baths and right on the tramway so can get into central Manchester quickly. There's even a new cinema down the road. There's a large recreation ground a few minutes' jog away with a decent quality cricket ground that occasionally hosts a big football match. Ray and Percy play there with mates from Hague Street Primary School in Newton Heath, not far from Manchester United's birthplace.

Before Ray's younger brother Percy is out of school for the summer holidays, Europe is on the precipice of war.

4

War

*'Our honour is said to be involved in entering
into the war. That is always the excuse. I
suppose our honour was involved in the
Crimean War, and who to-day justifies it?
Our honour was involved in the Boer War.
How many to-day will justify it? A few years
hence, and if we are led into this war, we
shall look back in wonder and amazement
at the flimsy reasons which induced the
Government to take part.'*

– Keir Hardie, House of Commons,
3 August 1914.

June 1914 – France have alliances with Britain and Russia which, in combination with the territories they control in North Africa and western Asia, have effectively encircled Germany. Add in an agreement with Italy and guarantees to Belgium and Luxembourg's neutrality and like popcorn in a bag, if one kernel fires, the rest will follow into war. Germany themselves have pacts with Italy and Austria-Hungary, and in turn Romania.

In late June, the first kernel pops. Archduke Franz Ferdinand, heir to the Austro-Hungarian throne, is assassinated by a Serbian-backed terrorist. Crisis follows. With German encouragement, Austria-Hungary declares war on

Serbia in late July. Russia's support of Serbia brings France into the conflict, and Germany declares war on Russia on 1 August and France two days later.

Britain has been largely preoccupied with other concerns: social, industrial and political unrest and a potential civil war in Ireland. Many in Parliament see the continent's tensions as a purely European affair that Britain should exclude itself from, but it is an argument that loses out. Britain enters the war after Germany invades Belgium.

Propaganda presents Britain as saviour to poor little Belgium, such moral arguments being necessary because, unlike other nations, there is no compulsory military service. Recruitment will be an entirely voluntary affair.

That being said, a young man like Raymond Walter Crickmer can't walk through town without being repeatedly slapped in the face by demands for him to join up. And patriotism genuinely runs rife. For young boys brought up at school and in the Boy Scouts with military language and jingoism, it's an overwhelmingly exciting affair. Many are keen to fight so they can see the world. Others are immune to the patriotism but it's a struggle to remain so.

'Life perhaps seems to go on as usual,' one newspaper warns. 'Do not be deceived, this is the most deadly peril Britain has ever met. You must strain every nerve or you will be crushed under the German boot.'

Try to keep calm and carry on with a threat like that.

***

Going against the patriotic fervour somewhat is the Players' Union, a move which once again sees the press eviscerate Manchester United's players.

'They once called themselves the Outcasts – they deserve to be!'

The FA has imposed a small tax on professional footballers' wages to raise money for those league clubs suffering from smaller war attendances. The union point out that it is not the players' responsibility to support these clubs. There is little sympathy.

There are some who criticise not the United players, but the sport as a whole. Unlike cricket and rugby, football persists with the league season. Its supporters believe it to be a crucial morale booster for those on the Home Front, while the government view it as a valuable recruiting opportunity. Hundreds of footballers sign up to fight within weeks, proving its worth as a propaganda tool.

It's a mutually beneficial relationship. Football flourishes at home and on the front lines. Cricket needs a carefully prepared pitch, and rugby means being thrown to the ground, which no one wants on their breaks from arduous training or fighting. Soon enough, leagues are formed and encouraged in the army. The main complication is inconsistent teams. It is hard to be consistent when the goalkeeper's been shot between fixtures.

***

Back home, 14-year-old Ray Crickmer sees the posters everywhere. 'Britain needs you at once', 'The Empire Needs Men!' And 'JOIN YOUR COUNTRY'S ARMY! GOD SAVE THE KING!' The one that seems omnipresent features Lord Kitchener's head and his pointing finger. Always pointing, always at him, Ray thinks. It seems to follow him as he walks past it.

Other posters target women like Ray's mum Alice.

'Women of Lancashire. Do you realise that if you keep back a son or sweetheart you are prolonging the war and adding to the peril of those who have gone?'

The daughter of a career soldier, Alice worries for her two sons, but she's comforted by the fact the war should be over by Christmas. In fact, that's why many young men have signed up so quickly. 'It'll be over by Christmas, you won't see anything if you wait,' is a common quip. But quickly enough, Britain's soldiers realise how well-organised the Germans are and how devastating modern weapons can be. Bayonets against machine guns? It's like taking a lemon to a knife fight.

Back home, the troop trains begin to come back from Mons. Trainload after trainload, filled with frighteningly wounded people. And the women and children of each man's village gather up all the comforts they can find, to meet them at the station and to feed them and to help them. But the patriotism and the excitement have faded away. The world has become distinctly grey.

***

The war is not over by Christmas. It has become clear that this is total war, a national war unlike any seen before; not several thousand men fighting in a land far away, but the complete mobilisation of the entire country, not just to fight, but to provide.

For now, though, football continues, providing a necessary distraction and sometimes charity, too. A keen patriot, Ernest Mangnall has sent 4,500 cigarette boxes to every man fighting in the Manchester Regiment's 4th Battalion. Meanwhile, his City side sit just behind Football League leaders, Charlie Roberts's Oldham Athletic, whose rise has been extraordinary.

Roberts began the season at Old Trafford in opposition to Billy Meredith's Manchester United, a little like the pre-season practice games of old. Oldham won 3-1 as Charlie played a masterly game, ever in the right place at the right time. United supporters shook their heads in wonder and envy, left thinking what could have been when he beat two men in midfield and expertly set up one of the goals. His quality was starkly contrasted by United's Irish centre-half Patrick O'Connell, who had a wretched 90 minutes.[24] The comparison drove United's supporters mad, and probably

---

24 O'Connell went on to manage several Spanish clubs including Barcelona, Sevilla and Real Betis, with whom he won the 1934/35 La Liga title.

Meredith, too, who endured a difficult game against Oldham's ever-improving back line.

Charlie and Billy reunite throughout the season for charity matches. Sometimes they play, other times they merely offer their faces as encouragement for donations, such as in March, when the County Police play the Special Constables. Charlie referees and Billy, toothpick in mouth, hops up and down the line with his slender frame, calling offsides. By April, Charlie's Oldham are in a rather brilliant position. Level on points with Mangnall's Manchester City and Blackburn Rovers, with a game in hand on both, Oldham have seven matches to play. Win the majority and they will be champions for the first time. The situation is a little different at Old Trafford. United have won only six games and may be relegated. So much for a distraction from misery.

J.J. Bentley's time as secretary-manager has been flawed and though he retains a role at the club, his day-to-day hands-on responsibilities are given to Jack Robson, who has done exceedingly well as Middlesbrough, Crystal Palace and Brighton secretary. At his first club, he was paid just £3 a week and declined to travel to away games to save the club's money. At Brighton, with more cash, he won the Southern League and the Charity Shield. He seems an excellent fit: prudent, but successful. His credentials are better than Mangnall's when he arrived at United.

A few months into the Robson era, United start April in the way they must – with victory – but the result is greeted with boos. It's not that the crowd are frustrated at a season's worth of poor performances. It's not a demand for more from the directors. They are not even showing their disgust towards a refereeing decision. They boo because they think they've been conned; they think the game is a fix. And they are right.

Several players from both sides arranged it pre-match and a large amount of money was then bet at odds of 7/1 for United to win 2-0. Those connected hardly tried to hide it. Liverpool's players remonstrated with a team-mate when he struck the crossbar late on when the desired scoreline had already been achieved.

Billy Meredith spent much of the first half suspicious, he said, as to why he was never being passed the ball. He asked what was going on at half-time and then spent the entire second half without getting a touch. His account was easily believed.

Unlike the distinctly principled Billy, the fix makes sense for his team-mates. It has become clear by now that the FA will suspend league football for the rest of the war, starting from the end of this season. Footballers, therefore, know that their careers at the top might be over in just a few weeks, especially if they are 30 years old like Sandy Turnbull. Perhaps they also thought the ongoing war would provide a distraction to their crime. Instead, it makes their wrongdoing worse. While others are fighting for their country, putting their lives on the line, here several men conned the public of their money and time.

That the fix seemingly had little to do with saving Manchester United from potential relegation prevents the club from receiving punishment for its involvement but the plain truth is that the fixed victory over Liverpool is crucial to United's Division One survival. The Reds stay up by just one point.

* * *

Ernest Mangnall's revived City have faltered at the last, dropping to fifth with three defeats. Victory once in three would have taken them level at the top. Had another been converted to a draw, they'd be champions. Late disappointment aside, Ernest is doing a fine job and appears, were it not for the rude intervention of war, on the precipice of replicating his United success.

Also faltering late on is another horse familiar to the Old Trafford boys. Charlie Roberts's Oldham Athletic have, like City, endured key defeats at the season's end, unaided by controversy over a director's suspension for 'ungentlemanly conduct' and a player's sending off which dampened the Boundary Park crowd's enthusiasm. Still, so good has their season been, they approach the season's final week level with Everton – who have snuck into top spot – but with a game in hand. Unfortunately, their falter turns into a complete collapse as they lose twice and thus must settle for second. Charlie went into the forward line for the last ten minutes of one match, clearly frustrated with his side's poor finishing, but made a defensive error days after in the second. He is left furious with himself.

Although those final two performances were substandard, it is Charlie's quality and leadership that has dragged Oldham to consecutive record-breaking finishes. Roberts is left pondering what could have been as the Football League takes its first pause since Saturday, 8 September 1888.

5

Futility

*'It is many years since Charlie Roberts
donned the green shirt of "Saints", and
his reappearance in the side brought back
memories of the past. Roberts remains one of
England's best half-backs.'*

– *North Star (Darlington)*, 22 November 1915.

June 1915 – When Ray Crickmer and his younger brother Percy spot a queue forming at one of Blackley's shops, one of them joins it and the other runs home to tell mum Alice to come quickly with some money. She does so and gets whatever she can because food is short and its availability comes in unexpected bursts. People are not starving, and the government is yet to introduce rationing, but everyone dreams of a little more food. It doesn't help that an entirely uneven distribution exists. Hoarding of food, most often bags of flour, causes great resentment in communities.

Britain's problems are unique. The country has celebrated its empire for many a year, but now reliance on colonial imports makes things tricky. Sugar is the first noticeable shortage, as beet sugar comes from opponents Austria and cane sugar from now inaccessible South America. Germany's unrestricted submarine warfare restricts things further still. In better news, shortly after Old Trafford hosts the English Cup Final – won by Sheffield United – Italy leaves its alliance with Germany and Austria-Hungary and joins Britain, France and Russia.

As for football, the league proper has paused but the sport continues with regional divisions. Billy Meredith is unsure whether he'll play. While he still loves scampering down the wing, he's deeply resentful towards Manchester United's directors for failing to hand over his benefit money in full. His old friend Charlie Roberts is certain to play. He's using his last few years – he is nine years younger than Billy – to further improve, and doing so as part of a high-flying Oldham Athletic side is an enticing proposition.

The old leading United pair meet repeatedly for charitable causes. Charlie, in particular, is everywhere: Fallowfield, where they had been Outcasts in 1909, to raise money for the local Red Cross hospitals; Oldham, Charlie deeming charity endeavour more important than an Oldham away match, playing with Billy, Sandy Turnbull and others to raise money for the Blackpool Soldiers' Home of Rest; and even back to Darlington, for a romantic and timely return.

The career of one of England's finest half-backs' is nearly over, though he doesn't know it yet. Turning out in the green shirt of his old St Augustine's club, where he last played a dozen years ago, Charlie puts on a show. He's denied once by a fantastic save and later juggles the ball towards and into the goalmouth before allowing his team-mate to finish it off. United winger George Wall joins Charlie for the match because his regiment is stationed nearby.

Meanwhile, Billy Meredith attempts to join the army and, remarkably, is passed medically unfit. Conscription is about to be brought in and there is a fairly significant expectation that all men should attempt to sign up before they are forced to. Conscripts will be viewed differently to volunteers by their comrades, senior officers and the general public, many of whom see those yet to sign up as cowards. There is little Billy can do, though, as he's passed unfit, and Charlie, too, will never go to war, even once eligible for conscription in April 1916, when all married men aged 18–40 are called up.

Despite losing many of their players, Oldham are once again challenging Everton, as with last season, for the title, although now just for the league's south Lancashire section. At Everton, the *Birkenhead News* suggest, 'It was Roberts here, Roberts there, Roberts everywhere.' In early February, Charlie plays a 'brilliant' game against Stockport County and prepares to take on Liverpool. The local *Echo* newspaper informs its readers, 'Oldham's team will produce England's centre-half, Charles Roberts, and that factor alone is sufficient to arouse great interest.' With football's younger talents away fighting, Liverpudlians are therefore eagerly waiting to see one of the game's remaining stars at Anfield, but Charlie doesn't play. And he may never play again.

Roberts is ill. It has set in quickly, as all illnesses do in this era. He has developed pleurisy, causing him sharp chest pains that worsen while breathing. It's evident that Charlie cannot play in such circumstances, and attention turns to discovering the cause. Often caused by flu, in Charlie's case, pleurisy is a sign of another bacterial infection: pneumonia. It's a serious threat to life.

Charlie has a narrow escape. The real dangers of pneumonia pass mercifully quickly, but its long-lasting effects are only beginning to set in across Charlie's body, and not just in his lungs. He is still struggling to breathe and his knee is seizing up with great regularity. Football is absolutely out of the question.

His old mate Billy can play, though, and does for the first time in a while. Manchester United have, like Oldham, continued playing in a regional league but Meredith has not turned out for them. Not even once. It is not a sign of a declining love for the game; Billy is as enamoured with football as ever. When acting as linesman in a recent charity match, he hopped excitedly on the side, keen to be involved. On a couple of occasions when the ball came near him, he passed it to help the weaker team. He's itching to get back into regular action, but not for United. Instead, Manchester City secretary Ernest Mangnall offers him the chance to return to the Blues. Eventually, United give Meredith their permission to 'guest' at Hyde Road and with that, for the first time in 13 years, the Reds are without either of their trail-blazing star duo of Meredith and Roberts.

It is symbolic of United's current philosophy. With Mangnall's great side fully disbanded, Jack Robson has been tasked by John Henry Davies with building a young team. The directors insist this is done on serious purse strings, so Robson seeks players not yet involved in first-class football who can be moulded into top performers.

Meredith returns for City against Liverpool in mid-March, turning out in blue for the first time in a decade. He starts slowly, with his legs a little cumbersome – very unlike him – but he works himself into some typically bright play. His centres are pinpoint-accurate. Such crosses demand a stocky centre-forward to bulldoze them home but Sandy Turnbull – Private Turnbull, that should be – is on the front line. Sandy signed up in November 1915, just a month before the commission into match-fixing concluded and suspended him. He had been working for the Manchester Ship Canal Company before joining the Middlesex Footballers' Battalion.

In April, with Billy now settled in back at his old stomping ground, the FA rule in his favour for once. They decree that he, and a selection of former team-mates, can sue United for unpaid benefit match receipts. He's pleased, and so is Mangnall because City have pipped Burnley to the league's Lancashire title.

Billy plays countless charity matches throughout the summer and J.J. Bentley leaves Manchester United after over a decade. John Henry has offered him a board position but with Bentley having now lost the league presidency, FA vice-presidency and the trust of United's players, it's time to back away quietly.

* * *

Quietness. Those on the front line have forgotten what that sounds like. The meaning of it has changed. In France, 57,000

British soldiers are killed in one day at the Somme. It is one of human history's deadliest battles and it will continue in this vein until mid-November. Such vast numbers of death numb Europe's population. When Alf Albut dies aged 67 in December, no one at Newton Heath or Manchester United notices. Death has become all too normal.

Alice Crickmer fears for her sons' futures. The war that was meant to be over by Christmas 1914 is about to celebrate its third Noel and Ray is not far off signing up as he celebrates his 17th birthday at the end of 1916. Alice tries not to read the death lists each morning, but every time she reads the paper, there is someone she knows, even if it's only a friend of a friend of a friend. She wonders what the future will be like for her and her children. It just feels like everyone will be dead. When a million are dying at the Somme alone, it's a hard feeling to shake.

Ernest Mangnall receives regular letters from his players throughout the war. Some report on their achievements in matches played behind the lines while others wish him well for the season but say, 'Sorry, I can't play this year, I've received a shrapnel wound to my wrist in an explosion which killed 13 of my comrades' or 'Sorry, my boat has been torpedoed, I won't be back for a while.' Just little things like that.

Charlie Roberts sends more letters than he receives. He is suffering from infective arthritis. Bacteria has spread to his knee from his lungs after pneumonia. It makes his knee painfully stiff and so he cannot play football and he cannot join the army. Instead, he looks after his children, attends charity matches wherever possible, talks to old team-mates and works at his newsagents and tobacco shop. He sends letters constantly, especially to Lance Sergeant Sandy Turnbull of the 8th East Surrey Battalion, who Roberts gifts cigars, cigarettes and tobacco from his shop, neatly wrapped into metal boxes. Sandy gleefully greets the contents when they arrive in the trenches, passed down the human chain through the mud.

With the sun still to rise on the misty morning of 3 May 1917, the 8th East Surrey advances towards the village of Chèrisy, ten miles east of Arras. They hope to catch the German front line off guard, and they do. The village is captured and Sandy and his comrades reach the banks of the River Sensèe almost fully intact. On the other side of Chèrisy, their supporting units have not been so successful. The 8th is isolated. Heavy shell fire rains down upon them mercilessly. Within a couple of hours, Sandy's battalion has been completely overrun by the German counter-attack. Many are dead or captured.

Several days later, Sandy's wife Florence receives an ominous-looking letter at her home in Gorse Hill. One of his comrades writes:

'I am writing to try to explain what has happened to your dear husband, Alec. He was wounded, and much to our sorrow, fell into German hands, so I hope you will hear from him. After Alec was wounded he "carried on" and led his men for a mile, playing the game until the last we saw of him. We all loved him, and he was a father to us all and the most popular man in the regiment. All here send our deepest sympathy.'

Florence does not hear from Sandy because Manchester's beloved, bruising centre-forward is dead.

Turnbull's leg was hit, by a bullet or shrapnel, early on in the capture of Chèrisy. His commanding officer ordered him back to the dressing station but Sandy refused and pleaded to continue. When the Germans began to surround the 8th, Sandy and co. came under heavy machine-gun fire. With typically excellent movement, he manoeuvred his way out of the fire and into the relative safety of nearby houses. His comrades believed him to have retreated successfully. But this was not a football pitch, war is not a game and Sandy did not return. The only explanation his comrades can muster is that he was picked off by a German, lying low amongst the houses.

News that Sandy is MIA reaches Manchester in the summer of 1917. Charlie is devastated. Billy is, too. They've lost one of their very closest mates. In fact, everyone associated with Mancunian football is deeply saddened. Just as in the 8th East Surrey Battalion, Sandy was a much-loved man and a brilliant player. His body is never recovered.

6

Crickmer's fight

'If you could hear, at every jolt, the blood
Come gargling from the froth-corrupted lungs,
Obscene as cancer, bitter as the cud
Of vile, incurable sores on innocent tongues,
—My friend, you would not tell with
such high zest
To children ardent for some desperate glory,
The old Lie: Dulce et decorum est
Pro patria mori.'

– Wilfred Owen

July 1917 – News of Sandy Turnbull's death travels across the Atlantic to Harry Stafford. The United States have just involved themselves in the war, drawn in by Germany's declaration of unrestricted submarine warfare.

Harry, approaching his fifties, leaves the US for Canada, where better jobs have opened up due to the war effort. Harry takes what is a promotion of sorts. His partner Alice and her brother, Tom, join Stafford in Montreal, a city in the midst of protests against conscription. Back home, Harry's son Harold Bown is entering the workforce, too. Aged 14, he becomes an apprentice fitter in Plumstead at the Woolwich Arsenal, near where his absent father once took on the local football team as captain of Newton Heath.

Old Trafford plays host to several charity matches, the latest a Belgian soldiers' team versus a Manchester XI. The money raised is given to Belgian charities. Ernest Mangnall arranges a donation on behalf of Manchester City, with another going to the Manchester Royal Infirmary Board for the treatment of military patients. At Hyde Road, Mangnall allows all soldiers in admission-free. Almost 60,000 visit the ground while on leave. The veteran secretary has developed another focus, too. He asks the football authorities to arrange benefit matches for the families of footballers, like his old centre-forward Sandy Turnbull, whose lives have been lost fighting. Businesses across the country have committed money to such an idea, but the FA are left offering their indebtedness to Mangnall for raising the issue within football. They duly create a £5,000 national war fund.

Although charity is gratefully received, it won't cut it and the government announces rationing will be brought in just after the New Year, when Raymond Walter Crickmer celebrates his 18th birthday. Now of age, he immediately joins the army and becomes Private Crickmer. Ray is just under 5ft 2in and of slim build. With brown eyes and brown hair, a mole on the right side of his neck, slightly flat feet and a history of bronchitis, he is passed medically fit.

Alice is scared for her son, understandably, but can't help but be proud as he emulates her father in his khaki uniform. She hopes his fate will be like her father's and not the many who have gone, never to return – men like United's Sandy Turnbull, Oscar Linkson or Thomas Wall, younger brother of George.

Ray undergoes a long training period and gains strength quickly, his chest growing by two inches. An obviously bright lad, he becomes a tank engineer and, after some months, is assigned to Manchester's 5th Battalion. The 5th is a Territorial Force unit that moved from Rochdale immediately to Egypt at the war's commencement but eventually joined Europe's Western Front. They were fighting in the Third Battle of

Ypres while Ray was completing his forms back home in Manchester.

In July 1918, Ray is ready for duty. He leaves his parents, who are becoming accustomed to rationing for butter, margarine, lard, meat and sugar, and heads to Warrington's Reception Depot where his service officially begins. He is slowly transported towards his battalion, now in the Charleroi area.

Crickmer eventually arrives in Charleroi, where Manchester's 2nd and 5th battalions are stationed, including the great war poet Wilfred Owen, who bemoaned 'the old lie' that it 'is sweet and fitting to die for one's country'. In early November, Owen is killed, aged 25. It is a bitter death, and ill-fitting in its timing. The war is nearly over.

7

Freedom

'The war is over, and in a million households fathers and mothers, wives and sisters, will breathe freely, relieved at length of all dread of that curt message which has shattered the hope and joy of so many. The war is over. The drama is played out.'

— *Manchester Guardian.*

November 1918 – It is a fine Monday morning and late autumn sunshine reflects off Manchester's wet, cobbled streets. The city is just getting into its routine at the beginning of a new week when the news comes out, first as a trickle, and then as a flood, speeding out from the floors of the *Manchester Guardian* and *Evening News* offices, on to the streets and far out into the suburbs. By 10:25am, flags fly and sirens wail for freedom.

Newspaper carts dart across Manchester spreading the news and, everywhere they go, the impulse of the British people is to throw open the windows. A dark, dense cloud of death and misery has infected the country's every nook and cranny and as the air of freedom and the wind of change sweeps across on this autumn morning, every Mancunian wants it to penetrate every room and drive into every gap. That cloud of death, misery and war has risen. A new world is here.

The *Guardian* passes from hand to hand. Flags come out of windows, offices and shops. There is no wind, and so they simply hang, as if already in memory of the dead.

At 11am, the war officially ends. Just as a football crowd takes in a breath before a goal, the crowd gathered in Manchester's Albert Square watches two flags rise, and then the uncontainable hum of celebration spreads. No one in this city has been immune from the overwhelming force of the Great War, and doesn't Manchester know it? For every man or woman leaping in delight, another is wiping a melancholy tear of remembrance. Soon enough, though, the jubilation triumphs. By lunchtime, female factory workers spill out in their work clothes, processing through town, growing in numbers and size. Songs break out, the streets thicken and soon throb with people and emotion. The Italian marching bands of Louis Rocca's Ancoats march and play. Bells ring out. American soldiers join in, and the Belgians, too. Shops shut their doors, schools open theirs, the recruiting office locks up and the tram service slackens as guards jump off to join in. Manchester is both at a standstill and moving without pause and with joy.

As evening comes, people delight in leaving their windows open with the lights on, even though the street lamps are still adorned by their 'mufflers'. Like a debutant celebrating his first senior goal, it takes the celebration some time to tire. It is as if everyone could run for miles, releasing every reserve of nervous energy.

***

When the glow dies down and the dancing, drinking, kissing, singing and cavorting ends, the euphoria yields to a sober, melancholy reflection on the lives lost and the lives ruined. The lives lost, and the lives ruined – pointlessly.

War has ended without a glorious knockout blow or even a great accomplishment. No one can truly explain the value of victory, other than that it ends the fighting. The Germans have suffered a losing draw, Europe's crisis is not over and this is no new world, but a bucket kicked down the line.

That cloud of death remains, too. In the weeks after November's great celebrations, hundreds of people in

Manchester die from influenza. 'Spanish' flu arrived in Britain in spring and only the fast-thinking preventative actions of Manchester's medical officer, Dr James Niven, kept the city's death rate stable. He introduced social distancing, encouraged handwashing and organised the mass provision of baby milk. In fact, he urged citizens to avoid mass gatherings, but no one could stop the population enjoying the Armistice, and the death rate spiked immediately after. Elsewhere in the country, things are significantly worse.

* * *

The Western Front is quiet now, but the millions of men serving cannot race home. They must stay and partake in a long, drawn-out demobilisation scheme over which there are real concerns because Europe remains sick, and not just with flu. Rationing is in place in Britain, Bolshevism has taken over in Russia and general unrest is bubbling, not helped by the slow demobbing process.

Although melancholy replaces euphoria for many, football rides that wave of joy for a long time still. It is now the indisputable national sport. The FA's controversial decision to persist with the league during the 1914/15 season paid off, for football was not viewed as unpatriotic or distracting, as rugby and cricket had claimed. Football genuinely takes some credit for victory, although the *Athletic News* are hyperbolic to the extreme in their editorial.

'Football was the great sport of our soldiers behind the trenches, at home and at the base, away in foreign theatres of war, and at home through the dreary months of training. It was the great tonic of the boys called on to train and fight, and it was also the great mental tonic and physical "refresher" of those at home who were working night and day and putting every ounce of effort into their work. The game answered a great purpose in preserving the pluck, the hope, the faith of the nation. In this great war of nerves, football was a great steadying influence.'

Football has indeed given the nation something, and in return it sits on a new pedestal, helped by the cross-class participation in the game as working-class and middle-class men engaged together in the same battalions. Heroes, the lot of them, and in the first post-war election campaign of December 1918, in which 8.4 million women over 30 can finally vote, the popular wartime Prime Minister Lloyd George – who counts Billy Meredith amongst his supporters – promises to make Britain a 'country fit for heroes'.

George is re-elected and thus represents Britain at the Palace of Versailles as the world meets to negotiate peace. As he does so, Charlie Roberts engages in his own back-and-forth. In the absence of Lieutenant Colin Veitch, still in France, Charlie is the Players' Union stand-in chairman.

After 1909's great controversies, the union's pre-war activities settled down. Day-to-day, their work was exemplary, helping footballers and their families by investigating appeals, covering funeral expenses, paying removal costs or hospital fees, and even bailing men out of prison. They made quick, on-the-spot assessments that made farcical the FA's slow-moving and tricky 'Benevolent Fund'. They also acted as an unofficial employment agency, finding new clubs for those out of work.

The union had, to Meredith and Roberts's disgust, abandoned attempts to join any national body, but continued to push legal boundaries, challenging clubs for unpaid wages, compensation or unjust contractual agreements. They had mixed success, limited by financial problems as the FA began to refuse to permit an end-of-season fundraising match. The union's secretary Syd Owen called them 'handicapping ... high-handed ... intolerable ... stupid ... and vindictive'. He refused to apologise, and the FA attempted to boot him out. Unlike in defending Broomfield in 1909, the union formally censured their own secretary so Owen told them where to stick it and left to coach in Budapest.

Over the final pre-war years, the union gave up its St Peter's Square offices, retreating into a spare room in the new secretary's own home – a visual manifestation of their diminishing power. Charlie Roberts grew increasingly frustrated and dismayed by matters. He called his fellow footballers 'a lot of sheep ... who cannot think for themselves'.

The war brought its own problems and Charlie held little back. 'The hypocrisy of the whole thing stinks in the nostrils,' he said of the decision to force footballers to play without pay while club secretaries continued to enjoy generous salaries and FA officials' generous expense accounts persisted. 'The player has been the MUG too long.'

Within days of the war's end in November, arguments began to rage about football's resumption. Within two weeks, the Football League announced professional players could receive £1 a week 'allowance', but no real wage. Passions were roused by this, and from a position of one nearly-dead union sprung two.

In mid-December, a meeting in London saw a new footballers' union formed with a distinctly capital-heavy taste to it. The founders had lofty ambitions not dissimilar from those touted in 1907 by Billy Meredith, but they had something else: the presence and support of experienced trade union officials. A meeting was duly set between players and the Football League for mid-January.

* * *

January 1919 – Ten years on from that cloudy, tense summer of 1909, the once radical Charlie Roberts now brings the players back into line. He is at odds with the new 'London' union, suggesting that any footballers' organisation should be run on constitutional lines with approval from the Football League and FA. The football elites approve. League president John McKenna says: 'We will not accept a players' union on trades union principles and whose strength lies in the strike clause.'

With this sticking point proving insurmountable and another 1909 on the cards, Charlie rises to announce that the old union is still in existence – though it hardly is – and they would be willing to deal with the league on constitutional lines, to renounce union methods and any links with the wider trade union movement. It is a complete departure from his pre-war argument.

A hurried meeting between the old and new players' unions follows. Within ten minutes, Charlie convinces his comrades. Perhaps all it takes is an explanation of just how scarring that 1909 summer was. He surprises himself with his persuasive tongue, and does so again when he returns to the main meeting to demand a doubling in the player's £1 'allowance'. The league and club officials meet and agree to a rise to £2. It's a rather successful day for Charlie. Perhaps a career in politics lies ahead, but he still just wants to play again.

'My left knee, which has prevented me from playing since I contracted pneumonia, the poison from which got into my leg, is showing signs of improvement,' he says. 'It is still stiff, and I require my walking stick; but I am hopeful.'

Football's return

*'Not stern, but actually punitive ... The
real crime is the reparations and indemnity
chapter, which is immoral and senseless.'*

– Harold Nicolson, British delegate at Versailles,
on the Treaty.

July 1919 – There is little to do for soldiers waiting in France
to return home. Football fills the time.

Ray Crickmer eventually travels back to England, to
Scarborough, where he undergoes a medical examination as
the Treaty of Versailles is signed to officially end the war. At
Heaton Park, Crickmer and several thousand other young men
are then dispersed from duty. Raymond relishes life back in
the comfort and safety of post-war Manchester.

Football's long-awaited return is greeted by enormous
crowds in September, but there is no such restoration for
Charlie Roberts. The 36-year-old outlined his intention to
play again only months ago and with so many young talents
killed, and others missing out on their development over these
last five years, there is absolutely still room for veterans like
Charlie, but his knee won't allow it. One of football's most
distinguished playing careers is prematurely and regrettably
curtailed. Manchester United and Oldham Athletic's greatest
captain must sadly retire.

Billy Meredith's longevity knows no bounds, however.
The Welshman has promised to never don Manchester
United's red shirt again due to his irreparable relationship

with the directors. It is sadly ironic, then, that the transfer system which Billy founded the Players' Union to combat prevents him from fulfilling his own wishes in the twilight of his career. United are unwilling to allow Meredith to re-join Manchester City, so he must stay. Almost exactly echoing his words of 1906, he describes it as, 'The blackest injustice to place a price upon the head of a player for whom they paid no transfer fee. The selling of players is a degrading business, and I will not allow a price to be put upon my head. I would rather end my career as a footballer than allow any club to sell me even for a packet of Woodbines.'

United are without Billy for the season's start, but under Jack Robson's stewardship, they combat negative pre-season expectations and start well. Without funds for transfers and with the financial and mental challenge of war hanging over the club, Robson has guided United excellently. With Louis Rocca's scouting assistance, United platform fresh-faced talent rather than ready-made stars: in goal, Jack Mew; in defence, Jack Silcock and Charlie Moore; at half-back, Lal Hilditch; up front, Joe Spence. None played first-class football before joining United, but they look good, drawing 3-3 at City before beating Mangnall's Blues a week later at Old Trafford.

Mangnall has taken on a new challenge of his own. Perhaps inspired by the Players' Union resurgence, or Charlie Roberts's derogatory comments towards club secretaries, Ernest founds the Football League Secretaries' and Managers' Association, of which he becomes chairman and treasurer.

City and United are level for much of the autumn, but the latter's form drops off greatly as the weather turns and the pitches grow heavier. A November encounter with Burnley ends in defeat and, such is the bitter cold, chairman William Deakin catches pneumonia. Unlike Charlie Roberts in 1916, Deakin cannot recover and the J.H. Davies-installed brewery man dies. Succeeding him is the knocked-over cyclist accountant, George Lawton, and United's form becomes first inconsistent and then experiences a dramatic decline before Billy Meredith finally returns, on Boxing Day.

Old Trafford's 45,000-strong crowd eagerly watches its hero, now 45, once again, but Billy can do little against a strong Liverpool defence in a disappointing festive stalemate. His game has changed. He excels when he's not immediately harassed by the opposition and so sometimes, he looks great, and other times, not quite so. For United, he is a luxury veteran, the opulent plush-covered chair sitting mainly unused in the corner. Those centres, though, those moments of skill, they are worth it in this post-war world. Who can fail to be enthused by a moment of joy from the boot of the Welsh wizard who had run the line before the Boer War, let alone the Great War?

Well, Billy is not without critics. After January's defeat to Chelsea, the *Football News* deems it 'almost pathetic to see him standing in idleness on the halfway line with his arms folded and chewing his indispensable quill'. These games of quiet impotence are growing in regularity and Billy finds little more chastening than hearing opposition fans ironically cheer a late touch after a particularly quiet game. He is not the answer to United's problems, despite some excellent moments, and the team stumbles onwards – or downwards, really. The Reds slump from fourth in November to fourth from bottom in February.

It's little coincidence that Billy's return comes just before plans are being made for the international fixtures because it's in Welsh scarlet that Meredith feels he has unfinished business, and he's ready for one final flourish.

* * *

Snow has fallen heavily in Highbury over this mid-March weekend. It is the first time Arsenal's stadium will host an international match, and it's a crucial one. A first-ever competitive victory over England in his final international appearance will secure Billy Meredith's Wales the Home Championship.

The teams are reflective of the time. England's oldest-ever XI, its average age 30, features mainly pre-war stars. Andy Ducat is making his fourth international appearance, almost a decade after his third. Similar stories litter the Welsh side which, of course, features 45-year-old Meredith, but also Lot Jones, 37, and a whole host of 30-somethings.

The feet of 21,180 spectators turn London's snow into sludge. It's hardly football's biggest crowd, but it is Billy's biggest dream: victory over England to win the championship. The Highbury pitch mimics the streets outside, with its plentifully distributed puddles.

Wales lead 2-1 at half-time but such is England's dominance in this fixture's past that for much of the second half, it seems inevitable that Meredith's Wales will fall under the might of their hosts. But they defy that might. Billy plays a key role in neither of the goals, but in this display, he gives more than just a glimpse of his once world-beating brilliance. England's Grimsdell is beaten by several dazzling dribbles from the veteran, whose team-mates maintain their lead until the end, at which point they jubilantly stride to their dressing room, the pitch's snowy water numbing their toes despite their strong leather boots. They clatter in with gusto, their victory's magnitude sinking in: a first-ever competitive triumph over the English. Billy sits down and cries, with unashamed joy and relief. His team-mates are delighted for the side's father figure, who has seen the 19th century turn to the 20th, won two English Cups, two top-flight titles and played through a global war. Through it all, he's never beaten England. Now, in his final international appearance, he has.

'Do you wonder that I am pleased?' Meredith says.

'We had a bit of luck alright: there is no doubt about that. But our fellows, especially the defence, played with grit and determination. All the boys did magnificently. I do not wish to make any distinctions.'

Upon individual praise from his interviewer, Meredith is dismissive.

'Oh me!' he replies, just before striding off with a grin. 'I'm an old man ... I ought to be in the Cardiff Museum!'

But no fan, spectator, journalist, player or director who saw the veteran Welsh wizard weave down the touchline, turning the English defence into knots, will agree.

9

Crickmer's new job

'THE KING SEES
FOOTBALL MATCH'

– *Leeds Mercury*, 29 March 1920.

March 1920 – King George V visits Manchester in late March, offering keen patriot Ernest Mangnall a proud moment equal to Billy Meredith's with Wales. Mangnall welcomes the king to City's Hyde Road ground where he watches the Blues alongside a 35,000 crowd.

George's visit is unfortunately timed for Manchester United. The Reds are playing away at Bradford City, and losing. United finish 12th, five places below Mangnall's City. There has been a slight relegation scare, but Robson's side end equally far from the drop as they are from the fourth spot they occupied in autumn.

At the start of July, 20-year-old Raymond Crickmer joins Manchester United, signing a postcard-sized document alongside Jack Robson, who, somewhat peculiarly, insists he won't remember Raymond, but he'll remember his middle name, Walter. And that's that.

Walter Crickmer, presumably still Ray to his old mates, trudges off to Preston's Fulwood Barracks to get his employment contract stamped off by his commanding officer. He's got himself an excellent job as a clerk. In fact, regardless of the job's quality, comfort and that it allows Walter to further develop his footballing passion, just having a job is good enough. The post-war employment boom has diminished entirely and unemployment is high, and still on the rise.

That being said, despite low food supplies and unemployment, Britons' lives are better than in many other post-war countries. Germans are suffering from hyperinflation, Russia is recovering from civil war, and the USA is under prohibition. Harry Stafford counts himself lucky that he moved to Montreal, Canada. He can drink the nights away as much as he likes.

And so can Britain's young men. Returned from the horrors of war, there are plenty doing their best to enjoy a society which is capitalising on the rise of cheap cinemas and dancehalls, in which ever-more liberal attitudes allow increasingly casual relationships. It's no surprise there's a baby boom. Walter, for his part, meets a nice girl called Nellie and takes her out with his new wage.

Football's boom continues, too. There's no sign of the British public's relentless football appetite declining; even United's reserves are attracting 10,000-plus Old Trafford crowds. Though positive, this does appear to be causing dangerous complacency among the club's directors. Some clubs are capitalising on the country's football fever, but United are not. They are no longer rich, owing several people money – John Henry Davies especially – and are wary of excessive spending. The directors claim there is little value in the market and if Mancunians are watching every week anyway, why spend money needlessly? Well, such a philosophy will only work if the team can maintain their top-flight status, and the squad looks unsuitable for such a task.

When United lose their opening game, the 50,000 crowd is large enough to surprise and move Davies, whose influence has necessarily declined since the FA's 1911 investigation and ruling. Now he intervenes. It's clear United need more than the high-potential talents Robson found during the war. With this one game alone generating £3,300, Davies duly gives Robson that much, and a bit more, to improve the team.

'When I saw that crowd,' Davies said, 'I made up my mind that if new players were needed, we would get them no matter what the cost.'

Davies has the right intentions when he speaks of having a 'duty' to United's 'magnificent supporters', but one may wonder why the directors couldn't have anticipated the squad's problems long before the season began. And a pessimist might view new signings William Harrison, Harry Leonard and Tommy Miller as incapable of turning the tide. The old Derby centre-forward Leonard is slow and the diminutive right-winger Harrison is substandard. Miller, however, Liverpool's Scottish international forward, might live up to his £2,000 transfer fee.

The expensive trio play in a late October goalless draw at Preston North End with Billy Meredith and Joe Spence dropped as Robson and the directors put their faith in the new boys. Indeed, Leonard's lack of speed appears irrelevant when he starts well with three goals in a week and back-to-back wins over Chelsea, but his performances tail off. Miller does the opposite, starting poorly before eventually finding his scoring boots. But it all tells a tale: United's defence remains excellent with Mew, Silcock and Moore, but the inconsistent Reds are reliant on individual quality in attack. Some fans demand Meredith's return to the team after, as far as they see it, the spending has been wasted.

It's nothing new. Robson and Rocca have found good talents locally or from lower leagues, but when United have invested since Ernest Mangnall's 1912 departure, they've spent poorly, and it's the old secretary J.H. Davies gets in touch with now.

10

Davies's unique offer

*'I have been greatly impressed by the
statements in the daily papers as to the
numbers that you have had to turn away.'*

– John Henry Davies, in a letter to Manchester
City's directors.

October 1920 – The visit of King George V earlier this year
was one of many occasions at Hyde Road when Manchester
City secretary Ernest Mangnall has faced overcrowding
problems. Upon reading of the regular crushes at his local
rivals' ground, John Henry Davies, Manchester United
president, offers City the use of Old Trafford.

Davies does not wish United and City to permanently
share a ground, only until the Blues can improve Hyde Road
or find alternative accommodation. City have long been
rumoured to be targeting a move elsewhere. John Henry
refers in his letter to 'the amicable relations which ought
always to obtain between the two premier clubs' but his
suggestion will in fact lead to the bitterest derby matches
yet to occur.

City reject his generous offer. Their directors are, in fact, a
little offended by Davies's suggestion given their recent £5,000
investment on the ground. They are also loath to commit
the same error as United in leaving behind their loyal east
Mancunian supporters.

In a cruel act of faith, just 25 days later, Hyde Road's
grandstand burns down. The fire's cause is unknown, but the

largely wooden stand blazes so furiously that by the firemen's arrival, efforts to save it are futile. The sky is awash with a golden glare and the thousands watching on have to take a collective 20 steps back to escape the burning heat.

Ernest Mangnall organises a heroic rescue mission. Before him the next morning lies a pitch scorched for its first 20 yards, black ash gradually easing into the muddy green of a November turf. Within an hour, he has a motley crew including out-of-work labourers, who turned up sensing the possibility of a wage, and a few City fans eager to help. The transformation they enact is remarkable in its speed.

John Henry's Old Trafford offer remains, but it is explained City would only be guaranteed the same gate receipts as last season. United would take any extra income. For the Blues, this seems askew, because post-war crowds are still swelling and with the ten per cent cut being taken by United – a standard fee for the use of another club's ground – the deal would make City worse off. City's directors request amended terms, but John Henry is sceptical. He believes he has offered something positive for Manchester to his neighbours, and is personally stung by rejection.

These sticking points create significant tension. The *Athletic News*, normally a United sympathising paper, criticise the board for rejecting 'the much-vaunted league spirit'.

Mangnall is not involved in discussions with his old boss. He is merely intent on providing a suitable ground for the forthcoming home match against Huddersfield Town. He has just three days. It's a mountainous task but, incredibly, Ernest and his crew are successful. An entirely new stand, with a 6,000 capacity, has been erected where ash lay just days before. Journalists write in disbelief as 35,000 cram into Hyde Road for Huddersfield's visit. Mangnall is delighted, and exhausted.

Just as ironic in timing as the fire following Davies's rejected offer is that two Manchester derby matches come a fortnight after the blaze, a fact which creates the fiercest derby atmosphere yet. There is a sense of bitterness and mistrust between these old friends.

Attendance records are broken at Old Trafford with a record-shattering 66,000 Mancunians passing through the turnstiles, to John Henry's great satisfaction. Fans of either side sit amongst each other and argue over recent events, but generally in good spirits. Tommy Miller scores a set-piece header to salvage an unlikely 1-1 draw for United.

At the Hyde Road return, spirits are stronger than they are friendly – the kind that burn the back of your throat. United travel expecting to find a half-built ground, but Mangnall now even has new dressing rooms and offices. All around the ground, the smell of varnish pervades the air. This is no reduced crowd; it's a bear pit, and the Blues bay for blood.

The City band's pre-match playing of 'I wouldn't leave my little wooden hut for you' has Hyde Road abrim with laughter, and the City fans join in. 'Home Sweet Home' follows, and garners the same response. Laughter turns to febrility and City flourish. They outclass, outpace and eventually overwhelm United – 3-0, in the end.

The emphatic derby defeat sparks team changes at United. The dropping of Harry Leonard and Lal Hilditch makes sense but supporters are left baffled when 22-year-old diamond in the mud Tommy Meehan leaves for Chelsea. In truth, he's a victim of the directors' financial concerns; Chelsea offered £2,000 and United's eyes glazed over. Their in-form craftsman with skill and versatility is let go.

However, despite Meehan's absence, United's other team changes pay off and four consecutive victories make the festive match against Aston Villa a must-see for the people of Manchester. A remarkable 70,000 attend, another new Old Trafford record and a testament to the ground's sheer size. Now Davies's eyes glaze over excitedly as he watches from the plush seats.

During the festivities, Manchester United's form declines greatly. They win once between Christmas and February, strengthening calls for Billy Meredith's return.

Indeed, Meredith, who has been playing for the Central League-topping reserves, gets his first opportunity since late September. He's United's best player in a midweek February trip at Anfield where a 2-0 loss is taken on the chin. Three days later, United welcome Everton. A little before kick-off at Old Trafford, the blackboard confirms a late alteration to the team and Billy's name is written out. A rejoicing cheer swells around the ground.

Again, he is United's best forward. He's knocked out cold after just a minute when a fierce strike connects directly with his head, but he comes to, recovers, and persists. His centres remain inimitably perfect and draw out urging pleas from the crowd, but they are too often left unstruck by his comrades in the forward line. He is, at the least, the equal of men two decades his younger, and better than many of them. Despite a loss of speed, there remain only two ways to stop this marvel of football: kick the ball into touch, or kick his legs, because clearly knocking him out with a ball to the face doesn't work. Billy pulls out his famous back-heel touch to escape a tight space, delighting the crowd, and then secures United's equaliser, dispatching a penalty with the inside of his right boot.

Meredith has come into the side due to injuries, but those famous crosses make him undroppable. He creates goals against Huddersfield and Middlesbrough and crucially, after an often uninspiring season of football at United, Meredith's late burst of form has replaced dull mediocrity with a personal exhibition.

'Meredith the Marvel' reads the headline. United finish 13th and the second of John Henry Davies's statement signings, Tommy Miller, leaves the club, just ten months after joining for big money. United only stay up because relegated Derby and Bradford were truly pathetic.

Billy has provided much-needed end-of-season sparkle and he's shown there's life in the old dog yet, as he promised friends he would at the start of the season when he said: 'As long as I'm fit, I'll still play.' He now says the same again.

11

Meredith's farewell tour

*'His league debut dates back to 1894. He has
appeared in 643 league matches – 345 with
Manchester City and the remainder with
Manchester United, while he has scored 226
goals in league football alone. These records
are unparalleled, and will probably remain so
throughout the history of football.'*

– *Lancashire Evening Post,* 21 May 1921.

May 1921 – Billy Meredith helped Manchester United's
reserves to the Central League crown and gave a smile
back to the Old Trafford crowd but it's no more than a
teasing farewell tour. Billy's time in this part of Manchester
is up. The Chirk boy is going full circle by returning to
Manchester City.

United's directors have finally granted him a free transfer
– he has been asking for some time – but with the stipulation
that he will not join their neighbours, but of course, Billy does.
Tell that man not to do something and do it he shall. The
silver-haired wizard departs United after 16 seasons and five
major trophies. He returns to City to work with, not just play
under, Ernest Mangnall. The Blues have just finished second.
Mangnall is doing an excellent job and he wants Meredith
to teach as well as play, to divulge his attacking secrets to
younger squad members.

United could do with employing some of their past great players to do the same, but when the great captain Charlie Roberts attempted to rejoin the Old Trafford club last December, hoping to secure a spot on the board, his enthusiasm was, remarkably, rebuffed. He has thus turned to his other team, Oldham Athletic, who need a new manager. The Latics have recently finished 19th in Division One after a late scramble to stay up and several significant players leave before Charlie's arrival. He will thus need to utilise his excellent knowledge of players, sourced from his latter seasons as a player, his days commentating on fixtures for newspapers and his role as Players' Union chairman. Fortunately for Charlie, his responsibilities beyond the transfers and tactics are limited because Oldham's ground needs no improvements and the club have a long-standing secretary and trainer in place. He is entering a decent infrastructure, albeit one with limited finances, reputation and crowd, three linked vices.

On the training ground, Charlie and Billy share similar philosophies, which is entirely unsurprising. They both think the old-fashioned ways are exactly that: old-fashioned, and in need of a change. Charlie desperately tries to improve his players' technical ability while Billy provides some modernity at City as Mangnall focuses primarily on off-the-pitch infrastructural changes.

Billy's City return is an emotional one. Twenty-six years, nine months and 29 days after his first debut, old Bill makes his second – or third, really, including wartime games – bow for the Blues, who beat Aston Villa 2-1. On the same day, Charlie manages his first match, a goalless draw against Bradford City at Boundary Park. He endures a tough start to management life, on the results side, at least.

'The advent of Charles Roberts hasn't proved an inspiration,' comments the *Liverpool Echo* after two points from four games and just one goal scored, but things turn around quickly. Oldham secure a pair of wins over Cardiff, and then the same against West Brom, all four narrow victories.[25] Mangnall and Meredith's City come next.

After a 2-1 defeat in the Hyde Road game, Charlie warmly welcomes his old friends to Boundary Park. Meredith quickly gets off to continue his pre-match preparation, but Charlie and Ernest can leave the details of the warm-ups to their trainers while they chat about each side's form, what they've made of their opponents so far, and if either of them knows of any good players who would be suitable to their teams. Meanwhile, Billy takes his dressing room seat. There are few places he loves like it. Not Boundary Park, but the 'dressing room', in general, how the buzz seems to gently vibrate and slowly crescendo towards kick-off.

It's a peculiar situation now because Meredith is old enough to be most of his team-mates' fathers, even if he's been kept young by his occupation. He's as keen a prankster as ever. He kidnapped and mummified Joe Spence's whippet in bandages shortly before leaving United, he lets ponies loose in the barmaid's quarters of his pub and he has recently taught his pet parrot to spout filth at his sisters, both nuns. On the pitch, Meredith is demanding. He can sulk like a teenager and his style makes his team-mates work harder than playing with any other outside-right might require. But he is a legend. Team-mates only speak positively about him. Jack Mew, United's goalkeeper and 15 years his junior, called him 'a jovial fellow and a real sport' before his departure.

Manchester City beat Charlie's Oldham at Boundary Park. Roberts watches on in continued wonder at this marvel of a footballer as Billy, in typical fashion, creates the only goal, running down the right and playing his centre-forward in. The Latics' defence has otherwise been good and the whole team's effort and enthusiasm are admirable, but there is little doubt

---

25 This system of playing teams home and away in succession is a post-war feature of utility that will soon fade out. Commentators are becoming increasingly concerned that it's creating rough games, with players seeking revenge for the first game in the second.

about where their weakness lies: in attack. When they get in front of goal, their finishing is dreadful. It's Charlie's biggest challenge, and he thinks if only he could get Sandy Turnbull in for a coaching clinic, because finishing was never Charlie's strongest point either. After 15 games, Oldham's record is symmetrical: five wins, five draws, five defeats. It's not bad.

Manchester United's is much worse. They are third from bottom after a turbulent season's beginning. The Reds' forward line has been further weakened since Meredith's departure with Miller, Hopkin, Hodges and Leonard all exiting for one reason or another. Some were sensible decisions, but the replacements for the quartet are unproven or veterans. Add to this poor management a slice of poor luck – top-class defender Charlie Moore getting injured in a pre-season charity match – and it makes for bleak reading. Moore is, or would have been, part of a formidable defensive trio alongside Mew and Silcock, two players shining so brightly in a bad team that they have attracted the attention of the England selectors. All in all, United seemed destined for the drop as the season began and as they live up to such expectations, those recent record-breaking crowds decline fast.

In the context of this, but also poor health, Jack Robson steps down as manager in October. The 61-year-old has led the team in strenuous financial times through the war and built a new, Meredith-less side. Perhaps most impressively, Robson has combined this with creating a vibrant reserve team set-up while keeping United in the top flight and attracting record crowds. This season has been less good, the side's quality affected by financial restrictions, but Robson's eye for a good player has been key, so he sticks around as assistant when John Chapman becomes United's first Scottish manager. Chapman joins from Airdrieonians, who he has almost single-handedly turned into a major footballing force. He's a widely respected man and it's a good appointment. Like Robson, John has a knack for finding diamonds in the rough while working on a tight budget. Well, which football manager doesn't?

This upheaval is rather poorly timed for a new father like Walter Crickmer, the clerk who's been at United for a year now. Like many young men returning from the front lines, Crickmer quickly met a girl and settled down. Nellie is her name, a blacksmith's daughter who works at a jeweller's in town. They married and moved in together and a month ago Nellie gave birth to their first child, Beryl. It's a busy time for this young dad, who is an increasingly important figure in United's structure.

John Chapman's talent-finding knack is far from evident early on. United's normally stringent directors somehow give him £6,000 to spend and John bets it all on two Scotsmen: centre-forward William Henderson – well, the team needs goals, don't they? – and centre-half Neil McBain, who might finally fill the Charlie Roberts-shaped hole. They make their debuts in late November against Aston Villa, with Henderson scoring the only goal of the game. That's a good start.

***

A fortnight later, Charlie Roberts is invited to Manchester's Grand Hotel. He has been a little distracted by recent results and is desperate for a couple of wins, but this is an opportunity for closure on his time leading the Players' Union. Charlie had to resign as union chairman to take on the Oldham job, both reluctantly given his great belief in the organisation, and willingly giving the hard, often fruitless work involved. In a flattering speech, the new chairman, Newcastle United goalkeeper Jimmy Lawrence, pays great tribute to Roberts's work, in recognition of which he receives a gold hunter watch and an intricate illuminated address, which says:

> WE desire to place on record our grateful thanks and appreciation of the great services rendered by you, Sir, to the Professional Football Player. Ever since you assisted to found the Players' Union you have

worked with **fearless and unselfish enthusiasm** to further the objects which were its ambition.

WE realise that **you made great sacrifices in the cause of the Professional Football Player** whom you leave on your retirement from the Championship with many advantages, privileges and monetary benefits which he did not possess when in 1913 you became head of the Players' Union.

IT was the desire of the Annual Meeting of Club Delegates for 1921 that your great services should be recognised and that there should be written record of our appreciation.

The sacrifices they talk of are many. Charlie was offered sizeable financial incentives to abandon his union comrades in 1909 and many are insistent that his union involvement deprived him of adding to his three England appearances. Charlie references none of this, instead telling those in attendance that he's proud to leave the union in a strong position both financially and in membership, and that he has always tried to do the best for the player without fear or favour, and certainly had never expected reward. He goes home to Clayton with a satisfied smile on his face. He's at Oldham the next day, readying for a game away at Birmingham. He's signed two new forwards but a 3-0 loss follows. Thankfully, consecutive wins against struggling Arsenal mean Oldham climb to 13th by Christmas morning.

***

That flailing Arsenal side is the only thing keeping United off the table's bottom. After five consecutive defeats, United's relegation seems certain and hope is hard to find. And then, Jack Robson is dead.

The United man has had health problems for some time, and Manchester's smoggy air has hardly helped. Great sadness and grief greet the news, for Robson was admired by players, officials, directors and supporters, who pass the house in which his body lies when the Reds play Newcastle at home three days later. It is a sombre and sad atmosphere, replicated at his funeral days later. Five of the youngsters Robson brought through and developed at United – Grimwood, Hilditch, Mew, Sapsford and Silcock – carry his casket. Hundreds are in attendance, including Ernest Mangnall in his role as chairman of the Managers' and Secretaries' Union, Billy Meredith and Walter Crickmer. Robson leaves behind a widow and young children, a fact that spurs Mangnall into action. He organises for March's international trial match at Old Trafford to be dedicated to Robson and his family and then manages the occasion, selflessly raising an enormous £2,000.

* * *

After a series of really poor results, Charlie's Oldham seem likely to join United in dropping down a tier. There is still plenty of football to be played, but the race is between them, Arsenal, United, Birmingham and Everton, and with fixtures against reigning champions Burnley and prospective champions Liverpool still to come, many tip Oldham as relegation favourites. Their weakness in finishing remains abundantly clear, described as 'woefully weak' (*Yorkshire Post*), the 'weakest in the league' (*Star Green 'Un*) and 'simply puerile' (*Leeds Intelligencer*).

'It is extraordinary how effective some of the forwards are tapping the ball and dashing it into the net – when at practice,' Charlie rues. 'Yet over and over again these same players, when given chances with the seniors in real encounters, have lost their nerve and thrown opportunities away.'

He tries new training methods to improve things, focused entirely on footwork and ballwork but, in the end, it seems more about confidence, and soon confidence comes. A month apart, with some decent results in between, Charlie guides

Oldham to two of the shocks of the season: victories against the champions and the champions-elect.

The latter match is particularly remarkable. Liverpool are seven points clear at the top of the table, and with a game in hand, when Oldham tear them apart and finish 4-0 winners. It's Liverpool's biggest defeat of the season, and Oldham deserve it. They play well above the class of relegation favourites, coming out with spirit and determination and earning an early goal on which they build strong foundations to get another three. The indelible impression left by the game is that they are too good to go down, and the points earned take them six clear of Charlie's old club, United.

His Oldham team lose to Tottenham on Good Friday and travel immediately north to face United at Old Trafford the following day. Once again, Oldham play like men inspired. Their first touch shows confidence, their passing is accurate and well-weighted and they are on their toes throughout. The opposite is true of United. Oldham lead within three minutes, an excellent feat given their efforts in London 24 hours before. Jack Mew plays well in the United goal, but even so, Oldham are 3-0 winners. Charlie's side finally appears to be learning from him, in attitude but also skill. They continually show control off their chest and thigh, something he's been teaching them in training.

Oldham finish the season a healthy five points clear of relegation. They'll clearly need to strengthen their forward line for the new campaign, but Charlie has done well. That being said, he has found the entire experience overwhelmingly stressful.

At Old Trafford, the mood is not one of stress, but of gloomy acceptance. The Reds are going down, relegated with a pathetic eight wins from 42 matches.

It has been 16 years since United were out of the top flight and their last relegation in 1894 led to a dozen years out in the cold, during which time Newton Heath faced bankruptcy and was relaunched as Manchester United. Taking that long while at the great, grand, expensive Old Trafford could lead to bankruptcy much more quickly and dangerously. What is clear is that a club with a stadium so magnificent should not have faced the drop: yes, they overspent in the halcyon years under Mangnall; yes, there was a war and an expensive stadium to upkeep; yes, there are debts to repay to John Henry Davies, but Jack Robson got United back on a sound footing post-war with good, cheap finds. The team's downfall has been that when the directors have finally loosened the purse strings, normally too late, they have spent money poorly. Almost every major purchase has been a failure and almost every major departure has been a mistake. John Chapman has a real challenge to restore United's top-flight status because every second-tier opponent will treat their trip to Old Trafford as a cup final.

In the real cup final, Huddersfield Town are winners under the innovative Herbert Chapman. From next year, the final will be played at the new Empire Stadium currently under construction at Wembley, built by Sir Robert McAlpine and Co, who are now in conversation with Ernest Mangnall because United president J.H. Davies was absolutely right: Manchester City do need somewhere bigger than Hyde Road. Old Trafford was not the solution, because Mangnall has another idea.

12

Mangnall's ambition

'The Manchester City club have
decided not to build their new ground
at Belle Vue after all.'

May 1922 – History is repeating itself for Ernest Mangnall, or rather, history is repeating itself *because* of Ernest Mangnall. The now veteran football secretary is moving Manchester City to pastures new, and once again, he's abandoning east Manchester.

Long-held plans to remove the Blues from Hyde Road to Belle Vue have dragged on and so Mangnall finds an alternative site at Maine Road. Belle Vue's backers are prominent and influential, and the complex has great advantages – in fact, two excellent and important sporting arenas, for speedway and greyhound racing, will soon be hosted there – but it is too small for City, with capacity limited to around 40,000.

Mangnall has instead secured a spot on the border of Rusholme and Moss Side large enough to build a stadium of up to 120,000 capacity. Ernest could never be charged with lacking ambition. Over several meetings with architect Charles Swain, he explains in great, specific detail his exact demands for the stadium, with a great focus on supporter comfort. Construction is slated to begin in June ahead of a 1923 opening date.

Across the city, Mangnall's old boss John Henry, whose influence at Manchester United is waning as his elderly years bring illness and mobility issues, receives a letter from Harry

Stafford, almost exactly two decades on from when they came together to save Newton Heath.

Harry writes of his dismay at hearing of the club's recent relegation and he mentions again the false 'serious illness' which he provided as his reason for emigrating in 1911. It is not the only lie he commits. Stafford claims he's been on holiday at a place so exotic it was possible to catch 100 trout before breakfast and that he's bought a grand hotel with pitches for football, cricket, baseball and tennis. There's even a dog-racing track. Well, maybe in Harry's dreams, there is. The only truth is that Harry is in Montreal and maybe – just maybe – he has caught trout before breakfast while on holiday. He is, in fact, still working on the railways.

One United man who does have a new project – Mangnall's Maine Road aside – is Louis Rocca, the dyed-in-the-wool Ancoats Red still working for the ice cream company his father founded. Louis and his brothers, especially Joseph, have overseen continued growth of the business, but it is, of course, football that stimulates Rocca more than anything. As the club's informal chief scout, he is always on the lookout for players to recommend to United. He has fingers in several pies and watches football most days, though not on a Sunday, when he attends Mass. Now, alongside other Manchester businessmen, he's invested in New Cross FC, a small club seeking to grow. As at United, Louis engages in every way he can, but always with one eye on potential talent to take to Old Trafford.

After several flopped major signings, relegated United cannot fail this summer, and they do not. Six-foot, 13-stone centre-half Frank Barson is a proper captain, United's first since Charlie Roberts. He's strong on the floor, a playmaker from midfield and a good reader of the game. He's a hardman, an enforcer whose nose points in three directions, who employs a powerful shoulder charge and who plays through pain in almost every game. Sending offs are common for Barson, and perhaps that explains his other similarity with Roberts:

that he has been oft-overlooked by his country. United have taken a clever punt on Frank, who has fallen out with Aston Villa after helping them to English Cup glory. It's a good signing, a transfer that reflects the original John Henry Davies philosophy of the early Manchester United years, one too often forgotten in recent times. Barson is a man to bring the crowds in.

The Old Trafford Pop Siders fall for their new man immediately. His aura of hardness pervades the place and seems to rub off on the team, who begin Division Two life fairly well in new white kits, with a red V, inspired by the colours of secretary John Chapman's previous club, Airdrieonians, and United's 1909 cup final shirts. The 'whites' quickly show their reliance on Barson, whose fitness cannot be guaranteed. He gets the most out of his body as he ages, but his combative style – and the devil on his shoulder – causes enough knocks. By Christmas, the Reds are bang in mid-table. Meanwhile, Charlie Roberts is about to enjoy his first adult Christmas without a footballing role.

He has found the management experience very stressful, especially alongside running a successful newsagent and tobacco business. Oldham Athletic began the season in good form. With 12 goals in five games and seven points earned, they were near the top of the table, but things lapsed. Once again, as with Charlie's first season, a lack of goals proved the problem. Despite achieving victory over PNE to end a long winless run, Charlie resigned soon after and not just because of the team's form. Roberts wanted to sign United forward Lochhead, but the Oldham directors did not. Add in Charlie's business commitments and the poor run of results and neither manager nor the directorship was overly hesitant to part ways. To the outside football world, though, it's a great surprise. Charlie has shown much of the skillset required, including learning from the creativity of Stafford, Mangnall and Rocca in his signings. But it's over, and Charlie enjoys a restful Christmas as a result.

United do not. The Reds are not out of the promotion race, but the United directors have shown an arrogance in assuming their side will bounce straight up and their complacency is drawing significant criticism. Nothing changes in the season's second half and United finish three points off second-place West Ham. Some proper investment, Barson aside, might have dragged them over the lip. Frank is becoming a hero in the same ilk as Roberts and Meredith, but it's insufficient.

Despite their relegation and subsequent failure to bounce back up, United as a club remain respected due to their history and stadium. Old Trafford hasn't changed a jot since its 1910 opening, but it's still a regular FA pick for big occasions, including this season's English Cup semi-final, the management of which provides an exciting challenge for the club's staff, assistant secretary Walter Crickmer included. This and replacing the donkey responsible for pulling the roller across the pitch are the two more unique tasks for Walter's season.

Bolton Wanderers beat Sheffield United in that semi-final and go on to defeat West Ham in the first Wembley final in late April. The match's official attendance is 126,047, but some estimate a quite ridiculous 300,000 are actually watching on. Whatever the number, it's immensely dangerous. The terraces became increasingly packed until thousands spilt on to the pitch for their own safety. It's a miracle no one dies, with over a thousand injured. The fixture's organisation draws significant criticism from Parliament and the press, but heads-in-the-sand FA administrators refuse to appear at an official inquiry. It's an unheeded warning for the sport's future.

Such problems have been painfully evident at Manchester City too – for which Ernest Mangnall has received some criticism – but these should now be a problem of the past because Maine Road is ready to go.

13

Old Trafford's curses

*'The assembling of so vast a throng quite
threw the good people of Moss Side and
Rusholme off their balance. There was a new
note of tumultuous excitement in the air, and
it penetrated to every corner of the district.'*

– *Manchester Evening News*, 25 August 1923.

August 1923 – Just like Manchester United's transition to
Old Trafford, Manchester City's move to Maine Road is the
culmination of an enormous endeavour for Ernest Mangnall
who has overseen every stage of the stadium from theory
and design to contracts and construction, and in the latter
stages, the invitation of tenders for programmes, refreshments,
chocolate, sweets and ice cream, as well as publicity in the
national press. Crucial, too, has been communication with the
Manchester tramway, the police force and the local council,
and then there's been the various press and public visits, for
journalists but also other sporting administrators, including
the Scottish Rugby Union who wanted a sneak peek as they
prepare to build their new Edinburgh ground at Murrayfield.

The move is overwhelmingly successful. Despite initial
shock at City's removal from east Manchester, supporters
are appreciative of the new ground's comfort and size. Just
as at Old Trafford, Ernest has the joy of seeing his baby,
his obsession for these last 18 months, come to life. It is a
wonderful thing, the erection out of nowhere of a stadium in

a community which had not been built around football before. It creates a new vibrance of life and an entirely new ecosystem. A thousand boots trample the ground of Moss Side, hawkers line Wilmslow Road with sweets, pies and black puddings, and an excitable buzz throbs around the area.

Even with a 60,000 opening day attendance, Mangnall does wonder after a few weeks if it could have been more. Maine Road is instantly one of the finest grounds around and Old Trafford remains a cavernous arena fit for the calendar's finest fixtures, but both are not even as grand as Mangnall originally wanted. His hugely ambitious plans have been somewhat scaled down due to space, finances and time.

It is a peculiar time for Ernest. With Maine Road, he has proved himself to be one of the game's finest administrators again. He is a passionate, forward-thinking organiser whose ambition and eager enterprise is visible in his everyday work, but he is beginning to be behind the times. The hands-on approach of tactical managers such as Herbert Chapman is beginning to pay dividends. His Huddersfield side, 1922 FA Cup winners, are on course to win their first title under his guidance. Perhaps Mangnall's skill is in delegating. At United, he allowed the players the freedom to concoct their own plans, over Ellen Meredith's hotpot suppers, while Fred Bacon led training and produced excellent fitness levels. At City, it's now Billy Meredith who Mangnall relies on to offer individual drills to developing players.

That is Billy's main role now, aged 49. United could do with similar insight from an old pro, but Charlie Roberts is focused on his business and, bafflingly, receives no offer to get involved from United. When the Reds earn only one point from four Christmas games, it's hard to shake the feeling that their second-tier stay might be decidedly longer than first anticipated.

Just as inconsistent as United is Britain's government, which has fallen a mere month after December's General Election. Conservative Stanley Baldwin failed to win a majority and after a vote of no confidence, King George V asks Ramsay MacDonald to form a government. In accepting, MacDonald becomes Labour's first Prime Minister and the first from a working-class background or without a university degree. But so clear is the likelihood of change that Baldwin prepares his Cabinet while still in opposition. It's Parliament's first-ever Shadow Cabinet. A time for change all round, then, and United are soon faced with the great footballing force of progress in the form of Herbert Chapman.

With Huddersfield renowned for their cup win two years ago and challenging for the title, a near-record crowd packs into Old Trafford: 66,678. It's the most for any home cup tie in England. Huddersfield lead after ten minutes and score three by half-time. It is an emphatic and not particularly surprising defeat, but it very much pricks the United balloon. Almost one in ten Mancunians were at the cup tie but only 15,000 attend the following league game against Blackpool. The chickens have come home to roost, freed from their cage by cup exit. Poor performances, players and management cause United's supporters to run out of patience and in a time of economic strife for much of the city, few can justify spending a shilling and their Saturday afternoon watching the Reds, playing in unfamiliar white. Unlike the new kits, the club's balance will soon be in the red, for the first time in many a year.

United's conquerors, Huddersfield, will go on to win the league, but are knocked out of the cup by Burnley. On the same day, Ernest Mangnall's Manchester City take on Brighton & Hove Albion and Billy Meredith is set to play.

'The City of Manchester took short breath and laughed in incredulous vein when it was announced.'

One could say they have every right to; 49-year-old Billy has not played a first-team game in more than a year. But Meredith is unperturbed by the public reaction. He knows he is as fit as ever. He has trained hard even when not playing because he knows little else. He is about to turn 50 and has not broken his football routine for nearly three decades. It's the same as it's always been. When official training has stopped,

Billy carries on by himself or goes home, gets some grub and heads back out on to the grass outside his house until Ellen calls him in for dinner. So, Billy is certainly not of the view that he can't play in the FA Cup, although even he might have been somewhat surprised.

'This is a wonderful day for me,' he says pre-match, 'and I hope I will justify my selection. I think I will, for I feel fine.'

Before the game, Billy reads telegrams from adoring fans who still remember his greatness, playing out one of his iconic run-and-centres in their daydreams while at work. Meredith represents a bygone era now, the pre-war football scene. He evokes deep emotion from those who watched him two decades ago, while for the younger generation, there is a sense of intrigue to see if their fathers and grandfathers have been telling the truth about this silver-haired wing wizard.

'It reads like a romance but Billy Meredith is not made of ordinary stuff,' says the *Topical Times*. 'The grey matter he has in his head belies his years.'

Mangnall's selection of Meredith is vindicated when he nets one of five City goals in a convincing victory. Mangnall thus sticks with his outside-right for the quarter-final against Cardiff City.

Maine Road hosts an incredible 76,166 as a 0-0 draw forces a replay. 'He was as useful as any of the Manchester forwards,' the *Guardian* comments, 'but it is a confession of weakness to play him.'

But the romance continues. Billy and company travel to Ninian Park, where he has donned the Welsh scarlet so many times before, for the replay. Confession of weakness it might be, but Billy starts again, and pulls a rabbit out of the hat. He's at home on this Welsh turf, and doesn't he show it. With both clubs' fans eager to see his talent, Meredith offers some typically exciting dribbles and teasing crosses in the first half. In the second, he makes the difference. He weaves forward with precise control, offers a hawk-like stare to his left which cons his opposite man into holding an inside position and then, with a flash of speed, he darts past the helpless defender and crosses to leave the Cardiff goal at Browell's mercy. Having duly tapped in for the winning goal, Browell rushes over to Meredith to offer his thanks and praise. They're soon joined by the rest of the City team. Forty-nine years old and the game-changer, would you believe it?

Billy is chuffed with his contribution. He takes a moment in the dressing room, cleans himself up and leaves Ninian Park for the final time as a player. 'See you at Wembley,' he says to an eager reporter waiting outside, and off he trots.

There's still a game to go before then, but after a goal at Brighton and an assist at Cardiff, Mangnall trusts Billy for the semi-final against Newcastle United. He gives him a warm-up game in the league to keep him sharp first, but he hardly touches the ball against Preston North End and, unfortunately, the same is true in a scrappy tie against Newcastle. A poor match goes Newcastle's way and unlike at Ninian Park and Maine Road, Billy finally looks a little too old for all this, with his gaunt figure and grey hair. In years to come, he'll joke that in his final years, you could grow mushrooms on the wings since nobody passed the ball to him out there, but it's not a jolly semi-final day. He claps his hands regularly as if to tell his team-mates he really is still here, but City underperform and Newcastle will go on to win the cup.

Defeat hits Mangnall harder than Meredith. Within ten days, it's announced that his time as Manchester City's secretary is over. The club are just 18 months into their time at the Mangnall-led Maine Road which has hosted some immense cup crowds. Just as with his United departure, this is a deeply unwanted shock. The 58-year-old has not won the same silverware with the Blues – he might have done had war not intervened – but he has set City up on sturdy foundations and Mangnall's legacy here will be just as long-lasting.

His esteemed secretarial career concludes on Saturday, 3 May 1924. At full time, the City players present Mangnall with a gold watch and the ground committee give him a silver cigar case and matchbox. When interviewed, the players describe Mangnall as a 'boss and a pal', which is some achievement given the near-40-year age gap between them.

* * *

Manchester United, meanwhile, have endured similar post-cup defeat deflation. Having been knocked out by Huddersfield, their poor league form worsened and they have finished a miserable 14th in Division Two. Matters are so bad that some believe Old Trafford is cursed. Some claim Liverpool's opening day win here in 1910 started it, ignoring the fact United won the title a year later, while striker Joe Spence suggests they should dig up the pitch to see if they could find 'the remains of a policeman or a Jew or something of the sort that was perhaps casting an evil spell over the club's going'. That particular suggestion is not taken up.

Admittedly, United have endured misfortune, including death. John Chapman's brother and father both died during the campaign and over summer, 24-year-old full-back Charlie Radford is killed in a motorbike accident. It's a devastating loss of a loveable giant. In less tragic news, key players Mew, Silcock and Barson have been hardly available through injury, playing just 40 times between them as United earned their worst-ever league finish. But Old Trafford is not cursed, United are just badly run and such fanciful excuses will not wash. Supporters are upset.

At the summer's AGM, the unofficial Supporters' Club, led by a taxi proprietor, George Greenhough, attempts a fierce grilling of the directors. The hard questions are conveniently avoided, but the re-election of two directors is made sufficiently tricky by Greenhough that John Henry Davies has to step in with a president's casting vote to ensure his friends keep their spots on the board. They have overseen a £1,500 loss because of low crowds, so United's debt is rising despite frugal spending. With little prospect of promotion next season, it feels like a true low point.

14

Barson's hotel

'Manchester United have their most
accomplished side since the war. I have seen
cleverer teams but none better equipped
for the battle for promotion. Every man
is a fighter.'

– *Daily Telegraph*, Friday, 2 January 1925.

September 1924 – Pessimistic pre-season predictions are wrong. John Chapman's side earn 18 of 22 possible points in the best start to a season for a decade. The visit of New Zealand's rugby team in mid-October is an extra cause for delight, both a boon for the club coffers and, for John Henry Davies, further vindication of the Old Trafford move. Even with the sparkling new Maine Road ground, it is United's ground that is chosen and Walter Crickmer duly helps organise the fixture.

Ernest Mangnall has retired to the seaside after a testimonial held at Maine Road. It is a rare thing for a club secretary to be awarded a testimonial, but Mangnall's unique contribution to Mancunian football means few begrudge him such an honour. A Manchester XI plays a Merseyside XI but only 10,000 attend. 'The football public have notoriously short memories,' United's programme reflects a week later as the Reds extend their winning run to seven with five goals against Coventry. 'The more's the pity,' the editor continues, but sympathy from the working man will be hard to find given Ernest receives a tidy £500 from the day. He can relax comfortably by the sea, should he wish, and if he picks up a newspaper, he'll notice his old club finally making some forward progress.

Such praise as above in the *Daily Telegraph* is deserving, but it will not be forthcoming by the end of a month in which factors aplenty threaten to topple United's promotion charge: injuries, including to the talismanic Frank Barson; poor finishing, which leads to three consecutive losses; and, crucially, boardroom lunacy, defined by the sale of Willie Henderson after scoring seven of the club's last dozen goals.

Reeling from Henderson's sale, United fall adrift of the promotion spots and, unable to find a suitable replacement, John Chapman and Walter Crickmer become responsible for one of football's most extraordinary signings. Albert Pape travels to Manchester with the expectation of playing for Clapton Orient against United but by kick-off, Crickmer has collected all the necessary signatures and wired off the contracts just in time for Albert to pull on United's shirt instead. Orient's players are understandably baffled. It's the quickest debut in club history, and, incredibly, Pape scores in a 4-2 victory. A good piece of business, then, but one followed by another nonsensical sale. *The Football Chronicle* describe 22-year-old Fred Kennedy being let go as 'astonishing'. Once again, United have sold one of their most talented young players, lured in by the offer of a little cash.

The directors' approach to transfers is the antithesis to the John Henry Davies 'ground and team second to none' philosophy, and the old man hasn't even left yet. Somehow, in spite of these decisions, United are promoted. Their form does not change drastically, but Derby County's does. The Rams' woeful end-of-season showing allows United to sneak into second place behind Leicester City, with whom they rise up back into Division One. The Reds celebrate at the Queen's Hotel, where Ernest Mangnall pilfered four of City's best players back in 1906. It was a seminal moment then; supporters and John Henry Davies hope it will be another now.

United's president emotionally congratulates the team on their great efforts. He is defensive, too, fighting back against the idea that the directors hadn't been desperate for promotion. In fairness, that Davies has promised a pub as a reward to Frank Barson demonstrates his keenness for success, and he has no qualms in delivering on that pledge. Barson makes a vow of his own, telling supporters that if the team 'cannot win the first division championship next season we will try to secure the English Cup'. And then he becomes a publican. John Henry gives him the keys to the George and Dragon Hotel in Ardwick Green, a fine establishment.

Frank despises flattery and so when, within minutes of his new career he receives a series of slaps on the back and handshakes and hears 'Good old Frank' from here, there and everywhere, he very quickly decides he's in the wrong place. It has been a matter of hours, if not minutes, when Barson calls over the head waiter. 'Phone the brewery – I'm handing the place over to you!' His belongings are still on the way from his old house. Back they go, and back he does, too. The publican life is not for Frank as it is for Harry Stafford and Billy Meredith.

The latter is enjoying his time owning a pub and has no such qualms with flattery. His farewell tour has hardly paused since those famous final appearances for Manchester City a year ago. He's enjoyed several testimonials. Recently, a 'Meredith XI' took on a combined Rangers and Celtic side. The ex-United winger George Wall played on the opposite side to Billy, just like old times. George ran along holding and occasionally puffing on a pipe, while Billy had his toothpick, of course.

In between such fixtures, Meredith writes newspaper columns, commentates on matches and works at his pub, which becomes known as both *Meredith's* and, for some, 'The Footballers' Pub' because of those who attend to chat with the old man. His wife Ellen works in there, too, and his daughters help out plenty. Billy keeps himself in excellent shape and offers advice to young players whenever he's asked, especially those he became acquainted with at City, such as Scottish wing-half Charlie Pringle, who has taken a shine to Billy's daughter Lily. His nephews receive similar advice, playing with him out the back, dribbling through bottles or finishing one of his famous crosses. So, there is plenty to do in this semi-retired life for Billy.

15

Meredith's film

'The film was voted on all hands a
film not to be missed.'

– The Bioscope, 17 June 1926.

May 1926 – Billy Meredith is not truly retired. One year on, his big project is a film, *The Ball of Fortune,* a silent picture based on a serialised *News of the World* novel. Billy was first contacted soon after its publication and began working in January, with scenes shot at Hertfordshire's Bushey Studios and two stadiums: Stamford Bridge and Elland Road. At the latter especially, Billy and the cameras' presence aroused significant public interest.

Filming wrapped up in March, although not before the film company's managing director tore a ligament while trying to join Billy in the football scenes. Meredith has no such trouble. He plays himself, acting as a football trainer for the Stapleford Football Club. His famous co-star James Knight plays Dick Hush, a boy from a wealthy family who finds that, upon his father's death, he is, in fact, practically penniless. Football is his route back to fortune.

Under Meredith's guidance, Hush progresses well and the pair soon turn out together on the pitch as Stapleford make a late recovery in a relegation battle. Billy, of course, is quite at home in the sporting scenes, while Knight is praised for his performance, too. Drawing particularly great acclaim is the climactic football scene in which Billy scores before the viewer is taken into the dressing room where a player receives treatment.

It is a fine representation of a football match, perhaps the first of such quality after many hashed attempts from American filmmakers. It is not merely a sports film, though, with an 'exciting undercurrent of intrigue' and 'a not too obtrusive love interest' which 'completes a thoroughly satisfying drama of sports life'. That's the *Lancashire Evening Post*'s view.

The film's first screening, in Leeds, is interrupted by May's nine-day general strike which brings much of Britain to a halt. While many invited consequently can't attend, those who do call it a 'film not to be missed' and a second screening is duly scheduled. The reception again is excellent, but most cinemas are waiting until the resumption of the football season to show it, at which point, Billy understandably becomes the film's most useful advertising tool.

Manchester United play their first home game in early September, after which leaflets bearing Billy Meredith's name in large letters are thrown and handed out, encouraging fans to visit Manchester's Winter Gardens Theatre and watch *The Ball of Fortune*. Many do. The advertising campaign is strong. Billy attends the Winter Gardens on several evenings to help put on a shooting competition. Elsewhere, he lends his Welsh caps, club medals and some photographs to a shop that is creating a window display for the film, which really picks up popularity as September draws to a close and continues throughout the autumn. Back home in Chirk, the locals crowd in to watch and cheer the appearance of their hero, the local boy done good.

While punters watch Billy's acting foray at the Winter Gardens Theatre in late September, just down the road in Manchester's Grand Hotel, an FA commission sits to investigate Manchester United. In early October, their decision is made.

***

It has been 17 months since United earned promotion. A lot has changed since, and a lot has gone well. In Paris in 1925, the offside rule was adapted to further favour attackers in an attempt to combat the growth of negative tactics. It created a remarkable start to the new season which United navigated well. Frank Barson had to change the most because the new rule caused new centre-half tactics. The W-M formation, so named for the shape it resembles when diagrammed, was quickly adopted by most teams. Where there were two backs, there are now three (two defenders, one centre-half). Where there were three half-backs, there are now two. Where there were five forwards, there are now three, the wingers and striker, supplemented by two inside-forwards who have moved deeper, more into midfield.

So well did United cope, in fact, that the Barson-led team were considered title challengers to Herbert Chapman's Arsenal, less than two years on from being taught a lesson by his Huddersfield team. Arsenal won that game, and later the title. United's league form declined because of a focus on the FA Cup, where the club reached a first semi-final since 1909 and faced rivals City.

Despite their status as favourites, United fumbled. Even Barson let himself down and City ran out 3-0 winners. The cup defeat preceded a five-game losing streak – including a club-record 7-0 loss at the hands of Blackburn – and United dropped to ninth in the league. Just four more points, and, more importantly, a bit of end-of-season effort, would have seen them in the top three.

Still, this was a cause for celebration: the club's best cup run since 1909 – and City lost the final and were relegated – and a best league finish since 1913, when Charlie Roberts left the club, all inspired by the first man fit to lace his boots as centre-half and captain, Frank Barson.

However, cynics suggested that things could have been better if only the club had been a bit braver, and taken a few more risks. Aversion to risk is the United strategy and, as the *Athletic News* pertinently warned upon the club's promotion: 'It is easier to slide than it is to climb.'

Nevertheless, United have started this 1926/27 Division One campaign safely enough. In fact, they have just started pulling a winning run together when the FA investigation concludes with the truly shocking suspension of United's manager John Chapman.

It is truly shocking, with just one caveat: Chapman's future at United was already decidedly unclear. The Scotsman signed a five-year deal upon joining United in 1921, and here is the end of the five years. The United directors appeared to have made a gaffe when, in mid-September, they advertised for applications. Chapman was understandably furious at this, especially when the directors encouraged him to apply himself, for the job he already had. Nevertheless, this little spat aside, it was expected that he would retain his job. That was until the dispute grew large enough that at one point a frustrated United director mouthed off to a member of the FA Council. As quick as a pickpocket glimpsing silver, an official inquiry followed, and the result is Chapman's suspension for the season.

As ever with an FA inquiry, a dark cloak is kept on proceedings, although to an even greater extent this time. Unlike Billy Meredith, matters will be not revealed in public. Chapman has no desire to air anyone's dirty laundry and graciously refuses to disclose any information. United's directors refuse to explain themselves to questioning supporters, who, furious and confused, take up the baton on Chapman's behalf and work tirelessly to try and glean even a slice of information to prove his innocence. Perhaps they might even be able to prove the guilt of United's directors and land a double blow. Club-to-supporter relations are severely strained, and the silence on display shows little but contempt towards the fans.

The players are equally surprised, which is particularly notable because the issue in question, although not revealed in its exact terms, involves some of them, and yet not a single one has been called in front of the FA committee. Only Chapman and the directors have given evidence. However, it's also stated with confidence that Chapman could clear his name by telling the story in public, but chooses not to because he doesn't want to compromise a player. Whatever their mysterious cause, these events deprive Chapman of the opportunity to continue building at United, and the rift between the club's supporters and directors widens further still.

* * *

Play must go on. Walter Crickmer is promoted to secretary, from assistant. 'Mr Crickmer knows more about the inside working of the club than anyone and his choice will be a popular one,' comments the *Evening News*.

Lal Hilditch is made player-manager. His first game in charge of United's shell-shocked team is a 4-0 defeat to Bolton Wanderers. It's a sign of just how tough a gig he's taken on. Although not abundantly evident at the start, Chapman was an Old Trafford success story, defying the odds to reach an FA Cup semi-final and help the club make a significant profit while maintaining healthy relations with all of fans, players and directors – up to a point. Hilditch is a player in an awkward situation, now having to direct his own team-mates. The form is up and down, but really, United are going in only one direction. By November, the Reds are two points above the relegation spots. They remain under a cloud and in limbo. Many supporters and commentators still expect Chapman to return upon expiration of his suspension, and the Supporters' Club even demands it, but it isn't to be. United are instead lulling along towards relegation without intervention.

* * *

In January of the new year, the first transatlantic telephone call is made and the BBC broadcast their first live radio sports event – England versus Wales in the rugby, followed a week later by their first football match. Medicine is leaping forward, too, with groundbreaking heart operations, the isolation of insulin and Alexander Fleming's discovery of penicillin. This is undoubtedly an era of innovation. In football, plenty of clubs are mimicking such progress in their tactics, structure and stadiums, but United are playing catch-up. John Henry Davies's well-established motto has been ignored: 'A ground and a team second to none.' United are pursuing little but a balance sheet in the black, and fans are duly trying out horse racing, rugby league or the greyhounds as a result.

It's the greyhounds that John Chapman moves into, becoming manager of Liverpool Greyhound Racing Club. This, and the appointment of Herbert Bamlett as manager, to put poor player-manager Hilditch out of his misery, makes it clear Chapman won't return.

United fans remember Bamlett as the referee from that 1909 cup quarter-final against Burnley, who made Charlie Roberts blow his whistle for him in the cold. Roberts later succeeded him as Oldham boss, and more recently, Bamlett has led Middlesbrough to promotion. Well, almost. He joins United before he could finish the job, and it should be pointed out that he had got them relegated in the first place before finding a gem in George Camsell, who has just scored a preposterous 59 goals in a season.

Bamlett arrives at a club in serious trouble. Whereas past derbies against Bury and Bolton drew in crowds of 40,000-plus, these fixtures now attract fewer than half that in the spring of 1927, and it's easier to hold on to fans than it is to win them back.

Fortunately, the change in manager has the desired short-term effect on United's league position. Inspired by a late run of seven goals from the team's most popular player, Joe Spence – an outgoing, mischievous, hard-running, hard-shooting, top-gear-only forward – the Reds move a safe ten points above the relegation zone. Add in a profit of £4,400, and on the face of it, it's no bad season.

But, as the *Evening Chronicle*'s respected reporter 'Casual' writes: 'The curtain is rung down on another season, and there can be little to create enthusiasm amongst the supporters of the United. It has, to my mind, been a season which will go down in the history of the club as one fraught with suspense, little enthusiasm, and numerous complaints.'

The new season arrives and the white-with-red-V shirt is replaced by the old red shirt introduced by John Henry Davies upon his 1902 arrival. A quarter of a century on, Manchester United's trail-blazing father figure is ill. The portly, bespectacled benefactor has watched his final match.

16

Funeral

*'There was a time when I could not stand
J.H. Davies, but I am inclined to think that
the truth was that he was too big a man for
us to understand.'*

– Manchester United's programme.

October 1927 – A Joe Spence hat-trick sees Manchester United thump Derby County 5-0 at Old Trafford. It's a fitting result to see the great John Henry Davies out. Two days later, United's founder, long-time leader, and ever-reliable shoulder to lean on dies.

United would be nothing without Newton Heath, but that old club would have dissolved into nothing without Davies. Manchester, as a city, has lost a great, proud friend.

John Henry's pursuit of success, within and outside the rules, was the founding rock on which United was built. His lavishness was unrestricted by regulation in those early days when his immediate assessment was a good one: build a ground and a team second to none, and success will follow. It did. Under his guidance and with his bulging sack of money, passed under the table more often than over, United won every honour they could and constructed one of the most magnificent stadiums in the world, which is exactly where their name spread.

The club never owed Davies less than £20,000, and it was once estimated at least treble this amount was due to him. He and his brewery companies have benefitted from this relationship, too, but not to such an extent that his ownership can be seen as anything other than charitable, whatever the motivations.

John's wife Amy finds the corridors and expansive rooms of their beautiful Bramall Hall estate so empty without her beloved husband, but she has become as great a United fan as he, and she will continue to attentively follow the team's fortunes. There are few better ways to maintain her connection with her husband. She and John travelled all over to watch the Reds play. Together, they loved talking to supporters and hearing their opinions, which is why fans are saddened by Davies's passing. Perhaps deliberately and carefully crafted by John, it is the United directors who the supporters take issue with. Davies was always at the centre of the big, fan-friendly moments and initiatives, while the directors dealt with, and put a face to, the day-to-day dirt. Crucially, though, Davies listened to supporters more often than not. He meant well. He loved to provide for them, and he delivered on the promises he made. When they showed loyalty, he showed it back.

Loyalty was a big part of John's life, and he showed it to his employees who he thought deserved it. On the other hand, he could be a ruthless bastard. He had enough enemies to show for it, those he'd taken to court, or shifted on after a falling out. There were those he shut up with money or a job, too. And how about the footballing authorities? Well, they and Davies had their fair share of coming-togethers. But this ruthless bastard was also immensely charitable and a much-loved Manchester man. Few clubs had a better record of charity than United under Davies and the general public genuinely appreciated his intervention to save Bramall Hall – the Tudor mansion near Stockport which later became his home – when it was set for demolition.

United wear black armbands in their next match, away at West Ham, where they win 2-1. The team are in good form, it must be said, but the death of the club's founder and benefactor begins an anxious period that threatens to spiral into a challenge of the sort not experienced since the old brewery man came in a quarter of a century ago.

The great and the good of Manchester United gather together for John's funeral. Billy Meredith wears a double-breasted jacket on a cold day. He looks as lithe as ever, his cheekbones visible from afar. He catches up with Charlie Roberts, who has developed something of a paunch, which protrudes respectfully outwards. Walter Crickmer, more of the Meredith figure, is there too, and Louis Rocca, Dick Duckworth, George Wall and plenty of others.

At December's AGM, the directors praise the club's 'present proud and secure financial position', as they honour John Henry. 'Today, Manchester United can go on and prosper without his support and guidance,' claims the club programme. These are easy claims to make, but time will be the judge.

***

Louis Rocca's wide-ranging volunteer role has become more firmly official. He has been made assistant manager to help Herbert Bamlett. Form is satisfactory on the face of things, but behind the scenes, not all is well. The Davies cycle of success has been replaced by a cycle of mediocrity, and just as the team was entirely reliant on its solid defence in the early part of the decade, it is now dependent on the increasingly injury-prone Frank Barson.

'Shall we say there is no team without Barson?' the *Athletic News* ponder. We shall.

Relegation appears so likely by April that Division Two sides have begun planning next season's trips to Old Trafford.

'Relegation was inevitable. The directors have sold the traditions of the club,' one miserable supporter comments, United two points adrift with three games to go. 'The ostrich-like policy of the directors will have a boomerang effect from which they will not recover for years.'

He is wrong on one point: relegation is not inevitable. The directors finally splashed some cash in mid-March. Veteran centre-forward Bill Rawlings cost them £4,000, an excessive fee caused by an aversion to spending earlier in the campaign, but the signing has paid off. Rawlings scores ten goals to keep United up.

The other crucial architect of their survival has been Hughie McLenahan, a West Gorton-born half-back who came into the team late in the season at the urgings of Bamlett's new assistant Louis Rocca. Louis signed Hughie a year ago, for the peculiar transfer fee of two freezers of ice cream.

Hughie is a product of a team at Gorton's St Francis Monastery, who also produced Herbert Burgess, the legendary United and City left-back now managing AC Milan in Italy. Rocca had been long aware of McLenahan's ability because the young lad showed his potential for Manchester Schoolboys, but McLenahan had a good job working at the *Manchester Chronicle*'s offices and, wanting to keep it, was loath to drop it all for football. He was convinced, though, by Stockport County's offer of an amateur contract, which he was told would be non-binding.

Louis later tried to sign McLenahan as a professional, but Stockport knocked him back. Still, Rocca's appetite for a player is as insatiable as a toddler's for ice cream, and he kept up this chase. When attending Stockport's late-season match against Darlington, he noticed a bazaar advertisement similar to Newton Heath's in 1901. While Rocca was reading the details, a hopeful Stockport director approached and asked, 'What are you going to do for us, Louis?' Rocca's answer was easy: 'A freezer of ice cream for every day of the bazaar if you release McLenahan.' The transfer was soon done and Louis got one of the lads from Rocca's Ices to take down the goods.

Now, McLenahan is showing his worth is far more than that. Just 19 years old, he's an intelligent player making an impact. 'He just requires a little more power,' is the *Athletic News*' only complaint, 'which will come with age and beefsteaks!' And maybe a portion of ice cream, too?

17

A threatening love

'MEREDITH'S NEW LOVE'

– Daily Mirror, 22 June 1928.

June 1928 – Manchester United stay up, then, but Old Trafford's hero Frank Barson bids farewell. Despite his contributions on and off the pitch, Barson is sold after an injury-hit 11-appearance season alongside a fellow Frank: McPherson, a forward who has drawn the Old Trafford crowd's regular criticism despite a decent record of one goal every three games. McPherson drops several divisions upon departure, but with good reason. He joins Manchester Central, a new club whose creation, existence and ambition are a direct threat to United.

Central's foundation is a consequence of City and United abandoning east Manchester. United left in 1910, and the Blues 14 years later. The boroughs of Gorton, Newton Heath, Openshaw, Ancoats, Droylsden, Clayton, Hyde, Denton, Ashton, Blackley and Harpurhey are now poorly served by first-class football, having previously been home to two of the nation's best. The large group of those frustrated by this includes Charlie Roberts, still living in Clayton with his increasingly successful business. Now 45, Charlie is perhaps the greatest living legend in United history and the marker of comparison for all centre-halves of the decade, yet he is rarely found back at Old Trafford. When he wants to see football, he often goes to Maine Road. It's closer.

Also irked by this is a former City director, John Ayrton. Having sought the opinions of many east Mancunians,

Roberts included, since his old club's removal from the area, Ayrton has been encouraged by the enthusiasm for a new team to serve the area.

In the summer of 1928, Manchester Central is founded, with ambitions of developing young talent as well as providing entertainment for the local residents. 'Manchester has the biggest sporting community in the provinces and is well supplied with playing fields for youths,' explains Ayrton, whose new team joins the semi-professional Lancashire Combination.

Charlie Roberts is highly enthusiastic about the project and immediately involves himself, and so does Billy Meredith. The 54-year-old has enjoyed many aspects of the celebrity, retired lifestyle – the massaging of an ego is never so bad – but relishes the chance to get stuck into the dirtier side of the game again; to get his boots on for something with a purpose. Central becomes his new love.

Reunited two decades after first playing together, Charlie and Billy watch from the touchlines as Central host a summer trial match. There are a few players who need not be watched to recognise their quality, for the mere presence of Roberts and Meredith – absolute heroes to most footballers – means Central have attracted some serious talent, such as McPherson, who steps down from top-flight Manchester United. His stay is a mere seven games – in which he scores seven goals before joining Barson at Watford – but Central have nine other players with recent Football League experience too, including ex-City centre-half Charlie Pringle, a former team-mate and now son-in-law of Billy Meredith, having married Lily.

Central curate a fine team over a few intense weeks and develop a status-defying 40,000-capacity arena on the very Belle Vue site rejected by City and Ernest Mangnall for being too small back in 1922. They will come nowhere near filling it for now, but support for the club is widespread from football fanatics in the area and also across Lancashire. Meredith and Roberts have been involved with coaching, scouting and spreading the word. Charlie's son, Charlie Junior, plays, although his dad is working hard on convincing him of the merits of business over football, which says a lot about how he sees the status of the professional footballer a near-decade on from his stint as Players' Union chairman.

English Cup holders Blackburn Rovers agree to play Central in the side's second home match and bring the trophy with them to encourage a good crowd. It works and is a damn sight better than what's on offer at Old Trafford, where United have started another season poorly.

The club's shining beacon of hope at the end of last season, Hughie McLenahan, has broken his leg. It's a bitter blow for him and United. Deprived of his exciting, youthful progress, as well as the crowd-pleasing Barson or any good new signings, Old Trafford crowds are declining dramatically. John Henry Davies has barely been laid to rest but his greatest legacy is finally becoming the white elephant cynics predicted it would.

Charlie does still attend some games there, but only in his capacity as a part-time newspaper commentator. He is dismayed by what he sees. United are bottom of the table in February before another late-season surge sees them finish 12th. It's another remarkable escape and so good has their form been that some hasty predictions of a title challenge for the new campaign are made – it's a fickle game.

Stanley Baldwin's second run as Prime Minister has come to an end as Labour's Ramsay MacDonald achieves the party's first election triumph, although it's their second time in power. It is momentous, and they hope this time it might last a trifle longer.

Central, an even newer force than Labour but one with equally high hopes, attempt their own ballot after an excellent first campaign. They seek election to the Football League. It's ambitious, but they have every right to try it. With businessmen and former footballing stars backing them, a huge audience on their doorstep and excellent facilities, they seem a good bet to be added in. But it's not to be this year. There are bigger forces at play in 1929. Labour and United will be rocked by one, and Central by another.

18

An Old Trafford boycott

'Wall Street crashes'

– Manchester Guardian, 24 October 1929.

October 1929 – Wall Street's crash heralds the start of a global economic depression. Its immediate impact is devastating in the United States and while significantly less so in Great Britain, the wave of poverty it brings will soon crash down on these shores, too.

In Manchester, the city's two clubs have made a Division One sandwich, United sitting bottom and City top, with a young Scottish inside-left called Matt Busby recently making his first start. But there is one more team in the city now, too.

A mere 9,060 spectators rattle around Old Trafford for United's match against Burnley, just a thousand more than Manchester Central welcome to Belle Vue for the FA Cup second round. The white-shirted rookies won two games in qualifying before defeating Mansfield Town away from home. Wrexham win 1-0, but the whole occasion is a marker of Central's success on and off the pitch.

Amy Davies, John Henry's widow, wonders why the respectable Charlie Roberts, someone she admires greatly, is involved with Central and has not been made United manager given the team's dire performances. But Amy doesn't interfere, with the exception of an incredibly generous Christmas present, the £4,000 transfer of Cardiff City's outside-left George McLachlan. Her role is quiet but crucial. John Henry's shoulder has gone, but Amy's vital safety net remains.

Ice cream boy Hughie McLenahan returns with a bang after 13 months out with a broken leg. He scores eight goals in six games to end the season, much to the delight of Louis Rocca, as United pull off yet another late escape, finishing 17th this time. But then another summer in which United's squad is weakened rather than strengthened comes and goes. The Reds lose their opening seven games and with no sign of a win coming soon, the media pressure mounts. By mid-September, even the conservative Charlie Roberts, who is more measured in his analysis than many others, has seen enough. He voices his dismay in a highly critical public diagnosis of the club's problems. The directors bear the brunt because United's form is not just relegation-worthy, but record-breakingly bad. The *Football Chronicle* call them 'the worst team in senior football'.

Crucially, the directors can no longer boast that their frugality is being rewarded by a bank balance in the black. With such poor crowds, they have made a £1,341 loss and the debt has increased to £11,000 while their usual 7.5 per cent dividend is paid out, a decision infuriating United's passionate Supporters' Club, led by a gruff, mid-40s taxicab proprietor living in Rusholme, George Greenhough. Football is a uniquely brilliant release from work stress for George. Or it used to be, at least.

Greenhough chairs a meeting at Collyhurst's Railwaymen's Club. A vote of no confidence in the board is passed. It's hardly the first criticism of the directors, but there is talk of a boycott, too, and that's new.

When United lose 2-0 to Grimsby Town three days later, the Supporters' Club hands out 17,000 leaflets to raise awareness of meetings. With three weeks until the team's next home match, against Arsenal, there is much time for strategising. Evening meetings are held in Cheetham Hill, Oxford Road, Bradford, Stretford and Salford on consecutive days. At each meeting, a further vote of no confidence is held. On most nights, the halls are overflowing with attendees.

Club secretary Walter Crickmer is pressed for an official response, but the directors wish to stay silent.

George Greenhough's demands are several but with two basic, overall aims: a change in the club's management and an FA inquiry into the 'inner workings' of United, with a focus on the rising debt and to who United owe money. He also wants a Supporters' Club representative on the board of directors. More radical demands include a new trainer and signing several ready-made players, demands which draw the ire of the less radical football fan or commentator. In fact, many reporters are more scathing of the supporters than United's directors.

Nevertheless, they continue to badger Crickmer for an official statement. The *Manchester Evening News* comments: 'I feel sure that the United directors have only to recognise the existence of their supporters for them to receive the public's co-operation and support.'

Eventually, Crickmer is allowed to respond.

'I placed your letter before the directors, and they instruct me to say that in view of all that has been and is being done by you, they do not think an interview with you should be granted.'

It's a blow, but Greenhough does convince one important United figure to chat. Charlie Roberts accepts an invite to speak at the final supporters' meeting before the portentous Arsenal match. Charlie's case is a particularly interesting one. The club legend has been actively prevented from joining the board several times across the last decade. Now, United's great captain is involved with a club challenging his old side's status, Manchester Central. The deliberate rejection of Roberts by the directors has been a complete own goal. Charlie could not only have provided valuable football expertise, and business acumen too, but could also have acted as a barrier between supporters and directors. As a spokesperson, he would have been an equally solid defence of the club as he was in his playing days.

Instead, Charlie is involved with a rival club and is one of those publicly speaking in opposition to the directors, but, even so, his speech at Hulme Town Hall outlines his unique position in the debate. He blames the directors entirely for the club's malaise and says he cannot understand how the management could call themselves businessmen and yet were losing a large sum of money every week simply through lack of enterprise. And yet, he calls for the boycott to be called off. His reasoning is that public support is against it. It's a valuable lesson he's learnt in his Players' Union dealings: always maintain public support.

United's Supporters' Club choose not to heed his advice. The boycott goes ahead, and without great success. More people attend United's match with Arsenal than any other. The cause is not helped by the opposition. FA Cup holders Arsenal are en route to their first title so the people of Manchester want to get a glimpse of their quality. While the boycotters stay at home – they choose not to picket at the ground due to fears over the legality of such action – the overall impact is small.

'The boycotters have thrown a boomerang and hit only themselves for the whole country is now anxious to cheer on Manchester United,' says the *Athletic News*, summing up the general opinion of pressmen across the city who deride the supporters' action. Unintentionally, the boycotters have created greater support for the directors.

But then United lose an 11th successive game, and then a 12th – a Football League record. It is now half a year since the Reds won a match and the common jokes in town, on the streets and in the music halls on weekend evenings are that United have signed two Chinese internationals: We Won Once, and How Long Since.

By December, the pressmen's belief that the big crowd for Arsenal's visit would see United turn a corner ... well, that has been proved woefully wrong. Bamlett's team have lost 4-1 at Ewood Park, 5-0 at Elland Road, 3-1 at Burnden Park and

7-0 – a record defeat – at Villa Park. And so now the pressmen repeat the words of the boycotters they once criticised:

'The position of Man Utd seems almost beyond hope,' comments the *Athletic News*.

'When the boycott was planned, and put into operation by a section of supporters people in all parts of the country cried "Shame". But should not the directors have done something? Should they not have answered their critics, and proved that they were not allowing the ship to sink?

'They have done nothing, and more than that, they do not seem inclined to say what they are going to do in future. Can it be wondered that the gates at Old Trafford are dwindling to under 10,000? If there is no immediate change, they will probably be smaller than that.'

United have fought hard to stay in Division One with several great escapes in a row, but now they are headed down without so much as a whimper. There is no last-minute saviour signing this year, no bright youngster to spark the team into life, and certainly no end-of-season good run of form. Two home games in March, against Portsmouth and Leicester, draw in a combined total of 8,000 punters to Old Trafford. Talk about a boycott.

Confirmation of relegation comes with a 1-1 draw at Anfield. Manager Herbert Bamlett's contract runs out the following week and with just a few days' notice, the directors inform him it will not be renewed. He is disappointed with their lack of decorum in doing so and Bamlett's temporary replacement is Manchester United's Mr Reliable, Walter Crickmer. The 31-year-old secretary has spent the last half-decade wilfully taking up every job given to him, no matter how strenuous, but this one is particularly challenging, maybe even impossible. His club have been relegated with the worst record in top-flight history. At this rate, it's unclear if they'll survive even the Second Division. The promising talents brought in by Louis Rocca to the reserve side have been prematurely exposed to first-team football due to injuries and underinvestment, the support has slipped to almost three figures, the debts are growing, and the board seem shell-shocked into inaction.

19

Dire straits

'I know perfectly well that the United chairman is against huge transfer fees. So am I, but if a child of mine were dying I would spend all the money I possessed to save it, and to you, Mr Lawton, I say, your club is dying, so, for the time being, cut out your objections to high transfers and spend some money.'

– Charlie Roberts.

July 1931 – Relegated Manchester United require another gift from Amy Davies to stay afloat. This time John Henry's widow loans £5,000 to cover the summer's wages.

In even more dire straits are Britain's finances which, when outlined in a July report, cause a sharp drop in the pound. Labour Prime Minister Ramsay MacDonald is urged to cut benefit handouts, but a powerful minority in his Cabinet refuses to betray 'their people'. With government stuck, MacDonald visits King George V to offer his government's resignation but the pair have a close relationship and the king encourages MacDonald to form and lead an all-party national government, rather than hand power to opposition leader Stanley Baldwin. The move temporarily decimates the Labour Party and MacDonald's reputation within it, but it does end the government's decision-making inertia caused by fears of election defeat. Presenting a united front, cuts are made and the pound bounces back.

United's directors have no king to advise them. King John Henry is dead, long live failure? This is United's second relegation under post-Davies leadership and they are sliding desperately.

A pathetic 3,507 watch the season's first home game, a 3-2 loss to Southampton. Division Two football need not limit crowds too much like this, as United know. In 1924/25, Old Trafford welcomed an average of 26,490 per game. The blueprint for a sensible route to success is there: play good football in the second tier to attract fans back and therefore bolster finances. But that is not the path taken. The directors remain risk-averse. They speak of pragmatism, not promotion.

'The United's first business and one more important than securing promotion is to build up an efficient side of youth,' they say.

Such sentiments might go down well for a club with a less glamorous history and with more proof of recent successes, but at a club just relegated after three dire seasons, it does not. Not only did the directors accept relegation last year, but now they are accepting second-tier status.

* * *

Club secretary Walter Crickmer remains manager. It wasn't meant to be this way. United pursued genuine managers during the summer but found very few serious applicants. Negotiations even broke down with Third Division Barrow's boss. The mighty Manchester United, rejected by a lad at Barrow.

Walter cracks on regardless. His time is predominantly spent putting out fires, waiting for a permanent manager to arrive to reduce his workload back to just the one full-time job. There is little prospect of big-picture changes right now, but there are a couple of smaller ones.

In early September, a decade after leaving, Billy Meredith is brought back in. He becomes reserve team coach. He has long wanted a role, just like Charlie Roberts, and why they have been kept away, no one can say. In addition, covered standing accommodation is finally brought into the main stand, and prices are reduced to the country's cheapest. The directors even suggest a half-shilling unemployed price, a genuinely excellent offer given the dire state of local unemployment and the undoubted impact it has had on United's crowds.[26] These measures are desperate and well overdue, but they are good.

The directors are finally responding, but they soon realise a painful truth: United has lost many of its supporters. It is far easier to keep a hold of them than to win them back, and many have enjoyed the speedway, rugby league, the horses or the dogs, watching better entertainment in better conditions. That United's board is finally throwing money around, exactly when it cannot afford to do so, will not help that. It's a Hail Mary, and what they really need is a saviour for their sins.

Louis Rocca searches far and wide for undervalued talent but also wonders if one of City's out-of-favour players could improve United. Louis has become well acquainted with a young Scot named Matt Busby due to their shared faith. Manchester's Catholic sporting community is strong, meeting regularly to help one another out. Louis calls City to enquire about Busby's availability.

'You can have him for £150,' City say.

'I can't afford 150 shillings, never mind pounds,' replies Louis. And so Busby stays on the fringes of City's team. He's a good inside-forward but will require a stroke of fortune to be discovered as an international right-half. Busby wouldn't have overly relished swapping blue for red anyway. In October, United are 15th in Division Two and Old Trafford's most recent match attracted a crowd of just 6,694.

Some crowds are actually larger a division below, but not at Wigan Borough, the Third Division (North) side who have just withdrawn due to financial difficulties. Their exit presents

---

26 FA regulations don't allow any tickets under a shilling, so that plan is scotched.

a uniquely brilliant opportunity for a club ready to take on Football League status, a club like Manchester Central, whose chairman George Hardman begins a charm offensive.

United's entire existence is under genuine threat now. Here is a team saddled with debt with declining quality, support and league position who are without a manager, a single star player or hope. Compare Central, a highly ambitious young club seemingly destined for the top flight. The concept of United being effectively replaced is not so far-fetched at all.

Unfortunately for Hardman and Central's many supporters, Manchester's big boys collude to keep out this threatening love of their legends, Meredith and Roberts. United still know how to get their way, and they have the right connections. For example, City's vice-chairman Albert Alexander Snr has a seat reserved in United's directors' box for every game. The neighbouring clubs' relations may have been tested by the Hyde Road fire debacle a decade ago, but on a personal level, they have remained generally very good, especially with John Henry Davies out of the picture, and United have another influential friend: John McKenna, president of the Football League.

Central make an official bid to replace Wigan, complete with a dossier of supporting evidence. A day later, despite the significant press support backing Central, Manchester City lodge a formal complaint on behalf of themselves and United, stating that gates were declining. There is at least a semblance of truth in saying City's gates have suffered since Central's foundation, but United's have not. Their gates have declined only because the team is so poor.

True or false, moral or immoral, City's complaint to help their friends at United is successful. Central's bid is rejected in a decision that appals the vast majority of football fans, including those of United and City.

'This is to be regretted, as we think there ought to be league football in the Belle Vue area, where there are 440,000 people within two miles, and a million people within four miles. This is surely enough for two Football League clubs in a place like Manchester. What about London? Their clubs have far more opposition than this and I don't believe even today London can compare with Manchester as a soccer hotbed,' remarks Central's chairman.

'There seems to be a sad lack of enterprise in Manchester so far as league football is concerned. We shall carry on. Given reasonable support we shall continue making applications for admission to the Football League. We shall get there before long.'

The press agrees. Pre-eminent journalist Stacey Lintott says, 'Manchester Central potentially are not merely a Second Division, but a First Division club of the future. There should be room in Manchester for three league clubs.'

Manchester United's once grand name – heralded as far as Vienna, Budapest and New Zealand in 1908 – is now the butt of a joke. Its mere mention draws laughter in the music halls.

* * *

Still without reprieve from his double-job life, Walter Crickmer continues to do his best. He moves Joe Spence back from the right wing into the centre-forward position and the 33-year-old responds brilliantly with 11 goals in ten games. It's a smart move but not enough to make up for a leaky defence. Spence's two goals against Leeds, for example, are meaningless in a 5-2 defeat, as is his one goal at Bury in a 2-1 loss and two goals when United lose 4-3 at Bradford. And so on.

United's directors' desperation has become frenzied. They beg the Manchester Brewery Company to delay mortgage payments, ask the Stretford Council to pay their road charges in instalments and send a query to the Inland Revenue to see if income tax payments can be postponed. After that, a circular is sent around Football League clubs asking for offers for players.

Finally, at November's Annual Shareholders' Meeting, club chairman George Lawton offers an element of transparency to supporters. Finally, finally, finally. Lawton explains United need money, can't buy new players and need some well-off gentlemen to get involved.

> 'I want it to be known that myself and my colleagues on the board of directors will certainly retire if there is someone who will come forward with cash and help the club.'

Again, it is the right thing to do, but years too late. Supporters are also suspicious as to where the last decade's £60,000 profits have disappeared. Lawton blames the global depression for smaller crowds, as well as bad weather and injuries, but nowhere do he and his partners take culpability for poor team selection, inadequate investment, unsuccessful signings, irrational departures and the until now closed-off relationship with supporters.

Financial help is not instantly forthcoming. Advent arrives and everyone involved with Manchester United faces a bleak winter period. Walter Crickmer, with his ten-year-old daughter Beryl at home, knows his very job is on the line. No United, no job. He visits the National Provincial Bank in Manchester's Spring Gardens. The bank clerk there tells him that Manchester United Football Club cannot pay their players. There is nothing left.

It has gone midday and Louis Rocca is back at the ground. After another hour passes, several players come to his office to ask if their wages have arrived yet. He tells them to go home, with a white lie that Crickmer has been delayed by a directors' meeting. The lads do as they are told, with a few offering the same parting remark: 'Don't forget our Christmas turkeys!'

20

United's Christmas turkeys

'We had our turkey after all!'

– Louis Rocca

December 1931 – 'I have long been interested in Manchester United,' 54-year-old Salford-born clothing magnate **James Gibson** says, having just gifted the club £2,000 and enough money to buy the players and staff their Christmas turkeys.[27]

'I am at the head of the United now and if the public will back me up and give me any justification for carrying on I will assure them that the United will not fail.

'I want to place Manchester United, if possible, on a level with the great teams in the country, such as Arsenal, and I also want to see the Pop Side people at Old Trafford afforded some protection from the bad weather. When I have been down at Old Trafford and have seen the shilling supporters standing in the wet I have felt heartily sorry for them. I want to get covered accommodation at Old Trafford. Of course, this cannot be done in a twinkling, but if the public will come forward then I will do my best; and I will also see that the United have a manager who will be one of the best in the country and will be paid accordingly. I shall then look at the first team.

'I do not blame the public in the least for staying away from Old Trafford. The United board of management have never taken the public into their confidence and they could

---

27 Equivalent to £175,000 in 2023.

not be expected to keep on rolling up at Old Trafford while a hush-hush policy was being adhered to.'

This admirable philanthropist has been formally introduced to United by Stacey Lintott, a member of his regular lunching group and the north's pre-eminent football journalist. Lintott, an ex-player, arranged a meeting between Gibson and United secretary Walter Crickmer. The result is the saving of Manchester United.

* * *

Gibson could be considered a Mancunian nationalist. He is a uniform manufacturer like his father and has been for three decades. But he didn't simply take his family's company. No, James endured a series of tragedies in his early teens. His Irish-born father John and Salfordian mother Eliza both died, followed by his paternal grandmother, who had been looking after him and his two siblings.

The Gibson children then moved in with their uncle and two aunts in Moss Side. James worked for his uncle's corn merchant company where he quickly demonstrated business acumen equal to that of his late father. After several years under his uncle's tutelage, Gibson returned to Salford to pursue his father's trade: uniform manufacturing. In 1900, he formed Briggs, Jones & Gibson Ltd. He was only 23 years old, but the company carried his name because his father's reputation had been a good one and just about lingered on. First acting as company secretary, he soon became director but was yet to escape tragedy. His sister Florence died, too, aged only 14.

James met Cheetham-born Annie, later Lillian, and they settled happily in Old Trafford. The immense heartbreak worsened. Their son, Norman, died aged three, twins died at birth and, several years on, in November 1915, Lillian gave birth to triplets. Once again, death ravaged the family when two of the triplets died. Thankfully, with the aid of cotton wool wrapping and constant nursing, one survived: Alan. His health was poor, with a weak chest and long-lasting effects from pneumonia which made ordinary life difficult, but Lillian cared for him, while still finding time to help nurse troops in the Manchester area during the war.

The needs brought about by conflict allowed Briggs, Jones & Gibson to flourish. They supplied military uniforms for young men like Walter Crickmer, then known as Raymond, and an unceasing demand was matched by endless expansion at Gibson's factory. Young men and women were employed at a rapid rate, trained as machinists, finishers, pressers, embroiders and trimmers.

Gibson took immense pride in employing so many local Mancunians and was desperate after the war to maintain the company's size and thus its staff's jobs. To achieve this, he convinced local corporations to buy into the idea of work clothing, and soon enough his company provided uniforms for police officers, bus drivers, tram conductors, postmen, and so on, as well as the army and navy. The company thus proved fairly Depression-resistant come 1929, by which point Gibson had taken over the company outright and moved to bigger premises on Lostock Street, near Miles Platting, the original birthplace of Newton Heath L&YR Football Club.

***

Although Gibson grew up at the height of 'Football Fever', he never became a football fanatic. He preferred rugby in his youth and regularly used a punchbag in the attic for those moments of frustration and anger that any young man deprived of his parents, grandparents and sister would have.

In recent times, though, Gibson has become an Old Trafford season ticket holder and he admires football's power to evoke such great passion and to distract from everyday life's grim reality during this economic downturn.

Gibson explained this to Crickmer at his Hale Barns residence, Alanor, named after the two Gibson sons: Norman, who died aged three, and now 16-year-old Alan, who hasn't attended school since his first day aged five when he contracted pneumonia and his tragedy-scarred parents decided he would never go again.

James and Walter got on with ease. Crickmer is an honest, straightforward man, and James likes that. For his part, Crickmer was impressed by Gibson's immediate, eager specificity. He asked exactly how much United bring in – with regard to gate receipts for the first team, reserve team and away games – and how much they spend, in the form of player and staff wages, bonuses, expenses, payments for benefit matches and tax. He also wanted to know how much United were overdrawn at the bank, and which positions Crickmer would strengthen if the club had some money.

Gibson bid Crickmer farewell with a promise to act. Shortly after, the wealthy businessman contacted United chairman George Lawton and offered to immediately deposit £2,000 in the club's account. He has done so.

This £2,000 is not a loan, but an outright gift, one which has lifted an enormous weight from Walter's shoulders.

By 21 December, the full directorship has told Gibson, who has offered intense public criticism of their behaviour, that they will resign en masse whenever he wants them to do so. But that time is not yet. James wants to see some proof, in the form of a bumper Old Trafford crowd, that United are worth saving.

What the public is not made aware of is that Gibson has realised exactly how critical United's condition is. He believes the directors have underestimated the debt, which he values as at least £26,000, but he is still willing to get stuck in.[28]

Gibson has the backing of the necessary people. The FA and Football League are keen to see him take over, and so is Amy Davies, John Henry's widow, the so-called 'Mother of Manchester United'. She's not the typical United fan, sat

---

28 Nearly £2.5m in 2023.

before a blazing Yule log fire in the oak-raftered library of her Elizabethan Cheshire mansion, but her message will be received well by supporters, who have enduring respect for the Davies family.

'Tell the public to rally round,' Amy tells a reporter.

'He knows what he wants and will get it. He has the spirit of the game in him and he loves the team.'

It is now, for the first time, that the public are made aware of Amy's £5,000 summer gift. She says she would have made it £20,000 if the directors had made Charlie Roberts manager and got some decent players in.

Amy is not the only key figure to offer support to Gibson. Supporters' Club head honcho George Greenhough, leader of the 1930 boycott, is enthusiastic about the changes.

'I know nothing,' Gibson says, talking about football, but what he lacks in football knowledge he more than makes up for in business and PR acumen. His first smart move is to turn down the opportunity of picking the team himself. Instead, Gibson wins supporters over immediately by asking for Greenhough's opinion.

Like Stacey Lintott, Greenhough is another external figure who backs Walter Crickmer's credentials while relentlessly slating the directors. So when the FA give Gibson the green light to start picking the team just before Christmas, Walter is one of those he turns to. United's team will now be selected by Greenhough, Crickmer, the trainer Jack Pullar and 'Navigator', the *Evening News* reporter.

These clever moves don't see Gibson hailed universally as a saviour. Concerns are raised that he seeks to be a 'dictator' and there is much criticism of his demand for fans to show up to earn his investment. 'It is too much like "jam tomorrow",' comments the *Evening News*, conveniently forgetting the £2,000 Gibson has already gifted the club.

'Why am I doing this?' Gibson patiently responds. 'Because I believe in football. It is the finest recreation for spectators that the country has.'

* * *

United's reserves are to play Wolves at Molineux. Louis Rocca and reserve team coach Billy Meredith arrive at Old Trafford at half past three on Christmas morning.

Gibson's money has got the club back on its feet, but there is still no excess money to spend. Whereas usually the reserves would travel to Wolverhampton the night before and stay at the Victoria Hotel, finances dictate the impossibility of that. Rocca and Meredith make preparations while awaiting the players' 5am arrival.

When the lads arrive in Wolverhampton, Rocca takes them to the Stafford Hotel, where they enjoy a reviving round of toast and a warming cuppa. On telling the hotel manager of their situation, Rocca receives great sympathy. The manager tells him to bring the boys back right after the game and he'll serve Christmas dinner for a bargain price.

The reserves play like men inspired and hold a strong Wolves team to a draw. Then they get that turkey they thought they'd missed out on this year, and Christmas pudding and a glass of wine, too. With full bellies and a smile, they make the journey home with Rocca, in particular, anxious to discover the fate of United's first team back at Old Trafford.

As the party nears Sale, they meet crowds of people walking away from Old Trafford with broad smiles on their faces. They stop to ask for the result and are told United won 3-2 against Division Two's best side, Wolves, and more than 40,000 watched on. Rocca leaps in excitement and the group cheer themselves hoarse. The local public of Cottonopolis has certainly shown that they believe in James Gibson, even if the cynics in the press do not, and so Manchester United will be saved.

The crowd was not quite 40,000, with an official attendance of 33,000, but Gibson has clearly got his message across, and the supporters have given him one in return. It's the biggest crowd – excepting derby matches against City – for three years and, like John Henry Davies back in 1902,

Gibson is genuinely moved by what he saw. At half-time, he went down to the Pop Side to thank fans for showing up. He promised them, in a fever of excitement, that United will go on.

After a quite exhausting few days, Wolves batter United's first team 7-0 the next day at Molineux. The result is nothing more than a healthy reminder of exactly how much work is to be done. Back at Alanor, the Gibsons are enjoying an unexpected Christmas with James utterly enthralled by his new project and his teenage son Alan equally excited. Lillian is unerringly supportive.

Before New Year, Gibson meets with the Football League and FA's key figures. They give his United takeover their blessing and offer all the assistance they can to help him complete it, but it will need a few weeks yet. Gibson is then co-opted as a director and takes on full responsibility for the club's liabilities, a figure in excess of £40,000.[29] By doing so, he will save United £1,000 in bank fees, but only at great personal risk.

Gibson wants to reduce some of that risk by raising funds with a 'patrons' ticket' whereby supporters will pay in advance to secure ground admission for four years. His main target is Manchester businessmen, and he emphasises that football is a place for businesses and businessmen to take friends, acquaintances and staff. The tickets offer a saving of a third but elicit a poor response. Only £500 comes in, with Gibson having hoped to create a transfer fund to help avoid relegation to Division Three.

Privately disappointed but publicly resolute, Gibson accepts the timing was bad, just after Christmas, just before the tax payment deadline and amid an economic depression. He was also not targeting the club's normal one-shilling supporter, so the poor uptake doesn't reflect badly on the main support's commitment. Regardless, any disappointment

---

29 Around £3.5m in 2023.

disappears when Gibson opens a letter at his new Old Trafford office.

The letter is from a United fan who explains that, due to work, he's unable to regularly attend matches, and that he can't afford the patron tickets on offer anyway. Instead, he attaches a postal order for sixpence. It's all he can afford, but he wants to contribute something. James Gibson is so humbled and moved by this supporter's action that the failed ticket scheme only doubles his determination for success.

A fortnight later, he finally accepts the directors' resignations, including Harold Hardman, George Lawton and another who has been there for decades. There will be an entirely new United set-up. Walter Crickmer and Louis Rocca are the exceptions. Those two valuable United men will, sensibly, be kept around, and in future years, Gibson will thank the heavens for that.

His new board is made up of an ex-lord mayor of Manchester, a Stalybridge woollen manufacturer, a cotton merchant and a company director at Horrockses Crewdson Ltd. All four have money behind them, which is helpful because Manchester's general public has precisely none.

Another week on and **James W. Gibson** is officially made president of Manchester United. A new era beckons.

Part Five:
Youth, 1932–39

1

The first 100 days

'This nation asks for action, and action now.'

– US President Franklin D. Roosevelt in
his inaugural speech, before pioneering the
100-day concept to combat the impact of the
Great Depression.

January 1932 – Walter Crickmer doesn't rest much. He is
a tireless and fast worker who takes steps two at a time and
hurries in and out of rooms.

It has been just a few weeks since Walter sat on the edge
of his seat opposite a reclined James Gibson at Alanor. Then,
Crickmer detailed Manchester United's finances and the
club was soon saved. Now, they stroll around Old Trafford
together, Crickmer efficiently lecturing Gibson on the
running of a football club. There are a few introductions, but
no manager for Gibson to speak to. He is in conversation with
the club's secretary, manager and, in these last few weeks at
least, its arm, leg and head. Nevertheless, Crickmer tells him
more about Louis Rocca, only five years' Gibson's younger
and evergreen in his deep enthusiasm for the game. Gibson
is far from sneering at such fanaticism but appreciative of it,
and he'll find himself whisked away into its clutches soon
enough. Rocca is a dedicated scout with decades of experience
and a wonderful eye for a youngster whose talent is ready to
be refined.

That line of conversation interests Gibson. 'Where does
he find these players?' he asks. 'All over the country,' is the

answer. Crickmer explains that when Louis, or one of the many scouts working beneath him, finds a good youngster, they can come on trial in the reserves before a decision is made. For those with the brightest prospects, an extra bonus might be needed like a house for the boy and his parents in Manchester, or, on a lesser level, for the club to pay for train journeys home when necessary. Gibson is intrigued by all of this and wonders why Rocca needs to go as far as Scotland to find good young players.

'Well,' Walter replies, 'Louis finds a young gem at a good price before every other club around here discovers him. That's what every team is looking for.'

But there are thousands of talented Mancunians on United's doorstep, Gibson thinks.

They move on to the short term and which signings could help keep the team in Division Two. Walter says he'll defer to Rocca's recommendations. Louis has followed Southport's English Cup progress and noted a good, young centre-half who could solidify United's side.

They discuss the supporters, for one of Gibson's main urges upon taking over United was creating conditions for greater comfort at Old Trafford. He has been to the ground many a time in wet weather and seen the poor buggers coming under a wet onslaught on the Popular Side. Walter agrees it should be a priority. Gibson also wants to gauge Crickmer's opinion on the Supporters' Club and its chairman George Greenhough, too. Walter is not overly enthusiastic about George but he believes the Supporters' Club could be a great power for good if it was operated on more official lines, in direct communication with the club.

They've reached the directors' room inside the main stand and after a short sit-down to continue the conversation, Walter retreats to his office, leaving Gibson to ponder for a while. The new president walks out into the covered seats at Old Trafford, ideas racing as he surveys the three uncovered embankments which stretch back from the pitch.

* * *

Gibson promised money for players and Crickmer gratefully receives. Rocca's number one recommendation is indeed a Southport lad, £1,000 centre-half Ernest Vincent, 24, who provides better speed, strength and stamina than his predecessor, Lal Hilditch, 14 years his senior. Vincent is no Charlie Roberts or Frank Barson, but United win all but one game in the first seven after his arrival as the team accelerates away from the table's bottom.

Although still primarily working for his own company, matters handle themselves much of the time there, so Gibson regularly greets the players before and after training, which he attends more than some managers. The players warm to him as a result. From Gibson's perspective, it's a privilege to observe. He might not have been the biggest football fanatic before, but he is in awe of sportsmen.

The supporters are finally feeling at home at United, too. George Greenhough ends demands for Supporters' Club representation on the board. He has been quickly won over and instead returns to old focuses: arranging away trips and helping to improve the ground facilities. Gibson is eager to help, for reasons genuine and self-serving. A new officially backed Supporters' Club is formed and Gibson is there to hoist the flag and open their new office near the tunnel on the Popular Side. After, the players contest a six-a-side billiards match with the supporters at the Dog and Partridge. The supporters win easily – a good sign that they spend more time in the pub than their heroes.

Greenhough is not alone in being convinced. United's entire fanbase is engaged again. Crowds of 7,000 had been the norm for autumn games and now that many are attending reserve fixtures. One Easter first-team fixture draws 37,000 while even a rain-soaked dead rubber against Bradford City attracts a nearly 20,000-strong crowd. The Supporters' Club is pushing things forward, too, by forming a Ladies' Committee. James' wife Lillian is happy to hear this and encourages him to listen to their requests for better ladies' conveniences.

***

Still inside his first 100 days as president, Gibson sets the cornerstone of the modern Manchester United. In March's final directors' meeting, he ponders whether the running of a nursery team from next season might be a positive idea. The matter is left in Crickmer's hands.

Whereas the reserve team hosts players equipped to replace injured first-teamers, with the occasional triallist and youngster being assessed, this new side, christened the 'A' team, will be a breeding ground for young players. It will allow Louis Rocca to assemble eager and coachable talent one day primed to rise into the seniors. Crickmer is especially enthused by this project, the birth of United's Academy. He heads to Altrincham and negotiates the use of their ground at a £25 annual fee, secures a spot for United in the Manchester League and convinces Lal Hilditch, the old player-manager from 1926/27, to coach the side.

Franklin D. Roosevelt is still a year away from emphasising the significance and opportunity of an American president's 'first 100 days' but already in that time span, United's new president, James W. Gibson, guided by Walter Crickmer, has secured United's Division Two status, stabilised the finances, trebled the Old Trafford crowd's size and laid the foundations of future success in the form of the 'A' team. He has, in Abraham Lincoln's words, left nothing for tomorrow which can be done today.

2

Gibson's cornerstone

*'Thousands of people in these last 90 years
have been touched by the academy's influence,
and the names of young boys whose talent
was honed at The Cliff and Carrington have
become known far and wide.'*

— *United Review*, August 2022.

July 1932 – After easily preserving Manchester United's
Division Two status, Walter Crickmer welcomes in the club's
new manager. Helen has made up the spare bed and got out
the Crickmers' best tea set.

'Welcome, Mr Duncan,' she says to the 43-year-old man
when Walter and his pristinely dressed guest arrive home. He
has friendly eyes that slant down, he is clean-shaven and when
he removes his hat, he reveals a receded and thinning hairline.

Scott Duncan has just arrived from Cowdenbeath. After
a decent playing career with Dumbarton, Newcastle United
and Rangers, he managed Hamilton Academical and then,
with shrewd financial management and regular use of local
youngsters, propelled forward Cowdenbeath's reputation
by avoiding relegation to the second tier in all of his seven
seasons, the club's most successful era.

After Duncan freshens up at the Crickmers', he and
Walter head the short distance to Old Trafford where they
are met by Supporters' Club members. They give Duncan a
hearty welcome and wish him all the best.

Crickmer's time as interim manager is up. His most impressive feat, aside from retaining United's second-tier status, was his ability to sustain squad morale throughout turmoil. It's a sign of the players' respect for him. Now able to return to his real job, club secretary, a demanding enough role as it is, Crickmer brings Gibson's new man up to speed.

After Helen serves dinner, Walter and Scott share stories over a drink. They are two passionate football men. Over the next couple of days, both at Old Trafford and at home, Crickmer explains which quality players the team has and asks Duncan what kind of assistance he wants. Scott is a proven administrator, not just a manager, and has been brought in with a specific Gibson-given remit to thrust forward United's youth policy. The 'A' team's creation predates Duncan's arrival but will only begin in earnest in August so he now has a month to assess United's players at all levels.

The 'A' team's opponents will be work sides like Ashfield and ICI (Imperial Chemical Industries, the major company who have just helped invent Plexiglass and Dulux paint), local outfits like Newton Heath Athletic, Pendlebury and Gloucester New Mills and the 'A' teams of Manchester City and Stockport County. On 27 August, Ashfield provide United, dominated by Louis Rocca discoveries, with their first competitive match. The 'A' team loses 5-4.

'I consider that we have some young players who are destined for high honours,' Duncan says on review.

'No junior need fear that he will not be given a proper chance. What success I have met with in the past I hope to repeat with Manchester United.

'To hurry along a youngster is a big mistake, but the junior must be assured his time will come.'

He talks a good game and, indeed, United are in no hurry, but the 'A' team's benefit is immediate. Within a month of their first match, Crickmer is filling out the paperwork to turn three of the most promising players into professionals.

George Vose, a 20-year-old St Helens-born centre-half, is the pick of the trio.

Meanwhile, Louis Rocca's relentless pursuit of talent continues. He watches matches as many days and nights a week as he can, always inquisitive, always pushing anyone he meets for a recommendation. 'Not a bad lad, that one. How old is he? Been with you long? Who do you say he played for before?' Louis then operates a policy of 'one home, two away' for any player of talent. He doesn't want to be left signing a 'homer'.

Unlike in England, where clubs scared of losing their best talent chase him off their grounds, Rocca is treated with the utmost respect in Ireland because the hosting clubs are fully aware that a good transfer fee from United will allow them to kick on in the developing Irish Free State footballing scene. His latest trip is to Waterford.

'Rocca proved to be a jolly man,' says the *Waterford Standard*. 'He enjoyed the great attempt of the players to display good football ... [although] on one occasion when Walsh was in action he passed a flying drive to Scurry who ran up the line trying to gain the mark. Mr Louis Rocca burst into laughter and said he could hear Scurry singing "if I had the wings of a swallow".'

Louis is impressed with one or two players and a Waterford boy arrives on trial with the reserves a few weeks later, but he doesn't quite cut the mustard.

***

Duncan's lack of hurry with the juniors is evident when George Vose and 19-year-old Failsworth goalkeeper Jack Hall, another 'A' teamer signed on as a professional, do not come into the first team all season. In fact, Duncan's immediate pledge to give young players time rather than buy ready-made talent has tailed off. He's instead used plenty of Gibson's money to strengthen the side, without great success. 'Better, but inconsistent,' is the verdict as he guides United to an improved sixth-placed finish in his debut campaign.

The 'A' team is the campaign's undeniable positive. George Vose has progressed at pace over 16 midweek league matches and several cup ties, and thus, 364 days after the 'A' team's first match, its first graduate Vose makes his first-team debut, away at Plymouth Argyle. This admirable achievement is largely overlooked, however, given United's woeful start to the season, a five-game winless streak.

Underneath the gloomy first-team surface, there are great positives. Louis Rocca is now bringing in talented footballers long before their 18th birthday. A devout Catholic, endless gossiper and reliable friend to many around Manchester, Rocca has built an entirely informal network of primarily Catholic priests and schoolteachers – sometimes PE leaders, other times deputy heads – from whom he receives recommendations for bright young players. St Wilfrid's School in Hulme is home to some such people and from there Louis signs Jimmy Hanlon, a 16-year-old who can play across the front line. Rocca knows his name already because he receives a big wad of local newspapers on his desk every Monday morning and sifts through the results, highlighting names, like Hanlon's, that regularly appear in prestigious circumstances, such as for Manchester or Lancashire Boys. It's a supporting safety net rather than an infallible system. Hanlon, an attacker, joins the ground staff at United and proves himself to be a conscientious bright young lad with a strong work ethic. He'll play in the 'A' team.

Walter and Louis, then, are dragging the playing infrastructure forward at the youth levels, but James Gibson's resolve is tested by the combination of high expenditure and sub-standard first-team form. For all the underlying good, Manchester United are far from revived.

3

Rocca's train supper

'After Christmas, the rot which had set in
became worse and the players were beset with
an inferiority complex.'

– Louis Rocca.

January 1934 – At the start of the year, Manchester United
are 20th out of 22 second-tier teams. Sides have been known
to canter up the table after Christmas, but it's still a bleak
outlook, made worse by boardroom unrest.

A disagreement leads to two directors' resignations and
privately, James Gibson is concerned. The idea of throwing in
the towel is not a Gibson characteristic – not in business, family,
health or hobbies – but United's future is unpredictable, the
club's overdraft is growing unsettlingly large and while James
made himself responsible for it back in 1932, he wonders if
that was all a rush of blood to the head. How was he convinced
to plough on by one supporter's couple of pennies in a letter?

Well, he remembers exactly why when he witnesses
the steadfast support of those inside Old Trafford, but
nevertheless, financial anxieties are justified. Manager Scott
Duncan has spent a lot of money with quite pathetic on-pitch
returns. The overdraft now stands at £17,705. Amy Davies is
responsible for £5,000 of that, Gibson the rest.[30]

---

30 Over £1m in 2023.

On the pitch, the players seem beset by an inferiority complex and the squad is undoubtedly injury-afflicted. Over the season, Duncan uses a quite ridiculous 38 players. However, when he claims to have received a management offer from a First Division club, some cynical supporters ponder whether it's a clever move to make him seem desirable at a time when the team is plummeting towards the Third Division for the first time in its history. Duncan tells Gibson he wants to see the challenge through at United, and the established football media and most well-known supporters don't doubt him for a second. George Greenhough, for example, has been fully won over by the close relationship the fans have been permitted with Duncan and Gibson.

'There is nothing wrong at Old Trafford,' Greenhough states. 'The players have been the victims of ill luck and have suffered from nervous depression. This is now over and you can be sure things will take a turn for the better.'

Gibson backs Duncan, too, and certainly never interferes with team selection. Invested figures like Walter Crickmer, Louis Rocca and Greenhough are further reassured by Gibson's obvious eye on the future. Any focus beyond these next few months indicate Gibson's fleeting worries are just that: temporary, and United's president is working on a scheme to improve Old Trafford's accessibility. The nearest train station is currently at the cricket ground, but Gibson envisages a new drop-off point right outside the football ground's entrance.

In March, the departed board members are replaced as the late John Henry Davies's old friend and 1908 Olympic football gold medallist Harold Hardman returns to the board after two years away. Born as near to Newton Heath's birthplace as someone could be, Hardman made four United appearances in 1908 as an amateur, shortly after winning Olympic gold for Britain. Davies invited him to join United's board in 1912. Hardman is now a successful solicitor with his own flourishing company.

United win three of six March games, bringing them up into a relegation scrap with Millwall and Swansea Town. Bottom-placed Lincoln City will definitely go down. The other three will fight to avoid going with them.

* * *

Five points from five April games keep United in the battle until the season's final day, when they play Millwall.

United have 32 points and Millwall have 33. It is effectively a relegation play-off match.

United require an unlikely away victory. In fact, so meagre are expectations that a Third Division manager has already phoned Walter Crickmer to arrange next season's games. Walter has politely told him to wait and see what happens.

* * *

As with many of the defining moments in United's recent history, Louis Rocca again finds himself away from the action due to his job. His days of leading the 'Rocca Brigade' to matches with their red-and-white-striped umbrellas are certainly over, and unlike on that fateful Christmas Day in 1931, Rocca is scouting rather than helping manage the reserves. In which division United will play next year is unknown so Louis looks for neither Second nor Third Division talent, just for young, mouldable prospects.

After watching and taking notes on several players 200 miles from east London, he races to try and locate a newspaper with the afternoon's results. There is none available in the small north east town he's in, so he travels to Newcastle. His nerves rattle along to the train's clickety-clack rhythm.

He arrives in Newcastle, finally, and spots a scruffy little lad selling the evening paper. He asks him to read the scores …

'Blackpool 1 Bradford 1, Bradford City 2 Grimsby Town 1, Bury 1 Brentford 2, Fulham 1 Oldham Athletic 2,' he begins.

'Come on, come on,' Louis mouths to himself.

The boy continues with increasing speed.

'Hull City 0 Burnley 1, Lincoln City 2 Bolton Wanderers 2, Millwall 0 Manchester United 2, Notts ...'

'YESSSSS!' Louis shouts, leaping about like Willy Wonka in his chocolate factory, or, as Rocca will later admit himself, an escaped lunatic. The surrounding public is utterly baffled by the sight of a man in his early 50s prancing about next to this at first baffled and then giggling youngster.

'Do you want the rest?' says the news lad. 'No, no, thank you, son,' Louis replies.

Louis returns to Manchester on the next train and indulges in a good dinner, before which he says a silent prayer.

Down in London, it has been a thrilling end to the tightest of relegation dogfights; thrilling for United, not so much for Millwall's 'Lifeless Lions'. Eight minutes in, United led when Jack Cape ended a sparkling run with a fast cross. Tom Manley – a Rocca find back in 1930 – headed goalwards and after seeing his first effort saved, thumped in the rebound.[31] Cape then scored United's second after half-time, side-stepping his marker and sending a scorching left-footed drive home. The United players went wild in celebration as the large baying crowd around them shook their heads in glum realisation of their fate. That United went down to ten men due to an injury to captain Ernest Hine did not affect their intensity and, with an incessant work rate that left Millwall panting, they prevailed.

'The most disappointed people over that win were the Third Division clubs who were having visions of good gates and a fine ground to come to, besides a holiday to good old Manchester,' Louis smugly says. He, James, Walter and everyone associated with United carry a jig in their step for the next few days.

---

31 Manley is officially United's first 'academy graduate', because he signed while under-18, he hadn't made a senior appearance before joining United from Northwich Victoria, and he played below first-team level at MUFC. However, he joined before the 'A' team began, which was the real start of the club's academy.

NEWTON HEATH.

Newton Heath FC ahead of the 1899/1900 season. Harry Stafford is furthest left on the very back row.

Ernest Mangnall, pictured as Manchester United secretary.

Charlie Roberts leads Manchester United out at the 1909 FA Cup Final

Manchester United pictured with the 1909 FA Cup, a couple of seasons later. Back (left to right): Ernest Mangnall (seretary/manager), F. Bacon (trainer), Jack Picken, Hugh Edmonds, Mr Murray (director), Harry Moger, John Henry Davies (chairman), Tom Homer, Mr Lawton (director), Alex Bell, Mr Deakin (director). Middle: Billy Meredith, Richard Duckworth, Charlie Roberts, Alexander 'Sandy' Turnbull, Enoch West, George Stacey. Sitting: Arthur Whalley, Leslie Horton, Harold Halse, George Wall.

*Welcome home for the victorious Manchester United team following their
1-0 victory over Bristol City in the 1909 FA Cup Final at Crystal Palace.
United showed off the trophy to cheering fans as they made their horse-
drawn journey through the streets of Manchester.*

*Billy
Meredith
pictured
with his cups,
medals and
caps.*

Billy Meredith in training, 1915.

Charlie Roberts, while at Oldham Athletic.

Manchester United's second team in 1924. Then-assistant secretary Walter Crickmer is on the right of the back row.

Louis Rocca, pictured as Manchester United's chief scout in the 1930s.

Billy Meredith in his elderly years.

James Gibson, Manchester United president, 1935.

Walter Crickmer, photographed as United club secretary in 1953.

Walter Crickmer celebrates United's 1957 Division One title with the players, including Bobby Charlton and Duncan Edwards.

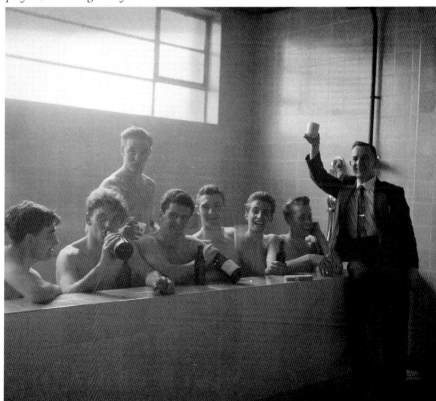

Walter Crickmer boarding United's plane to Belgrade, via Munich, for the 1958 European Cup quarter-final against Red Star.

4

Railway

*'Manchester United have created another
record in soccer history by arranging
that the railway should bring "fans" direct
to their gates.'*

– *Leicester Evening Mail*, 8 July 1935.

September 1935 – 'Now we've got the railway station – can we deliver the goods?' reads the cartoon in Manchester United's first matchday programme of the 1935/36 season.

Scott Duncan's Reds lost their first match away at Plymouth Argyle, but return to Old Trafford with expectations high for the upcoming campaign. After beating Millwall to stay up 18 months ago, the team enjoyed a pleasantly uneventful subsequent season, with George Mutch's 18 goals helping them to a decent position on the very edge of the promotion battle, and a £4,490 profit has removed James Gibson's concerns.

This time around, United should be closer to the table's top. In fact, they are considered promotion favourites, but commentators believe that is dependent on whether anyone can perform in the centre-forward position.

Gibson's long mission to improve the experience of the match-going fan has taken another step. The United Football Ground railway station has opened for this match against Charlton Athletic, and the programme's cartoonist George Butterworth – known as Gee Bee – has relished the opportunity for a pun, or ten. 'Stationmaster Gibson, inspector Scott Duncan and Porter Curry have trained a first-class team on the right lines, and right from the whistle will go full steam ahead,' it reads. Gibson loves these cartoons, and personally commissions them for each programme. He chuckles in his seat reading them before the game.

The station has a shuttle service of steam-hauled trains from Manchester Central which operates from an hour before the game until five minutes before kick-off. It's quick – just five minutes – and cheap, only two pence each way. It is Gibson's latest brainchild and another one for which he has taken on significant personal risk. To encourage the Cheshire Lines committee to permit the venture, United have guaranteed the construction costs. It makes it a win-win scenario for the Committee but requires courage and conviction from Gibson. It's brave, forward-looking and innovative. It drops supporters 15 yards from the turnstiles of the main stand, which is unique in English football.

United respond to their opening-day defeat to Plymouth with an excellent home performance against Charlton – 21,000 watch on, and they are surprised to see the attack in one of their most dangerous moods with Charlton struggling to escape their own half. Soon enough, the Addicks defence weakens under United's fiery onslaught and the Reds establish a firm grip of a fast game by half-time. The final score is 3-0.

Up next, Bradford City, and they too face the wrath of United's attack, with a 3-1 win this time as the start to the season turns positive. After six games, the Reds have settled into second and Louis Rocca feels great satisfaction when 22-year-old Bert Redwood makes his debut in the next match, a 0-0 draw with Tottenham Hotspur. Louis picked Redwood up from a relatively unknown club called Sherdley Albion.

A few years ago, as with the end of every season, Rocca attended a series of matches in the St Helens district of Lancashire where, occasionally, Louis finds a good player amongst the average. On this instance, he'd taken Ted

Connor, his long-time assistant, with him. Ted's role when travelling with Louis is either to approach a second player if there are two stand-out performers or to act as a decoy in times of trouble. At this particular competition in St Helens, trouble is never far away.

'The womenfolk have the last say and each club in the competition has a band of miners, whose methods of preventing their players being spirited away are entirely their own,' Rocca explains.

Redwood stood out in the semi-final, a slugfest between 21 hard-working scrappers and one with a bit of footballing ability. Bert was 18 at the time, but strong, sturdy and clearly possessing a football brain with composure and solid positioning. Louis and Ted split up in search of him post-match but discovered that Liverpool had got in ahead of them.

'Well, let's give Liverpool a real race to sign this lad,' Louis said.

After much asking around, silver-tongued Rocca found Bert's father. The pair got on well, and the father became keen for his son to join United.

'You never get a real player without trouble,' Louis knew, and here it came, for when he, Bert's father and Ted went into the players' room to meet with young Bert, they were thrown out with haste. Outside, a hostile crowd wanted them out of town, let alone the ground. Much like the Chirk locals with Billy Meredith 40 years before, these St Helens lads wanted to keep their best young player.

So, when Redwood eventually came out, he was accompanied by more than a dozen club committeemen who agreed that, at best, they could all go to the Redwood family home to discuss matters. Louis, Ted, Bert, Bert's father, Liverpool's representatives and 12 Sherdley Albion committee members elbowed their way through the crowd and home and there, with no one speaking alone at one time, Louis attempted his typical persuasion. Bert's father remained convinced but was unwilling to voice his opinion too assertively for a long while. When he did, they almost got the deal done, but just before Bert could sign forms for United, Liverpool's scout insisted Bert would be signing a death warrant by putting pen to paper on those. That it wasn't true mattered little. In fact, the lie aroused Louis' passions until he was bellowing in the Liverpool man's face. In this environment, Bert was nowhere close to signing. The meeting was over, but Louis made sure Bert's father wouldn't let his son sign for anyone else.

After the previous day's racket, Louis brought the typically professional, calm and friendly Walter Crickmer to Bert's house to complete the deal, and it was duly done. Louis finally had his man, but the trouble didn't end there. As they arrived at the nearest train station they saw the tail lights of the day's final service chugging away. They jumped into a taxi and ordered him to race like hell for St Helens Junction where there would be a service to Manchester. They rattled along the road with little care for safety and made it with a second to spare, sat panting and perspiring as the train pulled out of St Helens.

'You never get a real player without trouble,' Louis smiled at the normally unflappable Walter.

***

Bert drops back into the reserves after his debut but continues to develop nicely. Meanwhile, United attempt to convince another young talent's father to allow him to become an Old Trafford protégé.

Stan Pearson is a mere strip of a boy mentioned to Rocca by a schoolteacher, just like Jimmy Hanlon. Salford-born in 1919, Stan is a football-mad lad who's supported United since he was a nipper. He's played schoolboy football since he was nine at Predderick Road School and although he's a top cricketer, football is his passion and his heart is set on it as a career. He's clearly a wonderful talent, as shown in performances for the Adelphi Football Club and as captain of Salford Boys for two seasons.

Pearson left school at 14 to become a painter-decorator and then joined a firm of armature winders. That didn't stop him from playing, of course, and upon a series of recommendations, United manager Scott Duncan calls Stan's father, an electrician, to offer his son a position on the Old Trafford ground staff. The fact it's an open-air lifestyle is convincing and a deal is struck. It's another signing for the future as the 'A' team's ranks begin to swell with talent.

Up in the first team, George Mutch is leading the way again for United. On one occasion, Mutch scores United's first two goals away at Port Vale but has no recollection of them at all. After a kick to the face and heading the heavy ball, Mutch is concussed but he returns to training immediately. Football is not yet ready to have a conversation about the dangers of such behaviour.

From February, United go 18 games unbeaten to close out the season. A few too many draws stain the record, but crucially, they find wins against promotion contenders time after time, knocking rivals off like a pro at a coconut shy.

United are thus not just promoted, but crown years of endeavour with the Second Division title. With promotion secured and United's problems now behind them, Walter and Louis contemplate how the club's youth policy can be upgraded further still. They have fine talents in Hanlon, Pearson, Redwood and others, but many more excellent schoolboys are slipping through the net. How can they change the game?

5

Motor car of the year

'DUNBLANE BOY FOR
MANCHESTER'

– *Dundee Courier,* 10 August 1936.

August 1936 – Scott Duncan has made his own contribution
to Manchester United's talented youth ranks. He's spotted
a young 16-year-old outside-left from Dunblane, a Scottish
town virtually equidistant from Edinburgh and Glasgow. The
kid's got a wicked cross on him and an exciting, unpredictable
nature to his play. Raw it might be, but there's some serious
material to work with.

Charlie Mitten is the son of a physical instructor at
Dunblane's famous Queen Victoria School, where most
of the children are sons of Scottish sailors, soldiers and
airmen. Mitten plays the pipe in the school band, including
at international rugby matches at Murrayfield – a school
tradition – and he plays football with a local junior club,
Strathallan Hawthorn.

The whole Mitten family moves from Dunblane to
Manchester with Charlie, who is added to United's ground
staff, where he works with Stan Pearson and Jimmy Hanlon.
Aged 16, Mitten receives £2.50 a week, £1.50 of which goes
on his accommodation.

Charlie benefits from the advice and familiarity of the
club's Scottish boss. He had dreamed of playing for Arsenal,
but United will do, and so will Manchester. It's different to the
formal surroundings he grew used to at school. For a cheeky

young man, it's exciting, and his flamboyance shows early on in the 'A' team.

The mood at United is excitable as the Reds play top-flight football for the first time in five years, and the atmosphere becomes positively jumpy ahead of the first Manchester derby for half a decade.

The last meeting was on 7 February 1931, well before the United directors had even revealed the true extent of the club's financial woes. It's the longest the two rivals have gone without meeting in a league fixture and in the gap, United's very existence has been threatened not only by financial mismanagement but by the presence of Manchester Central, whose life has been fully snuffed out now. They have rebounded with James Gibson and the fans are delighted, but their meandering route to top-flight restoration has contrasted heavily with the success of their rivals. City have contested two FA Cup Finals, first in 1933, when they lost to Everton, and then the following year against Portsmouth, who they defeated to win their second cup, a full 30 years on from the Billy Meredith-inspired first. City have since proved themselves to be one of the country's finest sides and look good for a tilt at the title this time around.

A thrilling fixture unfolds in front of 69,000 Mancunians. Five years on from their last visit, City's supporters are impressed by the renewed Old Trafford and the new train service, while United fans are champing at the bit. They have waited five long years to show the Blues a thing or two. The chance is finally here and, boy, do they take it early on.

Tommy Bamford converts a Tom Manley cross after five minutes and after 30, the latter heads in a second goal. Giddiness flows through the ground. City's main man Alec Herd isn't his usual self and Jack Percival, who took the recently-departed-for-Liverpool Matt Busby's place, is off it, too. Nevertheless, City get one back in a fast, end-to-end match, and then score an equaliser after half-time, the game's third header – from Heale, ironically.

From there, it could be anyone's game. Both goalkeepers are kept busy in a frenetic half-hour of activity. Seven minutes from the close, William Bryant snatches victory for United in one of the finest displays at Old Trafford for many years. It is the absolute height of reward for five years' toil in returning to the top division. James Gibson feels great pride. After half a decade of tenacity and belief, the applause of 69,000 and the whole-hearted acclaim of the country's press is just reward.

Another famous triumph soon follows, with victory over the great Arsenal side. 'Perhaps I'm in the right place after all,' Charlie Mitten thinks.

United win 2-0, but after scoring in all of their opening eight games, and sitting level on points with rivals City, the Reds fall off. The top flight is unforgiving and will not indulge United's weaknesses. As the pitches get heavier and the schedule grinds on, the team find it tougher and by mid-November, they have plummeted to the bottom of the league. The youthful ground staff, Mitten and Hanlon included, regularly hear Scott Duncan and James Gibson bickering.

The club president finds solace from United's poor form at his home, Alanor. Family life there is very happy. His son Alan, against all the odds, has reached his 21st birthday.

In their idyllic Hale Barns mansion, Alan opens a few cards on the morning of 19 November, unaware of what waits outside. Several years ago, his father promised Alan that if he didn't smoke until after his 21st birthday, he'd buy him the best motorcar of the year. James knew full well, of course, that his son would not smoke – he'd had pneumonia five times – but it was a promise he always hoped he could deliver on. He and his son have a passion for cars. So the Gibsons enjoy breakfast and then finally James gets to reveal his secret. Lillian instructs Alan outside, and he goes out of the front door and on to the porch, just beyond which a sparkling Bentley, the best car at the 1936 motor show, is pulling out from the garage.

James enjoys it just as much as Alan. He adores the attention to detail and the quality of the finish. They go for a birthday drive and James savours it as one of life's great moments. So does Alan.

* * *

There is a young man Gibson will soon get to know who's enjoying a very different upbringing, in Dublin. Johnny Carey lives on Adelaide Street, adjacent to the city's Dun Laoghaire harbour. He, like Stan Pearson, was born in 1919. They are post-war baby boom boys, and Carey has two brothers and three sisters.

Johnny has only ever known his country as the Irish Free State, which came into being when he was four years old. The majority of Ireland, which has a population of about three million, works in agriculture in rural areas. Emigration to England and America is common, mainly because living standards are low and employment is becoming increasingly exacting to acquire. It's not always better in England, but discontent is hardly uncommon in Dublin, whose slums in their worst areas can be reminiscent of Manchester's Ancoats in Louis Rocca's youth.

Johnny's upbringing is, however, a positive one. He impressed at Gaelic football at school and then for Leinster College, but any future in that sport was restricted when he was banned by the Gaelic Athletic Association. He'd gone dancing on a Saturday night with a few friends to what was called 'An English Dance' and with intense hostility remaining over mingling with the English, the GAA suspended everyone who attended it. Johnny was baffled and stung by this decision, which proved counterproductive because Carey subsequently put his efforts and free time into his other sport, the English game: soccer. Johnny was a ball boy at the local tennis club, where he got to see talented stars like Fred Perry, and he swam as well, but soccer became his thing. He played in goal first, for Home Farm, and then as a winger for the same team as he played through the age groups, eventually helping them to the Free State Minor Cup in 1936. As a result, a bigger team,

St James Gate, showed their interest. Originally formed as the Guinness Brewery Works side, Carey is with the famous outfit to start the 1936/37 season when Louis Rocca pitches up to watch him.

It wasn't meant to be like this – because of the English Dance for starters, but Rocca hadn't even come to Ireland to watch Johnny Carey. He had, in fact, made the journey over to see Benny Gaughran.

Louis has been coming to Ireland for many years, ever since his early escapades with his tutor Harry Stafford. This time, he's there upon the urgings of Scott Duncan, who has sniffed out another player. He's heard, via some connections back home, of a talented young centre-forward. Many months ago, he communicated with United's unofficial Irish scout, Billy Behan, who had played with the club as a goalkeeper a few seasons ago and is now back living over the water. Few are better connected than Behan, who made contact, on Duncan's request, with this Benny Gaughran to see if he'd like to come to Manchester. As an amateur, a deal wouldn't be too difficult to make, and Gaughran was interested.

Louis has been sent over to watch him, make sure he really is the mustard, and then bring him back if so. The only problem is that upon arrival, Rocca discovers that United's move for Gaughran has been gazumped by Celtic. The Bhoys have been watching him for over a year and acted immediately once they heard of United's interest. Rocca can only respect their speed.

Rather than waste a trip, Louis asked Behan who else he should watch while there, and so they go to St James Gate to see them take on Cork. Seventeen-year-old Johnny Carey, who is studying to be a civil servant, scores within a minute. It's only his sixth game for his new side.

Rocca meets the committee post-match and they agree to a transfer fee. Louis has been convinced with ease, and now he must do some persuasion of his own, travelling with Johnny back to his family home to gain parental consent because of the young lad's age. There, Louis finds John Carey Senior to be one of the most warm and welcoming people he's encountered. It takes a few hours to get to matters of business, and then it's agreed that Carey can go to Manchester.

The next day, Louis returns to the smog-filled city with his latest capture, for whom it's all very exciting. United have paid around £200 to the Dublin club, who are chuffed with their lot. They only signed Carey a few months ago.

Johnny arrives in Manchester with this charismatic Anglo-Italian who has suddenly moved him to a new country. On their way from the train station to his new home, Carey sees the newspaper boards proclaiming 'A big signing at Old Trafford.' He can't believe it. He's very proud, but says nothing to Louis so as not to seem arrogant, or immature. It's only when he reads the newspaper that he finds out the big signing they're talking about isn't him, it's John Ernest Thompson, brought in from Blackburn Rovers for £4,500.

Thompson makes his debut in a 5-1 loss to Liverpool as the first team's winless run extends to 11 games. Carey is not involved yet. He begins United life with the reserves in the Central League. It's not yet time for most of Rocca's finds.

Elsewhere in the country, it is not time, and never really has been, for King Edward VIII, who has abdicated after just 327 days due to his relations with a divorced American actress. Having taken over from his father George V in January, now, in December, George's other son – George VI – takes over. It's for the best because Edward appears somewhat sympathetic towards the hate-filled language of Adolf Hitler's Nazi Party in Germany. That being said, there are a few in Britain like that, but ideally, none of them will be running the country.

* * *

United are stuck to the table's bottom and, soon enough, relegation is confirmed, the heady heights of victory over City and Arsenal a hazy memory. Back to the second tier they go.

6

Youth

*'I am convinced that United have one of the
greatest young players in the country.'*

– Louis Rocca on Johnny Carey.

September 1937 – As the new season begins, it is finally time
for Louis Rocca's most promising finds. Johnny Carey makes
his Manchester United first-team debut wearing the no.10
shirt in front of 22,000. He's come a long way from Home
Farm in a short time. Ironically, it is a final United appearance
for John Ernest Thompson, touted as the 'big signing' just ten
months ago. Perhaps Carey will prove to be the genuine big
signing after all because, despite losing 2-1 to Southampton,
his performance is highlighted on debut.

'The one bright spark was the play of inside-left Carey, a
black-haired Irishman, who used the ball thoughtfully, and for
forty minutes he played so well, it gave the impression United
were actually winning,' reports the *Manchester Guardian*.
'Carey at all events did not deserve to have so disheartening
an introduction to the Football League.'

Despite United's relegation back into Division Two,
the mood is sound. The supporters remained faithful all
throughout the relegation campaign and now hope United
will win their joust with the second tier once again. This
time, unlike in 1931, the club is not plummeting downwards,
it's more of an unfortunate step back, and the discussions
behind the scenes show as much. A calmness pervades the
club over the summer with board meetings focusing on small

steps rather than big overhauls. Ideas include devoting 'special attention' to 'coaching practice' – rather than just players' fitness – and considering 'having each team watched in the match previous to that game against this club', i.e. scouting the opposition.

However, that calmness is not so easy to maintain when the same streaky nature showed in Division One persists under Scott Duncan back in Division Two. The United boss wants a sharper forward line but he has turned to the transfer market before without great success. His side is mid-table after eight games. It's not good enough.

Once again, just like last season, Charlie Mitten hears Duncan and James Gibson loudly expressing their differences of opinion over who should be signed and for how much. Unhelpful in the extreme is the fact that, in a rare display of active interference with the manager, Gibson has gone and signed a player himself. He has a holiday cottage down in Bournemouth and whenever he's there, he's gone to watch the local team to get his football fix. After seeing the performance of one Jack Rowley, he handed the local club £3,000 and brought him to Manchester. Nineteen-year-old strong and skilful Rowley has bags of potential and the price is a decent one, too. Only weeks earlier, Duncan had bemoaned the fact that £2,000–3,000 players were difficult to source, and Gibson has found an excellent one, but it is the manner of the impulse signing leaving Duncan displeased.

* * *

Although he's returned to United's reserves for now, Johnny Carey's headline-making debut has earned him a first Ireland cap, against Norway in a FIFA World Cup qualifier.

The World Cup began seven years ago when host nation Uruguay triumphed. Italy did the same four years later. The upcoming 1938 edition is to be hosted by France and the Irish Free State are one of 37 teams vying for 14 qualification spots. France have their place sorted as hosts and Italy theirs as defending champions, while Spain have withdrawn due to the outbreak of civil war. The remaining teams have been divided into a dozen groups based on geographical considerations, but with England, Scotland and Wales refusing to compete, Ireland have been left with a fairly charitable challenge: a two-team group. They are effectively playing a two-legged play-off to earn qualification. They were beaten 3-2 by Norway in Oslo and so need a victory at Dalymount Park.

Carey scores with his first touch of the ball as an international, only for the offside flag to be raised. In the end, Ireland draw 3-3 in a thrilling match that sees them come from two behind before enacting a desperate chase in the final five minutes. Unfortunately, Norway hold firm and take the World Cup spot.

When Carey now arrives back in Manchester a year on from his first journey over, he encounters another dramatic headline slapped up against the newspaper boards.

'MANCHESTER UNITED RELEASE MANAGER'

After winning only five of the opening 14 fixtures, Scott Duncan has left the club. He has received an offer from Ipswich Town, a Southern League side with ambitions of earning a Football League spot. With tensions high at United, Duncan has taken an enviable £1,500-a-year, seven-year deal in East Anglia. Walter Crickmer announces to the press that the directors have accepted the Scotsman's resignation, and then he bids his farewells to Duncan, completely unaware that he is about to embark on an entirely new job at Manchester United.

Crickmer must first manage applications for the now-vacant managership and while there are many, few stand out. His second task is to deny reports that United's new boss will be Lance Todd, currently secretary-manager of Salford Rugby League Club. Crickmer's third job is to become manager himself. Again.

***

In interim charge of United for the first time since 1932, Walter takes his team to Chesterfield. Ominously, the 13th-placed Reds have scored only four away goals all season.

Crickmer immediately promotes 18-year-old Stan Pearson, Louis Rocca's find from the Adelphi Lads' Club. Pearson has played primarily with the 'A' team but has begun to appear more regularly for the reserves. On the night of Duncan's United departure, Stan received a presentation for cricketing success with his old Adelphi Boys' Cricket Club at the Manchester YMCA. Now he's set for an unexpected debut, and his father is buzzing. He quickly asks his electrician firm for the day off to head to Chesterfield to watch on.

The Derbyshire side have a strong defence, for whom United are not expected to cause many problems. What follows is quite remarkable. This flailing and underachieving United side appears freed from a cloud of doom and 18-year-old Stan is a sensation. He sets up four goals from inside-left in a 7-1 victory. His father is beaming with pride.

Pearson's inclusion in the next game's line-up draws great excitement from the Old Trafford crowd, who have heard about his stunning exploits on the road. Well over 30,000 come to watch United take on second-placed Aston Villa.

Pearson sees a low drive saved excellently early on in a fast and entertaining opening period which concludes with United's 15th-minute opener, scored by Tom Manley. Villa then miss an open goal and strike the upright before Pearson shows his quality again, playing a perfect pass to enable Bamford to score United's second. After the break, Pearson himself makes it three, his face erupting into a grin as Old Trafford vibrates with a tornado of cheering for the young Salfordian. When Villa get a goal back late on, United see the victory through to demonstrate resilience as well as goalscoring prowess. James Gibson notices how the noise for this local lad Pearson has something unique to it. The pride is palpable, and it's going to become pretty regular at United.

Gibson and others on the board are now convinced there is no pressing need for a new manager of Manchester United. The mood is good, the finances are stable and the players like Crickmer, and show it on the pitch. There seems little reason to upset the apple cart, and the truth is that everything's comfortable right now. Gibson and Crickmer are on the same wavelength, and so is Louis Rocca, trainer Tom Curry and everyone else. No one wants this happy family disrupted; they are satisfied with the arrival of one disruptive figure in Stan Pearson, whose irresistible rise continues with another goal, again the third in three, away from home at Norwich City. The attack's slickness is impressive and again the Reds survive a late onslaught.

The next week's *United Review* depicts a dark-haired young footballer playing a fairground game. Mallet in hand, striking it down, on 6 November, he reaches only the 13th-highest mark. On 27 November, he reaches the seventh, for that's how far United have climbed in the table. 'Now, sir, what about ringing the bell?' asks the operator.

Well, Stan Pearson's personal scoring run has come to an end, but Crickmer brings in another young star. Jack Rowley, Gibson's south coast signing, makes his second appearance, replacing the injured Tom Manley, and his introduction is even more extraordinary than Pearson's. The £3,000 man scores four times and only the post, which denies him once in each half, denies him a famous double hat-trick, a feat not achieved for United since Harold Halse in 1911. Rowley and Pearson combine excellently and with four wins and 18 goals in Crickmer's first four games, United appear renewed. As 1937 becomes 1938, the Reds have reached fourth in the table. They're not far off ringing that promotion bell.

All of Pearson, Rowley and Carey are becoming semi-regular first-teamers, but Gibson, Crickmer and Rocca want more. In the wake of United's February fifth-round FA Cup exit, United's board review matters at one of their regular Tuesday evening meetings. The main item on the agenda is 'the formation of a junior athletic club for cultivating young players after they leave school.' As with the 'A' team in 1932, the matter is left with Walter Crickmer.

Back on the pitch, an impressive string of victories over promotion rivals inspire hope for the Mancunians, but while they have left many of them behind, their ambitions for an immediate return take a knock with a 3-0 defeat at league leaders Aston Villa, and then a draw against Norwich and a defeat at Burnley. In the end, big wins like the Pearson-inspired 7-1 at Chesterfield prove crucial because it is United's goal average which takes them into second and back into the First Division.

Unfettered enthusiasm and high hopes for the future greet promotion and in such an environment, the Reds are linked with Stoke City's outside-right, Stanley Matthews, who would add some cultured skill to United's eager but inexperienced attack. 'PROMOTED, WANT MATTHEWS', says the *Daily Mirror*, and Walter Crickmer is hesitant to deny the story. United have indeed made enquiries and Matthews himself says, 'I don't think it would be a bad move for a player in my position.' The 23-year-old is in Paris on a continental tour with England.

7

The World Cup

'Our policy is to build a team.'

– James W. Gibson.

May 1938 – Johnny Carey, like Stan Matthews, spends late spring on the continent. Having failed to qualify themselves, his Irish side are offering World Cup warm-up games to those who need them.

Carey thus earns his second Ireland cap, aged 19, at Prague's Letensky Stadion. The opposition in a 2-2 draw is Czechoslovakia, who, though a relatively new country created after the Great War, come under great threat shortly after this match when Adolf Hitler demands the Sudetenland, Czechoslovakia's German-speaking region, be ceded to Nazi Germany.

Earlier this year, Hitler's Germany annexed Austria, the most overt example yet of German expansion and aggression in violation of the Treaty of Versailles. That followed the March 1936 mobilisation of troops in the Rhineland, the German-French buffer zone, which was itself encouraged by the weak response to Benito Mussolini's Italy invading Abyssinia. Add in intervention in the Spanish Civil War to Hitler's scorecard and this recent declaration is not so out of the ordinary, but just as with the Rhineland, Abyssinia and Austria, Britain and France feel unable to act. They are still rearming, something Hitler completed at a pace several years earlier.

British Prime Minister Neville Chamberlain has been following a policy of appeasement for some time, and you can imagine why one might tread on eggshells in Hitler's company. Football has done the same. While Carey's Ireland played Czechoslovakia, Stanley Matthews's England faced the Germans themselves, in Berlin. After major diplomatic discussions back home, Matthews and his team-mates received orders to give the Nazi salute as a sign of respect to their hosts. As with Chamberlain and most of Europe, the players followed the path of least resistance with peace in Europe teetering nervously on the brink. After saluting, United-linked Matthews scored a stunning solo goal in a 6-3 win but despite all the bluster and rumours, he will not join United. The price has proved too high.

Meanwhile, Carey's Ireland continue their useful World Cup warm-up service as they face another country increasingly concerned by their border with Germany: Poland. Hitler has not yet threatened invasion, but everyone knows it is coming soon.

Poland are cheered, for now, by a 6-0 victory over Ireland, and they head to France for the World Cup.

* * *

There, Italy make it a second successive crown with a 4-2 final win over Hungary. The triumphant manager is Vittorio Pozzo, and as he celebrates, he may cast a thought back to smoggy old Manchester, for it was there that Lancastrian skies made paler this travelling Italian in his younger days.

Pozzo is the lifeblood of Italian football who has an utter devotion to his team, which he treats as his own little army, the players his soldiers. They respond urgently to his commands, the majority of which he gives with an overwhelming quantity of patriotism, even to the three Argentinians in his squad, the inspirational centre-half Luis Monti, left-winger Raimondo Orsi and right-winger Enrico Guaita. 'If they can die for Italy, they can play for Italy!' Pozzo claims when challenged on their nationalities.

The bushy-haired Italian is from Turin, but much of his education was received on Manchester's football terraces.

After some time studying across Europe, Pozzo moved to London and then Bradford, where his father's influence – he had a wealthy family – secured him a post studying wool manufacturing, but Vittorio found the construction of football attacks to be more alluring. When recalled home to attend his sister's wedding, Pozzo refused. He was aware he might not be permitted to return to Lancashire and couldn't countenance such a thought. As a result, he was cut off from his father's finances and he taught languages to fund his life and love for football. He loved, in particular, one of the finest teams of the early 1900s: Manchester United.

The short, thin-framed Pozzo, who had a bobblehead-like cranium, adored particularly the style of captain Charlie Roberts. His long, sweeping passes and his ability to bring the ball out from defence made a long-lasting impact on Pozzo, who waited around after matches to chat to the stars of the day. He soon established a friendly relationship with Roberts, as well as other great footballers of the era like Derby County's goalscorer Steve Bloomer.

Pozzo's 'Il Metodo' tactics with Italy have Charlie Roberts in mind. Pozzo dislikes the tactics of new thinkers like Herbert Chapman who used a third defender. He instead supports the concept of an attacking centre-half like Charlie, robust and influential – a dispatcher of the ball rather than merely a carrier. First, it was Luis Monti who Pozzo told of Roberts's play, and then another Argentine converted to Italy, Michele Androlo, who spearheaded the victorious 1938 campaign.

***

When Charlie Roberts reads of Italy's triumph, he thinks of how the diminutive Pozzo used to wait outside Bank Street to talk football tactics a full three decades ago.

Just a few hundred metres away from United's old ground, Roberts cuts a rotund figure these days. His tobacconist business has grown in the same way as his stomach: out. His children have helped with that. Richard, born just after the war, is managing the shop on a day-to-day basis now, with Christopher acting as shop assistant and van driver. Daughter Hilda is a shop assistant too and eldest son William is the company secretary. Charlie's wife Mary gets stuck in as well. Charlie Roberts Ltd is a flourishing family business.

The shop itself is used for all sorts. They still sell newspapers as well as cigarettes, they still live above it, and it still retains football at its very heart. The Ducrobell brand of cigarettes, named after that famous Duckworth-Roberts-Bell half-back axis that Pozzo admired so much, remains on sale. Ex-United players pop in for a chat with their old captain, too, and journalists are often found inside Charlie's abode, stopping by to use the shop's telephone. Sometimes Charlie will be in there when the pressmen pop by, other times he'll be out at a game, but less often recently. He's finding himself suffering from intense dizziness and headaches with increasing regularity.

* * *

Two days after Italy's World Cup victory, United complete the purchase of The Cliff training ground in Salford. James Gibson has emphasised the necessity for a training pitch for practice games, for both the 'A' team and the new MUJAC.

'MUJAC! May I add a note about this mystic word,' *United Review* editor Sidney Wicks helpfully notes. 'It stands for Manchester United Junior Athletic Club.'

8

History

*'History was created in Manchester United
football circles today.'*

– *United Review*, 3 September 1938, referring
to five United teams playing on the same day
for the first time (first team, reserves, 'A' team,
MUJAC A, MUJAC B).

September 1938 – Within a seven-mile radius of United's ground are 250 schoolboy football teams with upwards of 3,000 players. The Manchester United Junior Athletic Club (MUJAC) has been created in order that none of these sides' most promising players' talent is wasted.

The Gibson-urged, Crickmer-led scheme effectively formalises what Louis Rocca has utilised for some time: recommendations from a network of teachers, priests, lads' club leaders and anyone else. The trio have been working on this for some months and near the end of last season, Walter and Louis sounded out local schoolteachers to help them with this unique initiative.

Rocca, of course, is crucial to finding the talent for MUJAC, while Crickmer is perfectly placed to set it up. He is not only a United man but a Mancunian football man, too. He's on the board of the League of Manchester and the committee for both Manchester Boys and Football League secretaries. His work ethic is indescribable, his knowledge wide and his contacts wider still. He and Rocca have an insatiable appetite for progressing the game onwards, and ideally propelling United forwards at the same time.

Aiding the pair is a 30-year-old United-supporting teacher, John Bill, who will lead a committee of teachers and educators. He, Crickmer, Rocca, scouts Jimmy Porter and Ted Connor, trainer Tom Curry, coach Jim McClelland and various senior United players soon gather at The Cliff because one of the first uses of Gibson's new training ground is the MUJAC's trial day. The countless talented youngsters present are whittled down to just 30 who will play across two teams.

The boys chosen are buzzing. Many of them have turned out for Manchester, Salford or Lancashire Boys while others are complete unknowns. Whatever their reputation before, it is clear that Walter, with the assistance of these teachers and his scouts, has brought the best young Mancunian footballers all together in one place. But what James Gibson makes clear is that these boys are not obliged to play. The only stipulation put upon them is that they will *consider* playing for United. Being a MUJAC is thus an opportunity to learn and to thrive. For now, those selected will compete in the Chorlton & District Amateur League against players significantly older than them.

It has been some years in the making, but finally, Crickmer and Gibson's brainchild is made and the MUJACs begin as well as one would expect a team of Manchester's finest young footballing talent to. They win their debut game 7-0, and it is no first-day anomaly. The lads involved are the cock of the walk and little time has passed before membership of this new elite side becomes the primary aim of all young boys in Cottonopolis, and their teachers too. They all want to be the man who sent the latest great youngster to Manchester United.

Gibson is absolutely thrilled upon hearing of the youngsters' progress. He is a proud Salfordian and Mancunian and it is his fundamental ambition for United to represent the two cities. He is immensely grateful to Walter Crickmer for his work on this and on every project, and he doesn't hide it. At a board meeting less than a year on from Scott Duncan's

THE MEN WHO MADE MANCHESTER UNITED

departure to Ipswich Town, Gibson pays a particularly glowing tribute to the 'marvellous' Crickmer who has 'more than replaced the energies that any manager could have put in'.

The day-to-day running of MUJAC is in the hands of the John Bill-led committee when Crickmer's first-team responsibilities take precedence as the season begins, and for this, he receives equally great plaudits. After a defeat to Middlesbrough and a home draw with Bolton open the campaign, a 5-1 thumping of Chelsea is indicative of the progress made by United over this past year. Walter knows he has good players who know how to play good football, so he lets them.

'I was surprised by Manchester United,' reviewed the *Sunday Chronicle*. 'Here at Old Trafford they are actually keeping the ball on the turf in attack, instead of thumping it all over the premises, and are running into position to receive passes.'

Gibson's old dining pal Stacey Lintott is convinced times are changing, too.

'We may now, I think, take it that Manchester United are a better class football team than they have been for years. They are really good to watch.'

The Carey–Rowley wing pair draws particular praise. They attack with such gusto, speed and verve that no one can fail to be excited by their play, which is as effective as it is youthful. The first 'A' team graduate, George Vose, is excelling at centre-half, too, and United's growing ambition is reflected in the persistent links with Stan Matthews. The Stoke man has handed in a transfer request and Arsenal are the other club most heavily linked, although several others are sniffing around.

That peace in Europe remains as uncertain as Matthews's future is demonstrated by the launch of a new battleship off England's south coast. HMS *Manchester* is the first ship to be named after the city and it thus draws significant attention up north. Crickmer donates shirts and shorts in United red to the team's crew, who will sail for the East Indies. Meanwhile, Prime Minister Neville Chamberlain is off to Germany.

Britain and France have finally offered up something of a threat to Hitler. They will go to war if German troops enter Czech territory without international agreement. An international conference to solve the Sudeten issue follows and the leaders of Britain, France, Germany and Italy meet in Munich at the end of September. Germany's annexation of the Sudetenland is accepted because Hitler gives a pledge of peace in return. Czechoslovakia have no say in the matter, but when Chamberlain arrives back in Britain at Heston Airport on September's final day, he feels confident enough to proclaim, 'peace in our time'.

The British people trust Chamberlain. The scars of battle remain deeply embedded and the echoes of guns still ring in many people's ears. Avoid war at all costs.

* * *

Walter Crickmer's father, Charles, has died, aged 72. There is little time to rest and contemplate, and so with the deepest condolences of the staff and players at United received, he presses on. Old Trafford is set to host November's international between England and Ireland. Crickmer needs to arrange the printing and distribution of tickets and liaise almost constantly with the two Football Associations. As for United, he manages the mood expertly as the squad, who haven't quite settled down in the First Division consistency-wise, copes with injuries and absentees. The Reds are near the table's bottom, but far from propping it up. There are clear foundations to be built on.

The MUJACs are continuing to dominate their league while Louis Rocca searches the country for next year's intake. In November, he travels to the north-east on a recommendation from his own scout, who has spotted an outside-left playing for the Seaham Colliery side. Rocca is unbothered by the outside-left but likes the team's captain, a centre-half, who he approaches to offer a trial at Manchester United. 'I've signed an amateur form for Liverpool and I'm going on trial there next week,' is the reply. 'Well, never mind, son,' Louis says, 'if George Kay doesn't want you, let me know through my scout and I'll sign you as a pro right away.' Allenby Chilton goes down to Liverpool a week later and doesn't impress sufficiently, so he signs for United instead. He looks the part immediately and is another one for the future.

Many of Rocca's signings are a little unorthodox like this. Another young Red who could sympathise with Chilton in that sense is Harry Worrall, a two-footed 18-year-old who plays without fear and with good positioning. Every club in the league had been interested in Harry, Rocca's assistant Ted Connor had told him, so Louis went down to Worrall's next game on a Wednesday afternoon. He had already seen him play and was confident enough to sign him, so he visited the family home pre-match. Harry was still out working as a bricklayer, so Rocca chatted pleasantly with his father. Worrall arrived back at 1:30pm to neck a quick lunch before playing. To Louis' amazement, the youngster pitched into a huge meal of steak, chips, bread and butter with rice pudding to follow. No one could play football after a meal like that. 'Go on Harry, that's the stuff to feed on – you'll show them all how to play!' said Rocca, fully aware that the more Worrall ate, the less mobile he'd be and the fewer scouts would have their interest piqued. Rocca left the house having witnessed one of the largest meals he'd ever seen and then saw the vast majority of scouts leave the ground well before the end due to Worrall's disappointing performance. Louis heard one manager cursing himself for having come such a long way to see such an average display. Rocca's only competition was a scout from Liverpool who approached the Winsford chairman to register his interest but declared that he needed a little more time. Rocca pounced and agreed a deal for a few hundred quid.

In the scouting game for a long time now, Louis knows this speed to be crucial. He reminds his scouts of this often.

'Always be alert,' he says. It has paid off recently when Jimmy Porter overheard two men on a train discussing the merits of a young player deemed to be the best junior they'd ever seen in their village of Radcliffe. His name is Johnny Morris, and he's only 14 years old. Porter changed his afternoon plans, went to Radcliffe to watch and Morris became a MUJAC.

* * *

Walter Crickmer manages the England versus Ireland international fixture hitch-free. He's used to such challenges now. It's not stress-free, but he is as well-versed in it as England's side are in winning. They dispatch Ireland 7-0. Stan Matthews has finally committed himself fully to Stoke despite United links and puts on a sparkling display that reminds those in attendance of Billy Meredith at his peak. He scores a sensational solo goal, just like in Germany a few months back, striding from the halfway line along the right wing, driving into the penalty area, hopping over a flying tackle, feinting to pull back to a team-mate before shooting in from the narrowest of angles past a bewildered goalkeeper. In the face of opposition like this, Johnny Carey's team-mates for Ireland face little chance. Perhaps Johnny could have made a difference, though, for although he has recently scored his first international goal – aged 19, just like Matthews was for his – Carey does not add to his five caps at his own club ground.

For his club, however, Johnny is ever-present now and the Reds have found some good consistency in December, avoiding defeat and winning three times in seven games. George Vose is never absent, nor are Jack Rowley and Bert Redwood – the St Helens lad who Rocca beat Liverpool to sign – but even after his incredible start to first-team life, Stan Pearson is back learning his trade in the reserves, and he's developing well alongside Charlie Mitten. You can't rush a young talent.

Coming into the team instead is another young kid on the ground staff. Jimmy Hanlon has scored in almost every reserve match he's played in and does the same for the first time, netting on debut, aged 21, in a 1-1 home draw with Huddersfield Town. It's a fast, low drive that the goalkeeper can't track well enough in the hail and it's a sufficiently impressive performance for Hanlon to maintain his first-team spot. He won't miss a game for the rest of the season and his goalscoring rate hardly drops.

The mood at Old Trafford now is the best it has been since the move to Stretford. The United team is becoming increasingly dominated by youngsters. In fact, the United club is now synonymous with youth, and there is talk of three titles in a single season.

9

Magnificent MUJACs

*'I hope to see the day when Manchester
United will field almost entirely a local
and district side which will hold its own
with the best.'*

– Louis Rocca.

February 1939 – The free-scoring MUJAC side top the
Chorlton Amateur League as the new year comes in. They are
yet to lose a game and have scored 131 goals, romping through
south Manchester without a care in the world. They have played
Manchester United's older, more experienced and bulkier 'A'
team and, although they lost the match, showed themselves to
be a quality side, only just off the level of their superiors.

Three players are standing out. Howcroft is a strapping
17-year-old centre-half from Handley Green whose
dimensions have been inflated by some time down the pit.
He follows in the footsteps of Hanlon, Mitten and Pearson by
joining the club's ground staff. Aston is an east Manchester lad
from Ravensbury Street School who represented Manchester
Boys and shone at August's MUJAC trials. He's hardly
stopped since. An inside-forward with excellent ball control,
he twins in the centre with Mears, who has tallied an equally
outrageous quantity of goals. While the MUJACs' relentless
run continues, Louis Rocca is lining up next season's cohort,
with the advice and help of John Bill and his committee of
dedicated volunteers.

As the MUJACs hit the 19-game mark with a 19th victory and 142 goals scored, 'A' team graduate Jimmy Hanlon scores a hat-trick for United at Blackpool in a 5-3 win. It takes his season tally to nine from 16 games and means that, despite the shaky autumn start, United now sit comfortably in mid-table, as close in points to third as they are to bottom. They will not contest for the title this year, but Old Trafford is nevertheless abuzz with talk of silverware, for the Reserves are flying in the Central League, the 'A' Team is excelling in the Manchester League and the Chorlton Amateur League is being dominated by the unstoppable force of the MUJACs. Eight years ago, United were headed for the abyss, and now the country knows few better-run football clubs.

Competing for that particular title are Division One leaders Everton, who have also placed great emphasis on youth recently. Everton 'B' features players mainly aged 15 and 16 and they are unbeaten in their own league on Merseyside. It's not an open-age division like with the MUJACs, but Harold Pickering's lads play some sublime football. He thinks his team are the best youth side in the world. Louis Rocca thinks the same of his. It's only right, then, that they should play off to provide each other with some genuine competition.

At Old Trafford in late March, United and Everton's first teams compete and Crickmer discusses arrangements for these junior games with Everton's officials. There will be two, one at each team's ground in the second half of April.

The accomplishments of these two young sides have not been kept secret. Newspapers have eagerly publicised their records and so two recent defeats for the MUJACs, once in the league and once to the McLarens work side in the Bowling Holmes Cup, feel like a necessary learning experience, while the Everton match will be an essential test in quality, but also environment.

These boys have become accustomed to playing home matches at The Cliff and away games on small pitches in Chorlton and the surrounding areas – Old Trafford is a different beast. Many of them have longingly looked upon that hallowed turf at their heroes in bright red shirts, dreaming of a career away from school, the pit or the factory and on the football pitch. Now they will play there, they being Higgins; Curless, Haslam; Cookson, Howcroft, Healy; Lockwood, Aston, White, Mears, Brennan. Their parents have rarely watched their games – with the exception of Harry Haslam's – and there have never been crowds of great size, whereas this fixture has garnered intense public interest.

Billy Meredith will be one of the many seasoned experts in attendance. The 64-year-old is a widower now, his wife and mainstay Ellen having died a few years ago. His daughters and nephews support him well. He gets a boost upon every moment of recognition in the street and he remains the idol of a generation, or maybe three. Just as his old pal Charlie Roberts has long been the benchmark for half-backs that followed, Billy is the historical tool with which to compare the great dribblers of this era and so Stanley Matthews's best acts can rarely be told without mention of old toothpick Bill.

The Welsh wizard remains remarkably fit. His face, with mildly gaunt cheekbones, never looked intensely youthful and so, in older age, it does not look excessively aged. His trimmed moustache remains and when punters walk into the Stretford Road Hotel and see Billy at work, they need no assistance in recognising the two-time title and FA Cup winner, the greatest outside-right in the game's history. Meredith busies himself with his hotel and he watches football wherever he can. Unfortunately, his real mates in the game are dying out. Charlie Roberts is ill and Alec Bell died five years ago.

Billy has enthusiastically helped out with the MUJACs wherever he can but without an official role at either Manchester club since the early part of the decade, Billy's true passion has focused on his homeland. He has become the unofficial king of Welsh football, knighting each new representative of Cymru before they first step out with their red shirt. He hardly misses an international match and never misses the opportunity to pass on some wisdom to his successors, talented footballers like Jimmy Murphy, a wing-half for West Bromwich Albion. Before Jimmy's debut at Wrexham's Racecourse Ground, on which Billy himself had played four decades before, Meredith sought him out to wish him good luck on his first cap. Jimmy will never forget it. For Billy, it is a way of connecting with the game that he still yearns to play. His body might be fit, but time catches up even with the greats and so the best he can do is take joy in the progression of young players, while still chewing that bloody toothpick.

He's watching on, then, as United's MUJACs condemn Everton to their first loss of the season. Centre-forward Jack 'Crasher' White takes his tally to nearly 80 for the season with a double in a 3-0 victory. In spite of the scoreline, Meredith deems Everton's lads better. United's team is fast and furious, with Everton's more composed. Billy is not one for modern, accelerated football. He believes the 1925 change to the offside rule has made it too easy for players gifted with speed to thrive, leaving players with artistry and weave on the roadside – or out unused on the touchline. It is a personal bugbear of his, but he is very impressed by the quality of the MUJACs, which is on show at Goodison Park in a return fixture of equal quality, a sparkling exhibition of clean, honest and excellent football which Everton win 5-3.

The Toffees' first team become English champions while United's top-flight status is secured early enough to maintain focus on the youngsters. It is clear that the Manchester United Junior Athletic Club has been an unqualified success, but there is no benefit in resting, so the Reds invite Preston North End to be their next challengers. The Lancastrians have even larger ranks of youth players than United or Everton and they play in a similar classically excellent style to Everton. United are big, powerful and sometimes unstoppably quick with their first-time football, but PNE manage a 2-1 victory and duly challenge Everton to complete an informal triangular tournament.

The MUJACs season is done, then, and they are champions of their division. Inside-forward John Aston's reward is a promotion to the 'A' team, who are champions themselves, of the Manchester League. The reserves, meanwhile, lift the Central League for the first time in 18 years – when Meredith played for them in his final United campaign – and they complete the set with victory in the Manchester Senior Cup.

Louis Rocca has long considered and publicly stated that United are 'the finest club in the world' and for the first time in many, many years, he's starting to have a point. The youth system is thriving, United have four trophies in the cabinet and the club's accountants are just as satisfied as James Gibson. This year marks five on the bounce in which United have made a profit.

The first team are the club's only trophyless side. They take on Liverpool in the final game of their campaign and use it to pay tribute to George Vose, who is taking his benefit. It is appropriate that alongside Vose, the first-ever 'A' team graduate, are fellow alumni of United's burgeoning youth system like Carey, Hanlon and Wassall.

Two Hanlon goals give United final-day victory and an eventual position of 14th, the best for a decade. Like a proud father post-match, Gibson presents Vose with a £650 cheque and, in a short speech, emphasises the splendid service George has given the club. He has, without a doubt, been the most consistent United player of the decade. Everyone in attendance cannot fail to be aware of the cyclical nature of the game. In Vose's debut season, Gibson had considered throwing in the towel until the Reds managed an inspired two-goal win away at Millwall to avoid dropping into the Third Division, making Louis Rocca jump for joy in a Newcastle train station before eating well on his way home. Six years on, the team are a top-flight club with three title-winning teams of talent ready to take the next step up. Crickmer, Gibson and Rocca have not simply dragged Manchester United off the lip of the cliff, they might well have set this club up for greatness.

10

Gibson's mission statement

*'We have no intention of buying any
more mediocrities. From now on we will
have a Manchester United composed of
Manchester players.'*

May 1939 – Johnny Carey played 34 times for Manchester
United in the 1938/39 season and Louis Rocca's Billy Behan-
aided discovery is increasingly seen by secretary-manager
Walter Crickmer as the team's lynchpin, and a movable
lynchpin at that. Utilised in several positions across the team,
Carey has proven his smooth footballing talent to be highly
adaptable.

The Irishman travels again to Europe with his country
for a post-season continental tour. Having scored his second
international goal in a March draw against Hungary in Cork,
the Irish are off to Budapest for the return fixture, and another
2-2 scoreline is played out. It's then to Bremen to take on Nazi
Germany. Ireland beat their saluting opposition at Dalymount
Park three years ago, 5-2, but the Germans have improved
greatly, assisted by the Austrians now in their ranks after that
country's annexation.

Neville Chamberlain's September peace proclamation has
aged like milk. One year after his invasion of Austria, Hitler
has broken his promise that he'd take the Sudetenland and the
Sudetenland only off Czechoslovakia. He has, in fact, taken
over the entire country. Britain and France have renewed their
entente in February, recognising now that Germany and their

leader will be stopped with nothing but force. Chamberlain has introduced Britain's first-ever peacetime conscription and it is decided that they and France will give a guarantee of independence to Poland, believing it to be Hitler's next target. The seeds of war have taken root. They will soon bloom.

Just like the English a year before, Ireland's football team faces Germany at a particularly difficult time. Their players have, like the English, been instructed to deliver a Nazi salute as a mark of respect, and they too are distinctly unhappy about such a prospect. As the swastika flutters alongside the Irish tricolour and the anthems play, Ireland's captain Jimmy Dunne reluctantly raises his arm in salute and shouts. He is heard right at the end of the line where Carey stands and listens: 'Remember Aughrim, remember 1916!'

The Irish cannot claim to be in the dark about Germany's expansionist policies and actions, but the dark truth of Hitler's country is still unclear, especially in Ireland, where distrust for the British media and government understandably remains high. In addition, Ireland's envoy in Berlin is sending back false reports. Charles Bewley, an outspoken admirer of Hitler, insists that Jews in Berlin are not under threat and his reports home rub off to the extent that the Irish FA are happy enough to play Germany and give the salute.

After a strange experience for all involved, a 1-1 draw is played out. It's a good away result for the Irish and they are much praised afterwards by the Germans whose leader now strengthens relations with Japan, the biggest threat to Britain's empire in the East. Plans for Hitler's invasion of Poland are well underway and a military alliance with Italy is agreed.

It is becoming clear to the people of Manchester and Britain that war is coming, but life can do little but go on as normal, and the same is true for football and Manchester United. The club is on a great high, ready to offer genuine competition for the Division One title, ready to bring through more of its reserves and 'A' team talents like Allenby Chilton, Bert Redwood and Stan Pearson, and ready to mould the talent of the new MUJAC cohort. Johnny Morris, signed by Rocca's assistant after hearing his name on a train, is one of them, and Joe Walton is another, from Queen's Street School in the north Manchester suburb of Bradford.

While there are signings to make, fixtures lists to manage, player registrations, tickets to prepare, pitches to improve, railings to paint and so on over summer, the sun is out, the schedule is less unrelenting and tiresome, so Crickmer enjoys himself. He welcomes new men into the United family and helps them settle down in Manchester, always with a warm smile.

The mood at the club's AGM is good because the future seems bright. With greater clarity than ever before, president James W. Gibson sets out his mission statement: 'We have no intention of buying any more mediocrities. From now on we will have a Manchester United composed of Manchester players.'

11

An era's end

*'They have found a growth at the back of
my skull which has developed as a result of
heading heavy balls so often over 20 years ago
and are going to extract it.'*

August 1939 – Charlie Roberts is talking to a *Daily Mirror*
reporter while sitting nervously in the Manchester Royal
Infirmary.

'I have been almost like the living dead for the last two
years, especially after my active life,' he continues.

'When I was told I was to have an operation I refused point
blank, but when I thought it over I decided that anything was
better than going on as I have for the last two years.'

Day-to-day life has become a struggle for Charlie. He
has been suffering from chronic dizziness and headaches.
He's only 56.

'A month in here and a few weeks' holiday,' he says, 'then
I will be able to go and see United play again.'

Charlie is visited by friends and family in hospital – he has
a grandson now – where he stays for a couple of days before
the operation begins. It takes seven and a half hours, and at
the end of an agonising wait for his children and his wife May,
Manchester United's greatest player is dead.

It is grimly ironic that the Players' Union co-founder has
succumbed to such a fate. It is 22 years since the death of
25-year-old Tommy Blackstock in a United reserves match
inspired a hurt Roberts and Billy Meredith into action and

though it has taken an additional two decades, Charlie is thought to have been a victim to his profession like Blackstock – a victim of the footballers' plague. For decades, he has helped support bereaved families and fought for better conditions for his colleagues, all the while unaware of the impact heading a stone-like object was having.

'Charlie was one of the greatest players who ever lived,' a devastated Meredith comments, 'and one of the finest sportsmen. Everybody liked him.'

Walter, who is great friends with one of Charlie's sons, can hardly believe the news, but he must offer a comment on behalf of United.

'His name will always live in football history as one of the finest players the game has produced,' he says. And so it should. Charlie had it all: technique, physicality, composure, character, passing range, a good long shot, great ball control and leadership. The first United player to represent England. The first United captain to lift the English title. The first United captain to bear aloft the English Cup. Co-founder and chairman of the Players' Union. Manager of Oldham Athletic. Proud and successful businessman. Kind and much-loved husband, father and grandfather. A great friend to many.

Billy is one of the pall-bearers at Charlie's funeral. He is joined by fellow 1909 English Cup winners Herbert Burgess, Dick Duckworth, Vince Hayes and Jimmy 'Trunky' Turnbull – a United front for a United man, for whom the tributes are endless.

***

For many of Charlie Roberts's later years, his former club resembled nothing of the team he so expertly captained in his playing days, but now, United are in his mould again. The Reds start the new season with a 4-0 home trouncing of Charlie's first league club, Grimsby Town. Stan Pearson and Johnny Carey are both on the scoresheet.

Walter Crickmer's boys then travel to London for an away double with Chelsea and Charlton Athletic. Walter leaves John Bill and Louis Rocca in charge of an extra set of trials for the new MUJAC cohort, where the evening sun casts long shadows at The Cliff, the host to a wonderful collection of youthful potential.

Two days after a 1-1 draw with Chelsea and the MUJAC trials, Germany's invasion of Poland begins. The next day, Louis Rocca is at Rochdale's Spotland ground to see them take on Wrexham, looking for talent. Crickmer remains in London where his side suffer a 2-0 defeat to Charlton.

Eight miles away in Downing Street, Britain's most senior politicians are preparing for war. In the early hours of 3 September 1939, the British ambassador in Berlin hands a final note to the German government stating, 'Unless we hear from you by 11am that you are prepared to withdraw troops from Poland, a state of war will exist between us.'

At 11;15am on crackling BBC Radio, the Prime Minister, Neville Chamberlain, speaks to the nation.

'I have to tell you now that no such undertaking has been received, and that consequently, this country is at war with Germany.'

Part Six: Courage,
1939–48

1

A little dynamo

'United's ability to do well in league football
was hit on the head by the action of a certain
Herr Hitler, former painter in civilian life.'

– *United Review*, Manchester United versus
Everton, 1 June 1940.

June 1940 – Walter Crickmer's season of burdensome toil
concludes with Manchester United's first-ever Football
League fixture in the summer month of June. Everton are
the visitors to Old Trafford, and the match exemplifies the
stresses United's secretary-manager has faced since war was
declared nine months ago.

The amicable Lancastrian has always taken two steps at a
time. If he were a little taller, he'd take four at once now. Life
has felt in a particularly relentless hurry recently, such is the
reality of wartime on the Home Front. Every man and woman
is required to find war-contributing employment as Walter
has, as a special constable in the Old Trafford police force,
but not all are then also obliged to, almost single-handedly,
guide a major football club.

Unlike in 1914, there was never an appetite to discontinue
football altogether. The role the sport played in the Great War
is fondly remembered. It still required proactive campaigning,
including by Crickmer, who was one of the most vociferous
voices in private meetings, to guarantee the Football League
resumed at some speed. Even before it did, Walter ensured

his United club wasted no time. The Reds were one of two dozen league clubs to play at the first possible opportunity when the suspension on all sports gatherings was lifted 12 days into what has become known as 'Hitler's War'. Thus in mid-September, details of United's line-up to face Bolton was found amongst headlines such as 'Ring Round Warsaw is Closing', 'HITLER SAYS "DESTROY EVERYTHING' and 'CIVILIANS GUNNED IN STREETS."

United lost several key players upon war's outbreak as men headed home to join the army. Jack Rowley returned to Wolverhampton, Allenby Chilton to Newcastle, Harry Worrall to Winsford, and so on. But United's pre-war commitment to building a team of talented, local youths paid dividends. Crickmer could turn to Salfordian Stan Pearson and Mancunian Jimmy Hanlon, as well as his ever-reliable Irishman, Johnny Carey. The latter has found wartime employment at one of Trafford Park's largest factories, Metrovicks, whose water tower tickles Manchester's cloud-heavy sky.

In early October, regional league competitions began and Crickmer decided to use as many of his young prospects as possible, rather than rely on 'guesters' from other clubs. Crucial to this was his insistence that United could not let the club's flourishing pre-war youth system stagnate. Instead, Crickmer entered the reserves into the Lancashire League and found friendlies for the MUJACs. The committee of teachers who had overseen the latter side disbanded entirely, with the exception of John Bill, who Walter made secretary-manager to alleviate his own overwhelming workload.

With the reserves back playing, Crickmer could give ex-'A' teamers like Charlie Mitten valuable game time, and ex-MUJACs like John Aston, too. Well-deserved senior debuts followed soon after. Mitten, the Dunblane boy, put in a distinguished performance against Crewe Alexandra, alongside Stan Pearson, 19, Johnny Carey, 20, and Jimmy Hanlon, 22. When a first-team spot wasn't available for

Mitten, Crickmer found him senior football elsewhere, at Hyde United on a couple of occasions and for Tranmere Rovers when the Birkenhead outfit came to take on Manchester City.

Similar schemes have been implemented for others. Harry Haslam, an outstanding ex-MUJAC, was loaned to Urmston on an informal basis, and so was George Curless, a gifted left-back tipped for big things. Walter knows the latter well, for George has worked under him as an office boy for some time.

All the while, Crickmer has been working two jobs and running United on a shoestring budget. Old Trafford attendances have suffered a ten-fold decrease, a consequence of the government urging its citizens to save their money. Worse still, despite Walter making special safety arrangements to encourage larger crowds, including constructing shelters beneath the stands, season ticket holders requested a straight, cash refund. Walter listened, but that meant £2,500 gone, just like that. United are reliant on their president James Gibson, the profit they accumulated pre-war, and on incoming rent from the government, who are using Old Trafford's offices and rooms for military storage and The Cliff training ground as a base for barrage balloons.

Administrating all this has been a gargantuan task for Crickmer and he has proved himself to be a little dynamo for whom nothing is too much. Now the season is nearly over, he is ready to breathe a sigh of relief, but there is still one game to go.

Everton are coming to Old Trafford and Crickmer has assembled a mixture of graduates from the blossoming MUJAC side and 'guest' stars who have been given short spells of army leave. Most excitingly, Stanley Matthews is to finally turn out for United.

'Well, well, well,' declares *United Review*, 'what a team!'

Matthews is described as 'a star in himself, the greatest outside-right since the days of Billy Meredith'. Together with Matthews, talented City forwards Alec Herd and Peter Doherty, plus the 'bewilderingly clever' Raich Carter, form an unfamiliar but star-studded and fear-inspiring frontline. It is expected that they will present a serious challenge to a very good Everton side.

For each of United's players, Walter has had to write and convince them to come and turn out for the Reds, or do so through a network of friends, Billy Meredith and Louis Rocca often proving helpful in this regard. Crickmer then has to send a letter to each man's army supervisor or commanding officer to ensure they're free to leave their camp or barracks for an afternoon, and then he has to put the team out and deal with the fact that, up until the day and hour of the game, it isn't known if they will all make it. Reserves must be ready in case.

For this game, Crickmer has negotiated through Rocca for former City defender Matt Busby to represent United. The Scot is a Liverpool player but has been guesting across the country since joining the army last autumn. Unfortunately for Crickmer and Busby, the latter does not get his army leave signed off, and so Walter must source a last-minute alternative.

Those attending Old Trafford hoping to see sparks from the illustrious Matthews-led frontline are sadly underwhelmed. Herd's shooting is off and Matthews is tightly marked. In fact, it is an 18-year-old MUJAC named Briggs who stands out for United. 'We have plenty of other lads equally as promising in our MUJACs team at the moment,' Walter proudly tells inquisitive Everton reporters, and he's right.

The Goodison lads return home with a 3-0 win, secured with a sudden hat-trick from Stevenson in the game's final five, and they will soon get to see more of the MUJAC talent. Between them, Crickmer, Louis Rocca and John Bill have kept this excellent initiative going during this wartime season and, having already played Stockport County at Edgeley Park, the MUJACs get more big stadium experience on Merseyside. The fixture proves a fine finale to the 1939/40 season.

It's been a strenuous few months for all involved in football, but they are all assuredly grateful to do what they do when Manchester is otherwise filled with stories of death and grief.

Two days after watching the MUJACs at Goodison, Louis Rocca is back in his hometown. Ancoats is shaken by a new update; the land of Louis' parents has entered the war.

2

Little Italy's horror

'Families Weep as Police Seize Hundreds of Italians'

– Manchester Evening News, 11 June 1940.

June 1940 – Benito Mussolini's declaration of war on Great Britain and France leads to anti-Italian riots across Britain. Mobs ransack, loot and destroy Italian properties, forcing families to barricade themselves in their back rooms in the most degrading manner.

Ancoats, Louis Rocca's home, is Manchester's Little Italy, and fortunately, the population here fare better than in Glasgow, Liverpool and London. Even so, the pockets of limited violence mean when Rocca walks through the place he has called home for 58 years, he sees ice cream wafer biscuits littered across the cobbled streets, interspersed with fractured glass. Overnight, the police were instructed to arrest more than a hundred Ancoats Italians. They successfully took 30 or 40, including 63-year-old Father Cajetan Francessi, the local priest who has lived in England for four decades, during which time he volunteered in the Great War. In fact, he volunteered to fight in this war but was rejected due to his age; too old to fight but suitable for arrest. The next morning, weeping wives seek solace by poking their heads into St Alban's Catholic Church to pray. They find the incense and candles still burning, but the little church is empty, its father lost.

Louis Rocca's people have become the enemy overnight. It matters not that there are few, if any, Mussolini-supporting fascists here, or that at least 60 young Ancoats Italian boys are fighting with the Allies. Their fathers are interned, nevertheless. Louis is one of the few men left behind, his friends like fellow street vendor Joe Monti and ice cream man Carlo Frezza carried away.

Many Mancunians are sympathetic, but to those who are not, the Italians do everything to demonstrate their loyalty. They have already sent their sons, and now they hang British flags from their windows, plaster signs reading 'This is a British firm' over their smashed windows, and paint their ice cream carts red, white and blue. This still isn't enough for small gangs of young men frustrated by the war and the disruption to their life. They march up the streets chanting anti-Italian songs and the bleary-eyed women gathered on street corners, whose husbands are now in internment camps, scuttle away when the chants begin. Their husbands soon discover these camps are unfit for human habitation.

It is a traumatic few days for a community shattered by distrust, confusion and anxiety. Manchester's Little Italy will never truly be the same again. Early in July, further tragedy hits. The SS *Arandora Star* is sunk off Ireland's west coast. Its cargo is Italian and German internees being transported to Canada. More than 500 lives are lost, with dozens of Manchester Italians amongst the dead.

* * *

For those not affected by such tragedy, the summer's intermittent sunshine makes wartime life easier because when the nights mean curfew and blackout curtains, longer days are an even greater luxury. Normal life has certainly veered from the ordinary, even for an unordinary person like Johnny Carey, a talented professional footballer. It's tough for Carey. He gets to show his talent once a week. The rest of his time is spent helping make bombers at the Metrovicks factory. He gets up at dawn in the blackout and cycles to Trafford Park. For a man used to exercise and fresh air, the factory experience is a taxing one.

Fortunately, Johnny's appearance isn't too jaded when, aged 21, he meets a local girl called Margaret at a weekend dance. She calls him Jack, and always will. They hit it off immediately and life seems brighter all of a sudden. His mother wants him to return home to relative safety in Dublin, but he has no interest in that. He is enthused by Margaret, and the football.

Crowds are still relatively meagre, but United get decent numbers in for the new season because the team is a good one. The break has been revitalising for Walter Crickmer. He has made arrangements for United's various teams to compete in local leagues and attended London meetings with the FA, discussing how clubs can help the war effort. Old Trafford will thus become, on certain days a month, a training centre for 'broomstick men', those being readied to fight but for whom there are insufficient weapons to train with. They simulate gunfire with broomsticks instead.

Crickmer has also been constructing a squad of options. He'll need them. Even reliable men like Carey's availability is declining as the war intensifies. John Aston, the exciting MUJAC inside-right, manages a goalscoring debut in the season's first game as United beat Rochdale. There's something about these MUJACs and debut goals.

A little behind Aston in development is Johnny Morris, brought in by Rocca's assistant Jimmy Porter years ago. He has been promoted from the MUJACs to the 'A' team, and reserves appearances follow as soon as September, shortly before his 17th birthday. Even younger is Joe Walton, 15, who's shining for the 'A' team.

Youth remains the name of the game at United, even during the war, and United's young first-teamers are enjoying themselves at home, too. With most young men away, it's 'take your pick' for those back home like Johnny Carey. But he has settled on just the one girl. Margaret is for him and the pair are married in Chorlton-cum-Hardy in October. It's only been a few months and were it peacetime, they wouldn't have dared tie the knot after so little time and with so little money, but it's not. It's wartime, people do these things, and even their parents understand. Margaret is flabbergasted when her mum and dad are pleased rather than furious at her sudden marriage. In fairness, she's chosen a good 'un. Her parents think the world of Johnny because he's a true gentleman.

Within days of his marriage, Carey is back on his bike at dawn. Winter is closing in and Johnny arrives and leaves the factory, its water tower jutting skywards, in darkness. The 12-hour shifts change his appearance. The only time he really sees daylight is on a Saturday when he plays for Manchester United, let out early by the Metrovicks bosses to play. From Monday to Friday, it's darkness only. He has developed purple bags under his eyes and his weary cheekbones are thinning out. When he returns home to Dublin to see his family, his mother is deeply upset, but Margaret cleverly plays his appearance off as a result of a rough boat journey.

Theirs is not the only recent marriage. Young couples are being wedded at a pace before the men head off to fight or when they return on leave. Irene Turnbull is married to Alfred Journauex at Gorse Hill's St Peter's Church. Irene has recently welcomed Alfred back from Dunkirk, where he was one of the last to leave. She is the daughter of United legend Sandy Turnbull and so she knows all too well to appreciate your time with a loved one fighting over in France.

Just as in the Great War, death has become a numbing factor. In Canada, a year on from Charlie Roberts's death, the October passing of United's other great captain, Harry Stafford, goes almost entirely unnoticed. Manchester's people are too busy avoiding the Luftwaffe's bombs to remember the saviour of one of the city's great institutions. He has died unemployed, in poor health – that old ankle playing up – and without much to his name. Harry was a mischievous attention-seeker who acted with excessive bravado, left wives and mistresses with 'legitimate' and 'illegitimate' children alike, and lied about his own achievements. He needn't have. Few did so much for Mancunian football as Harry. That really would have been enough. Those who learn of his passing in spite of the cloud of death hovering over the world remember, despite his many faults, a generous, captivating and enthusiastic character who demonstrated loyalty to his football club, if not his wives; loyalty which means Manchester United still stands today after two near-bankruptcies and two global wars.

3

The Luftwaffe

*'The Manchester people have bought their
turkeys for Christmas, but they won't be
cooking them.'*

– German radio, December 1940.

December 1940 – The terror of London's 56-day Blitz has
concerned Mancunians, and when Liverpool suffers a three-
night bombardment five days before Christmas, it is clear
Manchester's time has come.

Guided by the Ship Canal's reflection of the moon,
the Luftwaffe's snarls compete with sirens' moans just as
Mancunians finish Sunday dinner on 22 December. Cutlery
is left scattered on tables as the city's population scuttle into
bunkers. Four hundred and fifty people squeeze into a Hulme
shelter built for 200. Within an hour, debris has trapped
them inside.

German aircraft drop more than a thousand bombs in
one night. That Metrovicks cast iron water tower at Johnny
Carey's place of work acts as the Luftwaffe's guiding point.
The bombers line up on the tower and hit targets around it.

While London's Blitz was psychological, Manchester's
specifically targets industry. Albert Square takes the first
bomb. A minute later, the Royal Exchange is ablaze. The
Victoria Buildings adjacent to the cathedral follow and fire
gushes out of a gas pipe nearby. Buildings collapse and fire
spreads. It has only been five minutes.

THE MEN WHO MADE MANCHESTER UNITED

Firemen scurry around doing what they can, a network of hoses interlocking through the city's main streets.

News comes in from Eccles; a stray bomb has killed a dozen first-aiders hosting a Christmas party. Thirty-one are injured. The family next door are all dead.

Fires of impetuous rage fill the city centre. It is night-time, but you could read a newspaper the sky is so bright. Some believe it to be England's biggest fire since 1666.

The focus turns to Stretford, Hulme and Salford. A manic half-hour begins absurdly when a bomb falls into a playground paddling pool. The following hundreds will not be so fortuitous. Huge craters bruise the streets. Six policemen are killed at a police station near Old Trafford.

With communication lines destroyed, bicycle messengers weave through fires, craters and rubble. Trafford Park Hotel's bowling green is hit. A neighbouring resident suddenly finds the bowls flying through his kitchen window. In Salford, two fractured water mains flood the burning street. It's apocalyptic. Finally, a blast at Manchester Cathedral ends the bombing, lifting the entire lead roof up. It somehow lands perfectly back in place, but everything inside is utterly destroyed.

The next day is chaotic. Fires are gradually brought under control and the sun rises to reveal the true destruction. A stray bomb has chipped Old Trafford football ground. In the surrounding area, 130 people have been killed. The total in all of Manchester is 684. It's unimaginable.

A soldier on leave approaches a Stretford church with his fiancée. Their wedding will have to be rearranged because where once a church stood is only rubble.

Old Trafford football ground survives that small hit, with only minor damage. Remarkably, Walter Crickmer does too. He is buried in the rubble of another building while on patrol in his police day job. Colleagues are dead. Walter says his prayers with little but darkness above him. He wrestles around in the bricks and mortar. Thankfully help is soon forthcoming, and Walter is carried out with injuries to his back and legs. The pain will not last too long and he will recover and, crucially, unlike many in Manchester, Walter will have his Christmas turkey, despite what the German radio might have said.

The Luftwaffe take their leave as United's Christmas Day fixture against Stockport is switched to be played at Edgeley Park instead, which also plays host to United versus Blackburn three days later. The Reds bring some much-needed Christmas cheer with two victories, the latter a 9-0 romp. Blackburn only managed to get seven players together, so some amateurs filled in the gaps.

February sees the focus turn to cup action and United are beaten by Everton over two legs even though Jack Rowley scores in each. He's back playing regularly due to being stationed nearby, and Walter is delighted with that. So is Jack. He's been guesting down south but it's good to see his mates again.

On 8 March, he and Johnny Carey both score hat-tricks as United beat Bury 7-3 at Old Trafford. And then the Luftwaffe come back.

When Carey begins his early morning cycle to Metrovicks, the Irishman sees a huge ball of flame hovering over the Old Trafford football ground. Such flames are hardly rare. Johnny has been on fire watch once a week for the last few months, staying in the Rusholme Public Library overnight, but this one gives him a particularly strange feeling. The positive is that hitting an empty football stadium might save hundreds of lives compared to a row of houses, but there is a pang in Carey's stomach as it becomes clear that things are in a bad way. This hit will be irreversible.

The main stand is rubble. Carey doesn't know it, but just a mile or so away Walter Crickmer is bravely running towards the dressing rooms hoping to save the kit and boots. It's futile. Offices, players' dressing rooms, giant stands and electrical and medical apparatus costing thousands of pounds lie amongst the rubble.

When James Gibson receives the news at his Alanor home, he simply breaks down and weeps. He is not a regular crier. He has seen enough tragedy in his life: the death of his parents, his sister and several of his own children. But all that was a long time ago, so for the first time in many a year, he cries.

The essence of opportunism

*'He'd had ten years of rebuilding the club to
see it all smashed by bombs.'*

– Alan Embling, great-nephew of
James W. Gibson.

March 1941 – Old Trafford's demise is as symbolic a blow as
they come. Just a decade ago, Manchester United teetered on
the brink of bankruptcy. Walter Crickmer, James Gibson and
Louis Rocca built the Reds back up. They now face the gut-
wrenching reality that their club has been turned to rubble.
The club, to its core, it feels, has been destroyed. The 'soul'
remains, of course, but as Walter stands amongst the debris,
hands on hips, his back still aching somewhat from his own
recent personal near-tragedy, it is a heartbreaking sight. The
shirts are gone. The shorts are gone. The balls are gone. The
boots are gone. The club records are gone. The gymnasium is
gone. The pitch is gone. The end of this famous Manchester
institution seems possible once again.

But Crickmer and United plough on. The club's next six
league fixtures are played away from home, during which
time, Walter negotiates with neighbours Manchester City
over the use of their ground. One of those six fixtures is at
what is about to become United's new home: Maine Road. A
Jack Rowley quartet and a Stan Pearson double contribute to
a 7-1 thumping of City. Rowley's lethal shooting – 17 goals
in ten games – is a grand help to Crickmer in these times of
strife. His plate is sufficiently overcrowded without having to

agonise over draws and defeats. Every football club is losing money through this war, and fast, but United's unique and fresh disadvantage is that they are not only paying their rivals to use their home, but they are also no longer gaining anything back in rent from the Ministry of Defence, apart from a small fee for the use of The Cliff.

In spite of such strife, no team plays more games than Manchester United. Unlike the first war season's 'Western Division', this year has featured just two regional leagues: North and South. To alleviate stress, clubs have been told to play as many games as they can, with the league ranked on goal average rather than total points. It is remarkable, then, that Walter Crickmer's side have, despite seeing their stadium blitzed to dust midway through the year, played more than any other club. It is a grand testament to the diminutive Lancastrian's immense organisational abilities and determination.

***

Bringing a smile to every Red, Walter included, is Johnny Carey, who scores in the season's final match to crown United Lancashire Cup champions with victory over Burnley. A near-10,000 crowd pay £500 odd, which is of great value to Crickmer and United, who have finished this campaign playing in kit borrowed from other clubs.

These are the unique challenges of war. United have sufficient cash reserves, but this doesn't mean they can simply buy new kits; they must instead purchase clothes with relevant coupons, just as Britons can only obtain food with food coupons. This situation has very few obvious solutions. United have no kits. Other clubs have generously donated theirs, but they have done so only temporarily. They need them back now.

Walter begs the Board of Trade to allow United an exemption to buy kits with cash, but they reject his pleas. Their suggestion is to instead ask the club's supporters to donate clothing coupons. Crickmer can see the sense but is hesitant. He doesn't want United to rely on the kindness of needy strangers.

Thankfully, the kind strangers do not care for Walter's pride. They hear of United's struggles and into Crickmer's possession come coupons donated by the local community. In fact, it is not merely a local matter. The first two come in from a Leicester woman who supports Aston Villa. 'The best of luck to Manchester United,' she writes to the *Manchester Evening News*. She has seen United play her own team in Birmingham some time ago and was upset to read of their plight. Her generosity inspires others, and another dozen coupons arrive the following day.

'It is very kind of these women to send the coupons,' Crickmer replies. 'I, too, have received some direct. It is still possible, however, that the Board of Trade will grant a licence for us to buy new outfits.'

Walter is clearly not one for grandiose, over-the-top statements despite this remarkable situation. For the first time since 1901, when Rocca and Harry Stafford went knocking on doors across town, United are kept afloat by the local community.

With this wind in their sails, the Reds commence their season in fine form. A Liverpudlian reporter, writing after Crickmer's lads have defeated Everton 3-1 at Goodison Park, explains, 'United frittered nothing away and were the essence of opportunism.' One could say that about matters off the pitch, not just on it. The stresses of war are exposing the insatiable brilliance of Crickmer's administrative skills, most notably in his retained commitment to youth. Over the summer, he and Rocca have devised an innovative scheme. The latter is acquaintances with a set of football-mad brothers who live near him around the Oldham Road area. Abraham, Clifford and Frederick Gosling sell fruit and fish for a living. Since the war began, they have been working in the Trafford Park industrial estate, just like Carey and thousands of others, but they also run a football team, under their own surname, which also adorns their shops. Crickmer and Rocca's proposal is a simple one: United's youth players, whether newly discovered or graduates of the young MUJAC teams, will play for the Goslings. United will fund the side and consistently send in fresh prospects while the Gosling brothers, passionate United fans and keen to help out, will handle the administration, coaching and organisation.

The opportunity is a much-needed one for young lads like Joe Walton, who made his 'A' team debut aged 15, and others yet to make such a name for themselves like John Anderson or Jack Roach. The scheme is the absolute essence of opportunism and the positive results will be seen quickly enough.

Meanwhile, the same is true in the first team. Jack Rowley is banging them in for fun. His season sprang into action with a rare seven-goal haul in an annihilation of New Brighton and before October ends he manages three four-goal performances. A five-in-one follows in November and another hat-trick in early December, helping United to finish fourth in the pre-Christmas table. This season's league is split into two titles, before and after the festivities. Rowley has scored 32 of United's league-high 79 goals with 14 from Smith, ten from Carey, seven from the only-just-turned-18 Johnny Morris, and five from Mitten. Walter's management is certainly one of mood-handling rather than tactical genius but he has a great eye for adapting a man's position to drag the best out of him, and if he needs support, he can always turn to Rocca, the Anglo-Italian's long-serving right-hand man Ted Connor or the ever-present director Harold Hardman.

5

The Goslings

'GOSLINGS FC, THE UNDEFEATED
CHAMPIONS of the Manchester Amateur
League, and winners of the Manchester
Amateur Cup and the Manchester Junior
Cup.'

May 1942 – Manchester United win the post-Christmas league championship, trumping Blackpool by 0.445 points.[32] Jack Rowley's goalscoring form continued and when his availability declined, Walter Crickmer used 'guester' Harry Catterick, normally of Everton, who proved himself an excellent replacement by scoring seven goals in as many games across March and April. Johnny Carey has hit another 14 since Christmas, but Stan Pearson and Charlie Mitten are no longer playing so much for the Reds. Their army training has intensified.

While on leave, Private Pearson of the South Lancashire Regiment becomes the latest young United man to tie the knot. He and Lily Wood move in together in Lower Kersal before Stan heads off on duty.

When the 1942/43 season begins, Crickmer's ranks have been depleted but retain some depth because United are running four teams now. Walter is responsible for the first team while overseeing the reserves, the Goslings (acting

---

32 Each team's total was adjusted to points per 23 matches. United played 19.

as the 'A' team) and the colts (the MUJACs). Joe Walton is progressing very well with the Goslings, for whom two additional players of note are beginning to hatch in young goalkeeper Jack Crompton and defender Henry Cockburn.

It's all too well these youngsters are coming through because Crickmer is now faced with the reality of a new absentee every few months. His team finish fourth again after another stunning goalscoring showing. In one five-game sequence, they score five or more in each match and that record is cuddled by a ten-game winning streak. By Christmas, they've scored 58 goals in 12 games and conceded 26. Wartime football is entertaining because what else can it be? Nobody wants to see a 0-0 draw before they go home to listen out for the air raid sirens, pull the blackout curtains across and scuttle into shelters midway through their tea.

***

Johnny Carey, of course, is a mainstay through this time. Ever reliable, that man, but even his wartime footballing career is at an end. After Christmas Day's 4-0 win against Bolton at Maine Road, in which Carey scores a double, the Irishman joins the British army. He leaves on the highest of notes, scoring five goals in a ten-game winning streak, and the decision has not been made lightly. Not only is Johnny – or Jack, as his wife still calls him – to leave United and Manchester, but his six-month-old son Michael, too. He doesn't know when he might return, or if he will return at all, but wartime factory work has ruined him. He is a man attuned to the outdoors, a natural footballer who needs fresh air and exercise. Three years inside the Metrovicks factory has taken its toll and the army represents the starkest of alternatives. Carey heads to Algiers in North Africa, leaving United having played 112 times during the war alone, scoring 49 goals.

Even if not with pleasure, Crickmer can replace Carey. United's deep ranks of players, a consequence of pre- and mid-war commitment to youth, are keeping them going. It is clear they are one of the country's best sides, not just from the consistent positivity of their results, but from the lack of 'guest' players they require. It helps that Crickmer's boys are desperate to play as soon as they return to Manchester on leave, or train nearby. Mitten and Pearson write to Walter regularly to update him on when they'll next be back. Even Carey manages another match on his first time home.

United finish sixth in 1943's post-Christmas league table but reach the Lancashire Cup Final, where they'll take on champions Liverpool. Crickmer is delighted to welcome Jack Rowley back for the big occasion, and Stan Pearson, too. George Vose might be around, and Bert Whalley and Johnny Morris definitely are. The subsequent scintillating performance and 3-1 victory at Anfield sees Crickmer showered with congratulations by local reporters and officials. The display has earned United the title of the North's best team. The Reds play with skill and art, speed in defence and attack and intelligence in possession. Pearson is outstanding. The ex-'A' teamer is 24 now. Were it not for war, he would be approaching his peak in the Football League, and he's showing his best regardless, though in front of only 12,117 spectators, rather than 80,000.

The 1943/44 season brings with it the return of a five-team set-up at Manchester United. The first team star in the regional Football League, the reserves in the Lancashire League and the Goslings in the Manchester Amateur League. The Rusholme Amateur League hosts the colts and the South Manchester Wythenshawe League welcomes the MUJAC B side. The players making up the latter two sides were nowhere near the club at the start of the war. They are newly scouted talents, evidence, if you really needed it, that Crickmer and Rocca are not just helping United survive this war, but readying their club for the future by scouting and then rearing dozens of potential stars.

There is great public interest in such matters and Louis is more than happy to oblige with tales of his great finds when reporters inquire. On an October evening in 1943, he is regaling one such journalist with the story of signing Bert Redwood, United's talented left-back. He recalls the near-fight in St Helens, being chased out of town and bringing Walter back the next day to complete the deal, before their mad chase for the last train home. A fortnight later, Bert is dead having contracted tuberculosis while with the forces. He's buried in his hometown. Louis is distraught upon hearing the news.

United finish second and then ninth in their two 1943/44 campaigns while the colts and Goslings win some silverware. Crickmer's conviction in retaining United's focus on youth is paying dividends, his first-team ranks bolstered by graduates signed pre-war like Johnny Morris and Joe Walton, but also Gosling products Henry Cockburn, Jack Crompton and Albert Mycock.

6

Rocca's old pal

*'I have a great job for you if you are willing
to take it on.'*

– Louis Rocca, writing to Matt Busby.

November 1944 – Ex-MUJAC Charlie Mitten and ex-
Gosling Albert Mycock score in a 5-2 defeat to Liverpool at
Maine Road in mid-November. It's been a testing encounter
for the young forwards against a defence including Scottish
veteran Matt Busby, who enjoys the match on his old
stomping ground.

It's a rare return to the north-west for Busby. Even when
'guesting', he's turned out primarily for Chelsea, Reading
and Hibernian, rather than his actual club Liverpool, who
therefore excitedly welcomed back his 'magical influence
on the defence'. Walter Crickmer enjoys the goalscoring
performance of Billy Liddell, one of his favourite footballers
to watch, even if he plays in Liverpool red.

It is a satisfying month for Manchester United's club
secretary. After three years of his campaigning and persuasion,
the War Damage Commission has finally granted a licence
of £4,800 for the demolition of the Old Trafford grandstand,
which must be torn down before it can be rebuilt. It is the
first sign of progress in three years and, like Andy Dufresne
developing his Shawshank prison library, Walter only doubles
his efforts now.

For a few days, though, his focus is elsewhere, for his
own gosling, his only daughter, Beryl, spreads her wings

in marriage with Third Engineer Officer Reginald Wilton Norman in the grand setting of Manchester Cathedral. It is a happy day for the Crickmers.

Liverpool defender Matt Busby, meanwhile, has enjoyed his time back in Manchester on leave. It's a city he loves and he's used the opportunity to catch up with some old friends. In mid-December, he receives communication from another old pal who he didn't bump into the month before.

* * *

Dear Matt,

No doubt you will be surprised to get this letter from your old pal Louis. Well Matt I have been trying for the past month to find you and not having your reg. address I could not trust a letter going to Liverpool, as what I have to say is so important. I don't know if you have considered about what you are going to do when war is over, but I have a great job for you if you are willing to take it on. Will you get in touch with me at the above address and when you do I can explain things to you better, when I know there will be no danger of interception. Now Matt I hope this is plain to you. You see I have not forgotten my old friend either in my prayers or in your future welfare. I hope your good wife and family are all well and please God you will soon be home to join their happy circle.

Wishing you a very Happy Xmas and a lucky New Year.

With all God's Blessings in you and yours
Your Old Pal
Louis Rocca

* * *

Louis and Matt are members of the Manchester Catholic Sportsmen's Club. They are, indeed, 'old pals' who have talked football, faith and life since Busby's 1928 arrival in the city, at which point he found the Catholic community a helpful settling factor while he struggled to break into Manchester City's first team.

In fact, City were willing to let Busby go in 1930, when Rocca inquired about a fair price. '£150,' was the reply, but Louis had little more than a penny. Matt soon established himself as a regular and key player, dropping back to right-half, where his composed, intelligent play stood out. When later negotiating a new contract at Maine Road, it was Rocca who Busby turned to.

'You want my advice, you want my opinion?' Louis asked, in typically semi-dramatic style. 'You do your job and the money will come to you,' he explained, and Matt listened. He respected Louis greatly.

The war has disrupted the finest years of Busby's distinguished playing career, but hope remains for the resumption of said career soon. The 35-year-old has worked as a physical training instructor throughout the war and played regularly, guesting for league clubs, leading Army sides and captaining Scotland's side in their unofficial fixtures, which was as great an honour as they come, particularly as, much like Charlie Roberts, Busby's talents had long been overlooked by his country.

With the Lanarkshire lad developing his coaching ability, Liverpool offered him a deal to become assistant manager on a five-year contract, starting at £10 a week, as soon as war is over. However, Matt has little intention of becoming an assistant, and Louis has heard as much. Of course he has, he's a perennial gossip.

So when Louis refers to 'a great job', Matt is in few doubts about what it will entail. What he is less knowledgeable about is just how long he has been touted as a potential future boss by the Old Trafford hierarchy. It was James Gibson who first heard rumblings of Busby's fine coaching abilities. On a 1942 visit to Dorset, Gibson chatted with an old friend, Captain

Bill Williams, now sports officer for the Southern Command. With an eye always on the end of war, Gibson asked if Bill knew of any young officers who might be suitable to take on the United job and Busby was the subsequent recommendation. Gibson didn't leave it there. He wanted to see Matt play and get a sense of his character, so he went to watch Bournemouth, for whom Busby 'guested', and was very impressed.

Contact has been non-existent since, but as soon as Louis got a sniff of Liverpool's advanced talks with their player, he acted, telling Gibson to 'leave matters with me'. With inherent trust in his closest United allies, Gibson did.

Busby now promises Rocca he'll stop in Manchester when next on leave. So it is that in February 1945, when the Scot travels north again, he breaks his journey in two at Birmingham to play an international match and then arrives at Manchester's Cornbrook Cold Storage, the Gibson-owned premises acting as United's offices since the Old Trafford bomb. Inside 14 Hadfield Street, about 150 metres from the Bridgewater Canal at the north end of Chester Road, James Gibson and Matt Busby are formally acquainted. And then it's down to business. Matt has decided that he would very much like to be the manager of Manchester United, but he has several demands.

This is not quite the plan he had anticipated. Busby had expected to work his way up from a smaller club outside of the top flight, but he has faith in himself and he cannot turn down the opportunity to work and live in Manchester where he and his family have been settled for many years. His demands, still, are several, and fairly unique. Gibson is taken aback by some of them, but not by others. He has heard about Busby's character, from Bill Williams, Louis Rocca and Walter Crickmer, and knows he is meeting with a confident, single-minded man.

Busby is happy to stop playing football, but if he is to be manager, he wants absolute control over anything at the club he thinks is relevant to playing success, including coaching appointments, player recruitment and changes to the infrastructure. Gibson admires his conviction. He suggests to Busby a contract of three years. Busby requests – or demands, rather – five. Gibson accepts. It is a significant commitment, a brave chance taken on a young, unproven coach.

The khaki-clad Busby and suited Walter Crickmer make for an interesting pair, separated by eight inches in height. They sit down; Crickmer explains the contract and where Busby needs to sign. He does so. And so does Walter. And just like that, the war-beaten baton of Manchester United is handed over.

Busby has inherited a club from Crickmer that appears, on the face of it, to have very little – not even a stadium. But underneath the surface, Walter has prepared something wonderful for his successor, a team ready to be moulded into England's finest.

7

The Busby secret

'The Busby "secret" is out.'

– *Liverpool Echo*, 19 February 1945.

February 1945 – The Busby–Crickmer–Gibson trio agree that news of Manchester United's new appointment will not yet be made public, but that proves difficult.

Matt – who has received offers from other clubs, but prefers the United one – travels to Scotland after his brief Mancunian stopover. Watching a game at Hampden Park, he lets his mouth run a bit and it's everywhere soon enough.

'We are all very happy about it,' says Crickmer, as United are forced to confirm the news. 'We are looking forward to Matt taking up the reins here in due course.'

Busby's Manchester return delights the city's footballing population. Matt is remembered in Cottonopolis as a stylish and classy player and an absolute gentleman. For now, though, the 35-year-old must return to his army service, although not for much longer. War is coming to a close, that much is clear. The Germans are retreating with speed. British and American troops will soon cross the Rhine and the last bomb of war falls on Britain in late March.

In Manchester, Walter is enjoying his final few months of management, relishing the excitement of the cup. In the second round, the Reds provide the day's biggest surprise by smashing Stoke City six goals to one. Despite the rapid rate of scoring at the other end, young Gosling graduate Jack Crompton earns the plaudits for his performance in the United net. Jack Rowley scores two and so does little 5ft winger Bill Wrigglesworth, recently returned from two and a half years' RAF service in India. Crickmer's lads defeat Doncaster in the next round with ease, setting up a semi-final against Chesterfield.

The concentration and death camps at Buchenwald, Bergen-Belsen and Dachau have been liberated, the Red Army has surrounded Berlin, Benito Mussolini has been executed by the Italian resistance movement and now Adolf Hitler has committed suicide with Soviet troops less than 500 metres from his Führerbunker. Shortly after, Matt Busby arrives in Naples on an RAF flight. With him are 18 British army footballers who will tour the Mediterranean to provide entertainment. They will see Naples, Rome, Rimini and Bari, and Athens too.

Back home, United get their tactics wrong in the cup semi-final first leg. The ground is wet and dense, poor for passing, but United persist in such a style. Only Bert Whalley's excellent defensive work prevents a defeat with the score 1-1. Ominous is Chesterfield's record thus far: they have drawn away from home in the first leg of every round before winning at home to progress, but the mood is one of glee and optimism despite the result. Just three days ago, Berlin surrendered to the Russian army. While United and Chesterfield have been battling it out in Manchester, formal negotiations for Germany's surrender have begun in France.

8

Crickmer's final

'WAR IN EUROPE ENDED TO-DAY'

– *Manchester Evening News*, VICTORY
SPECIAL, 7 May 1945.

May 1945 – 'We may allow ourselves a brief period of
rejoicing,' says Prime Minister Winston Churchill, 'but
let us not forget for a moment the toil and efforts that
lie ahead.'

War is over. On 8 May, the Allies celebrate the defeat of
Nazi Germany.

Throngs of people fill Manchester's streets as a national
holiday is declared. They have been out the day before, too,
when victory was established, but this is the day of celebration
proper. Copious amounts of bunting flutter across every street,
beer is sunk, bonfires are lit and long tables stretch across
streets and in parks as communities come together to celebrate
the resumption of peace. Women from the factories dance
down the streets, waving their Union Jack flags, knowing their
husbands and sons will soon return home, safe and sound.
Manchester's people dance, in Piccadilly Gardens and all
across the city. 'Bless 'Em All' is the message on many a flag.
They will be home soon. Home at last.

Included in all of this are Walter Crickmer, James Gibson,
Billy Meredith – who has only just finished collecting his caps
and medals, blown across Stretford by a German bomber –
and Louis Rocca, who hopes 'Little Italy' will soon return to
what it was.

Four days after Victory in Europe day, United travel to Chesterfield. Crickmer has spent the last few days desperately seeking permission from Allenby Chilton's commanding officer for an additional day's leave to play in the second leg. The good news arrives only just before the game.

Watching on at Chesterfield is 46-year-old long-retired Joe Spence, the old United hero.

'Who is this Walton?' he asks the reporter he sits with.

Well, Joe Walton, that's who. A 19-year-old former Gosling, like Jack Crompton in goal, he is some talent. Walton plays his finest game yet in United colours in a brilliant display of collective defensive football. Chilton does superbly at half-back alongside Bert Whalley and Major Roy White, a Spurs 'guest' player who is lucky to still be a footballer. He'd suffered temporary blindness at Dunkirk only a year before. In defence, Walton and Roughton are excellent, and Crompton too. The pitch is better this time around, as is the weather. Chesterfield pursue their straight-down-the-middle tactics again, but with less effect because on a better pitch, United's more methodical passing game on the wings pays dividends. They win 1-0. On the same day, Busby's British Army team beats a combined Mediterranean Forces side 10-2 in Rome. Crickmer's United are to face Bolton Wanderers in the North Cup Final. The winner will take on Chelsea or Millwall in the overall final.

* * *

Housewives with shopping baskets, overalled men and servicemen alike queue up from the early hours of a spring morning to secure tickets for the Maine Road second leg. Walter Crickmer is enthused by the experience. It's like a pre-war match. A fervent anticipation fills the air and before the first leg has even been played, Walter must make a public statement to explain that there are no tickets left.

Three of Crickmer's team remain from that which began the war: John Smith in attack, Bill Wrigglesworth on the wing and George Roughton at the back. Two more are Gosling graduates in Crompton and Walton, and again, Chilton's availability is uncertain.

Excitement for the final and the war's end is hampered significantly by the news that George Curless, former MUJAC and highly talented left-back who worked as a clerk under Crickmer on the ground staff, is reported missing, presumed dead. He left Manchester United some years ago to undergo RAF pilot training in the United States, but on his very first mission, his aircraft disappeared on a bombing raid on northern Germany's Kiel canal.

Kick-off is at 3pm in Bolton.

***

Wanderers' manager Walter Rowley has endured a week as taxing as Crickmer's. A crowd of some 40,000 are expected for the first leg but Bolton's Burnden Park stadium, like Old Trafford, has played its role as a storage facility for the Ministry of Supply. Stacks of baskets are occupying space on two sides of the ground, which could otherwise be filled by 20,000 people. After many phone calls, half of the baskets are removed. Lofthouse scores the only goal of the game in front of 30,679 supporters. Bolton take in more than £5,000. Crickmer hopes United might have a similar crowd and a similar income. They need it.

Special trolley buses are put on to serve Maine Road from across Manchester. A band of the Loyal Regiment plays before kick-off and the two teams are paraded for introduction to the president of the Football League. Across Europe, the match is broadcast on BBC General Forces radio. Busby's boys in Bari could have listened to it if they weren't so busy enjoying the sunshine. Busby himself has made a valuable discovery. He has been bowled over by a stirring team talk delivered by Jimmy Murphy, the former Welsh international half-back.

A pulsating struggle between United and Bolton is ongoing back home. United are without Chilton, refused leave of absence from his army unit, leaving Crickmer with some late decisions to make. Jack Crompton makes some fine saves, and Walton's tackling is superb, his passing too. Wrigglesworth draws the tie level after 23 minutes but by half-time, it's 1-1 on the day and Bolton lead on aggregate. Bryant scores a second for United on the hour mark and extra time appears certain until, with one minute remaining, the ball hovers over the goalmouth and Barrass heads in a dramatic late equaliser that proves the winner of the North Cup. Bolton will take on Chelsea in the national final.

Back in Bolton, the whole town turns out to celebrate the team touring on an open-top bus. There is more revelry than on VE night. But regardless of the score, the occasion has been a wonderful one for Manchester. A 57,895-strong crowd played witness, and walking away from Maine Road, a soldier decked out with his medals – including the Africa Star, amongst others – turns to his pal. 'I've enjoyed every minute of that.' He spoke for everyone there.

9

Busby's final

*'Walter Crickmer, our secretary, was a great
help to me. He had been through the mill
and had tremendous experience of all sorts
of situations. His suggestions, advice and
guidance were of great value to me.'*

– Matt Busby, writing in the *Liverpool Echo*, 16
November 1957.

April 1948 – Three years since Walter Crickmer handed Matt
Busby the war-weathered baton, Manchester United are in
their first FA Cup Final since 1909. Busby's magic touch
has propelled United forwards, but this team has Crickmer's
fingerprints all over it.

> Crompton; Carey, Aston; Anderson, Chilton,
> Cockburn; Delaney, Morris, Rowley, Pearson,
> Mitten.

All but outside-right Jimmy Delaney, signed from Celtic,
can be considered talents bequeathed to Busby by the trio
of Crickmer, James Gibson and Louis Rocca – Rocca found,
Gibson bought and Crickmer nurtured.

Captain and right-back Johnny Carey and centre-half
Allenby Chilton are Rocca finds. Gibson was responsible
for sharp-shooter Jack Rowley. Goalkeeper Jack Crompton
and left-half-back Henry Cockburn are Gosling graduates
while the MUJAC set-up produced John Aston (left-back),

John Anderson (right-half-back) and Johnny Morris (inside-right). The 1932-launched 'A' team provided the magical wing pairing of Stan Pearson and Charlie Mitten.

* * *

When Busby arrived at United three years ago, he worked out of a petite room at Gibson's Cornbrook Cold Storage, squeezed in alongside Crickmer and his staff. He took training in the shadow of the bombed-out Old Trafford terraces, on which moss and weeds had begun to grow. But while tested and tried they might have been, United's wartime stalwarts had grown more than weeds. Busby gratefully received some of the country's finest players and the blue-eyed Scot was pleasantly surprised with the quality he found.

It is no surprise, then, that in many of the team photos snapped during Busby's first seasons in charge, there are two men sitting centrally amongst the red-shirted players, not one: manager Matt Busby and Walter Crickmer.

Of course, Busby provided that magic touch. Upon commencing, after being demobilised in October 1945, Busby leaned on Crickmer as his essential guiding hand. As the club's heartbeat through which every important decision and incident passed, Crickmer advised Busby on a daily basis. He'd give his opinion on a player's temperament or aptitude for changing position, he'd explain United's pre- and mid-war youth system and enact Busby's requests to revitalise it. It had been well-maintained in wartime, but it needed an elite 'oomph' added. And he'd advise on anything else Busby needed, but not on training, because Matt had utter conviction in his ideas there.

With the assistance of trainer Tom Curry, the squad's father figure, and his assistant Bill Inglis, Busby made United fitter than ever before and yet, the emphasis was not on conditioning. It was on ball work. Only 36 and still a better player than some of his charges, Matt participated in training with great vigour. His quality commanded respect and his philosophy was quickly established. He froze practice games and demonstrated how better to do things, and it rubbed off.

The pre-war MUJAC sides, Billy Meredith complained, were too reliant on power and pace. Busby retained those attributes, but introduced a Meredith-pleasing, box office, fast-flowing attacking style, the cornerstone belief of which, captain Johnny Carey said, was that 'the ball should never stop'. United played first-time passes into open space. It was magical when it worked. When it failed, Busby didn't mind. He wanted his team to entertain, and they did.

United proved the season's surprise package when, with Jimmy Murphy now involved, the Football League proper resumed in August 1946. Mitten and Rowley scored the goals in the opening day victory at Maine Road, still United's temporary home seven years on from Old Trafford's destruction. While ex-City player Busby is comfortable there, Crickmer's priority is to restore United to their true home. For symbolic reasons, of course, but City are also demanding £5,000 annually and 10 per cent of gate receipts.

While Crickmer worked on that, Busby and Murphy moulded the team bequeathed to them. Cultivating a family atmosphere, they secured United's highest finish since the 1911 title, ending just one point behind Busby's old club, Liverpool. It was an immense achievement given the Reds made only one major signing post-war in Delaney.

A mini player wage revolt combatted over summer, United slipped into a nine-match winless streak that left them teetering above the relegation zone in mid-October 1947. To some, it appeared the regression to the mean after the previous year's heroics.

A concerned James Gibson urged Busby to 'go and sign someone' and suggested several names himself. Busby said no.

The subsequent argument ended only when Gibson stormed out of the room, but United's president returned later that day to apologise. In doing so, he gave Busby his unequivocal active backing. 'Is anyone interfering with you?' Gibson would ask his manager. 'If there is, he'll have to go.'

Busby had insisted he had the right players and wanted to build things properly, as they had agreed back in February 1945. He was proved right. By the start of the 1948 FA Cup campaign, United were 13 matches unbeaten and had climbed to fourth. They travelled to eighth-placed Aston Villa to begin their cup run. A remarkable 6-4 victory followed. Entertaining, certainly, but a little unpolished from Busby's Reds. The same could not be said in the next round.

With City also drawn at home, United had to play elsewhere. Facing Liverpool, Busby cleverly took his boys to Goodison Park. After a dominant 3-0 victory, the newspapers' reaction said it all: 'This sort of soccer is more like sorcery.' Charlton and Preston North End were both beaten and then a Stan Pearson hat-trick blew Derby County away in the semi-final.

United have thus reached a first final since 1909, when Busby was not yet born, by beating sides who will finish the season placed fourth, sixth, seventh, 11th and 13th in England's top flight. With 18 goals scored in five matches, three clean sheets and just one match at even their temporary 'home', it's widely regarded as one of the FA Cup's most extraordinary runs and it has made United the country's favourite club. Journalists are calling them the best footballing side since the First World War.

With their final berth secured, captain Johnny Carey – gentle in his methods, but unerringly effective – reads a letter addressed to him in the *Manchester Evening News*.

'On behalf of my sons and myself I would very much like to convey my good wishes to yourself and the boys of Manchester United, and trust they will bring back the cup,' a Mrs Mary Roberts writes. 'I well remember the last time the cup was won by United and brought back to Bank Street, Clayton, by my late husband, Charlie Roberts, then captain and colleague of Duckworth and Bell. What a great day it was! They rode from the station in charabancs drawn by four white horses. Crowds of men, headed by brass bands, carried torchlights all the way up Oldham Street and Ashton New Road. Then the team played a match and afterwards – with their wives and friends – went to a grand dinner in the Midland Hotel, given by the chairman, Mr J.H. Davies, who I think made Manchester United what it is to-day. Good luck to you all.'

Walter Crickmer, meanwhile, has more than just one letter to deal with. Several vanloads of mail, containing 30,000-plus applications for tickets, have pulled up at Old Trafford. The FA have given Crickmer a quota of just 12,000. He and an especially bolstered staff work through the nights, wading through an ankle-deep flood of letters.

Managing this cup run has been a strenuous task for Walter, exacerbated by the need to play at other teams' grounds, as well as Maine Road, and by United's augmenting popularity. Yet even this overwhelming responsibility has been a mere side matter for the little dynamo. His unrelenting focus has remained on restoring United to Old Trafford, and he has finally received good news.

In the seven years since the Reds played a first-team game in Stretford, Crickmer has not once stopped his campaign for its reconstruction. It has been a long battle.

Walter has been supported by James Gibson, of course, and a United-supporting Member of Parliament, Stoke's Ellis Smith, who raised the matter in the House of Commons last November. Crickmer was disheartened at the lack of action which followed but in mid-March, shortly after semi-final victory, confirmation arrived that United could proceed with their Old Trafford repairs.

Walter's greatest grudge against the universe is finally to be fixed. Interviewed after the announcement, he admits himself to be 'tremendously pleased'. For a modest man of measured language like Crickmer, that says a lot.

* * *

United's flowing football has inspired Manchester as it still reels from war. Hundreds of buses depart the city for Wembley, with an eight-hour journey time, while others are on the train, including the team. Red-and-white scarves abound, others pin huge rosettes on to their Sunday best and wooden rattles clack endlessly.

It is United's first Wembley appearance. For those who attended in 1909, it is an even more remarkable sight, the imperial stadium living up to its expectation, recently embellished by the newly constructed walkway towards the twin towers in preparation for the summer's Olympic Games. It's London's first since 1908, the year United won their first title with Davies, Mangnall, Meredith and Roberts. Now it is Gibson, Crickmer and Rocca who got them here, having passed the mantle on to Busby, Murphy, Joe Armstrong, Bert Whalley and their supporting cast. That includes 47-year-old Abraham Gosling, who sends a good luck message to his old players Crompton and Cockburn.

The sunlit Wembley turf is pristine and the densely packed terraces produce a slow and moving rendition of 'Abide With Me'. Just three years ago, the world was at war. Lying in graves across the continent are men and women who would have otherwise stood shoulder-to-shoulder with their brothers, fathers, grandfathers and friends, about to watch their football team compete for the highest honour. Khaki-clad young men on the terraces are a reminder of this. National Service remains in place.

King George VI strides out, greeted by the national anthem. Wearing royal blue, Johnny Carey takes immense pride in introducing His Royal Highness to his team-mates.

Blackpool punish United's slow start by taking a 12th-minute lead. Chilton tripped Stan Mortensen, seemingly just outside the box, but a spot kick is awarded and converted. Crompton should have saved.

Jack Rowley's deft touch past the goalkeeper allows him to finish into an empty net but Blackpool lead again seven minutes later. Busby's tactics have cleverly nullified the threat of Stanley Matthews, but double-goalscorer Mortensen is thriving. At half-time, Busby adapts slightly and Carey gives a simple but inspiring team talk. Rowley scores his second equaliser, a fantastic header directed back across goal, after which United's force appears unstoppable. Stan Pearson's excellent right-foot finish in off the left post finally puts United ahead and John Anderson finds the top corner with a wonderful long-range effort to seal a victory of simply immense meaning to United and to Manchester and to its people.

United have triumphed in the best final yet played on this Wembley turf. Back home in Lancashire, Reds rejoice as they go down at the Empire Stadium. Across Britain, young kids listen to United's glory and fall in love. Amongst them are Ashington's Robert Charlton and Glasgow's Patrick Crerand. Two decades on, this pair will don royal blue for United at Wembley and lift the European Cup. There is some toil to go before then, but the legacy of this Crickmer–Busby team is clear.

* * *

Busby is rightly celebrated having achieved cup glory a mere three years into his first job. Here is a young manager responsible for the country's most entertaining football team. He deserves every bit of praise he receives. There is an awareness, though, of what has come before. The vision was in James Gibson's head. Louis Rocca found the talent. Walter Crickmer masterminded the mechanics. Busby provided the magic touch.

Missing from the celebrations, sadly, is James Gibson. United's president, now 70, is not well. Doctor's orders have kept him at home.

United celebrate down south before returning to Manchester, where an immense crowd awaits. But they will have to wait a while longer. United's train stops short, the players disembark at Wilmslow and they make their way to Gibson's home in leafy Hale Barns. The victorious squad gathers on the lawn below Gibson's bedroom, captain Carey the only exception. He and Busby carry the cup upstairs and present it to a giddy old man, who rises from his bed and comes to the window. Down on his lawn he sees what he ambitiously envisaged a decade ago: a victorious Manchester team made up of Manchester players. All his efforts, sacrifices and risks made worthwhile.

'I'm proud of you boys,' Gibson says. 'This is a moment I have been waiting for.'

The players go upstairs one by one and receive warm congratulations and thanks from an elderly, ill man who has achieved what became, as late as his mid-50s, a lifelong ambition. He bids them farewell and they are soon in Manchester, greeted by a tumult of waving arms. Billy Meredith insists the crowd isn't as large as it was in 1909, but anyone present amongst the estimated 300,000 would disagree.

Walter hurries about to ensure all is going to plan but enjoys the thrill of the occasion. Few are more excited than 66-year-old Louis Rocca, all those years on from 1909.

Once the buzz has died down and he has a moment to pause, Crickmer enthusiastically writes a letter to Gibson which demonstrates his admiration for his boss.

'The players as you know put up a great show,' he says.

'The crowds in their own way put up even a greater show when we arrived back in Manchester – one which I shall never forget.'

But there is something else.

'Midst it all, without you sir,' Crickmer says, 'the party was not complete.'

Epilogue

'Louis was the encyclopaedia of the club and always ready to give guidance,' Walter Crickmer said. 'We will all miss him.'

The death of Louis Rocca, whose passion began as an 1890s child, preceded that of James W. Gibson, who fell for United in his mid-50s, by a little over a year. These two Manchester United titans died soon after witnessing their beloved club achieve FA Cup glory and finally return to Old Trafford a year later. When Rocca succumbed to illness after a short hospital stay in the summer of 1950, his 'old pal' Matt Busby was touring the USA. Busby and his United team were floored by the news. Everybody loved Louis, whose enthusiasm never dimmed in his final years. Nor did his contributions to his club, nor his ability to make an excellent brew, his first job when he joined Newton Heath half a century before.

Rocca's final finds joined a revitalised United youth set-up, spearheaded by Busby and Jimmy Murphy. Kids like Mark Jones from Wombwell or Mancunian striker Dennis Viollet were hotly pursued by other leading English clubs, but won over by Rocca's unerring passion, United's burgeoning reputation and the opportunity to play for Matt Busby. Louis' final discoveries were complemented by those of his brilliant successor, Joe Armstrong. Another of Matt's old mates, Armstrong was less bold than Louis but equally kind. Small and bushy-haired, Joe expertly manned the Old Trafford telephone lines and, on weekends, used his excellent Rocca-esque eye for talent.

The enormous support for the Rocca family upon Louis' death demonstrated the 67-year-old's essential role in

Manchester's wider community, but United, of course, did dominate. At his funeral, red and white wreaths flanked the congregation before James and Lillian Gibson, Walter and Helen Crickmer, Jimmy Murphy, Jean Busby and Billy Meredith then watched Rocca's coffin be laid to rest in Moston Cemetery alongside a piece of turf specially cut from the Old Trafford pitch.

Gibson, though beset by bad health, continued to attend Old Trafford. Nearly blind, he listened to the crowd's reactions to understand what was occurring in front of him. Being at his spiritual home gave him life until another damaging stroke led to his death in September 1951. His 74-year-old wife Lillian inherited her husband's share of 51%. She was not permitted a place on United's board due to her gender, but all decisions had to pass through her approval, nevertheless.

Sadly, Gibson missed United's first title in 41 years by mere months. The team hadn't changed a great deal since the 1948 FA Cup victory so Walter Crickmer's fingerprints remained, but behind the scenes, Busby and Murphy had enacted a revolution. They revitalised, reconfigured and fine-tuned Crickmer's pre-war youth system to such absolute perfection that they could take their 1952 championship-winning team and still say, 'let's rebuild', because they were so convinced by the greatness coming through. The FA Youth Cup's initiation allowed United to exhibit the fruits of their labour. They won the first Youth Cup in 1952, and the second, third, fourth and fifth. Murphy and assistant Bert Whalley sculpted young boys with talent into good men with brilliance. These lads were the club's sons, educated in the ways of the world, not just of the football pitch.

With Gibson and Rocca gone, you might think United's family atmosphere would disintegrate, but the opposite was true. With characters like Busby, Murphy, Armstrong, Whalley, Arthur Powell, Bill Inglis, the laundry ladies Irene and Jean Ramsden, and many others, it developed further still. Walter Crickmer took United's youngsters shoe shopping, or organised their first-ever trips overseas. At other times, Jimmy Murphy sent them to Withington. There, an old hero of his lived: Billy Meredith, who presented Murphy with his first Wales cap two decades earlier. And the Busby Babes, as they had become known, would listen to his stories and advice.

The result of all this was dominance, the magic of which truly began in 1956 as United stormed the league. As they did, Busby thought back to Louis Rocca. He wished his old pal could have seen it; there was no bigger United fan than Louis – the man was utterly obsessed. Crickmer thought of James Gibson, too, who would have been overcome with Salfordian pride if he saw a wee lad like Eddie 'Snakehips' Colman come through, having been brought up within a goal kick of Old Trafford. 'A Manchester United made up of Manchester players,' he wanted. Will Salford do? Indeed it will.

United had great courage in these years. It flowed through the club. Gibson showcased it when he appointed an unproven Busby, when he gave him a five-year contract and when he prevented any interference with his management. That took courage. It was worth it for Busby's own conviction, demonstrated best when he abandoned the 1952 title-winning side in favour of his young charges and then, as title winners again in 1957, when he took United into Europe.

Crickmer was the man to organise it all. He'd got United back to Old Trafford, and now he could be found personally building the stadium's floodlights which soon illuminated the great white shirts of Real Madrid. Walter's role had changed greatly post-war, but it was his first-class secretaryship that necessarily matched Busby's enormous ambition. He had to deliver on trips to Zurich's Blue Stars tournament for Murphy's young talents, on tours of the USA, Ireland and elsewhere, and soon enough, he had to manage the arrival of Madrid's mighty *Blancos*. He welcomed foreign teams to Manchester, organised post-match banquets, liaised with British Airways for United's own trips abroad, and negotiated carefully with the Football League's bitter chairman who wanted the Reds out of the European Cup.

It was easy for many to forget how young Walter remained, in his mid-50s, because he had been at United for nearly four decades. Everyone was pleased to see him receive a most well-deserved gold service medal from the FA because fans, players, coaches and officials all respected someone who was quite clearly one of the nation's finest footballing men – Walter had helped everyone out at one point or another.

Real Madrid triumphed over United in the 1957 European Cup semi-final, but the Reds still won the league, while an injury to goalkeeper Ray Wood ruined their chances in the FA Cup Final. In 1958, Busby wanted to go one, or two, better. United knew they had the quality to win an unprecedented treble.

Crickmer's organisational skill continued. The demand for tickets for games like Real Madrid outdid even the 1948 FA Cup Final, but he and his loyal staff managed it. United navigated past Shamrock Rovers, Dukla Prague and Red Star Belgrade. Walter watched his side draw 3-3 in Yugoslavia to finish 5-4 winners on aggregate. With a semi-final berth secured again, United celebrated long into the night in Belgrade, singing, eating, dancing, chatting and making lifelong friends with the Red Star lads. On Crickmer and Busby's mind, though, was the pressing need to return and prepare for Saturday's league game with title rivals Wolves. United were aware their punishment for missing a match would be severe.

On 6 February 1958, Busby and Crickmer gathered the squad to return to Manchester. Their take-off from Belgrade was delayed by an hour or so after Johnny Berry misplaced his passport.

United's flight landed in Munich to refuel and the travelling party, Crickmer's good friends from the press included, disembarked on to a slushy runway. Snow threatened to thwart United's route home.

Successfully refuelled, United tried to take off, but twice, they turned back again. Walter and Matt were fully aware of the pressure to get home in time for United's Saturday fixture and, on the third attempt, the plane crashed.

Walter Crickmer was one of 23 fatalities. Only a year before, he had perched on the side of the bath in United's Old Trafford dressing room. Holding up a cup of champagne, he celebrated with Duncan Edwards, Bobby Charlton and the rest. The atmosphere bubbled as much as his glass; this group of young men were en route to achieving greatness. It was everything Crickmer had wanted to see from his favourite football club.

On 14 February, eight days later, three Manchester United youth team players were altar boys at St Ann's Roman Catholic Church in Stretford for Walter's funeral. He was buried at Stretford Cemetery.

Walter's absence left a complete void at Manchester United. He was the link to the club's past, but more than anything symbolic, he held the keys to the engine in his head. He was Mr Manchester United, Mr Reliable, the man anyone could turn to. He had lived it all. And so while Jimmy Murphy kept the red flag flying as Busby lay in a Munich hospital, what he would have given to have had that calming presence of the quietly charming and modest, religious man who always had a cheery word for all – a man of integrity with a quite incredible work ethic. No one had the tools to deal with Munich, but if anyone did, it was Walter. Tragically, he instead gave his life for Manchester United, just as he had for the 38 years before.

* * *

Billy Meredith read the news of Munich with immense sadness and, two and a half months later, while the country focused on United's extraordinary ability to recover under Jimmy Murphy's direction, Jimmy's old hero died. Meredith was the last of The Men Who Made Manchester United to go. So it was that, in the most tragic of ironies, the man whose stardom originally lifted this club to football's summit passed quietly, nearly penniless, and lay in an unmarked grave for almost half a century.

* * *

In 1968, a decade after Munich and the year in which United finally won the European Cup, survivor Bill Foulkes remembered his old friends.

'Walter Crickmer, the secretary, always reminded me of a little dynamo. Nothing was too much trouble,' he said. 'Today, a decade later, they are far from forgotten. Nor will they ever be.'

The same should be said for all these men. They differed immensely in character, appearance and in the contributions they made. Those early figures, Stafford, Davies, Mangnall, Meredith and Roberts, inspired that gene of courage and determination in United. They forged a sense of rebelliousness, and, of course, an expectation of success. They birthed United, and they made its name known across the continent. Those latter men, Crickmer, Gibson and Rocca, imbued that gene of youth into the club, doing so with the most colossal and unimaginable effort. Matt Busby took on this mantle in the most glorious way. And beyond the contributions of these men, whatever their characters, appearances, religion or wealth, they had one thing running through them with absolute, enduring certainty: a deep, implacable love for Manchester United.

Bibliography

NEWSPAPERS

Aberdeen Press and Journal – Athletic Chat – Athletic News – Barnet Press – Barnsley Chronicle – Barnsley Independent – Belfast Telegraph – Bexhill-on-Sea Observer – Birmingham Daily Post – Birmingham Mail – Birmingham Suburban Times – Birmingham Weekly Mercury – Blyth News – Bolton Evening News – Bradford Observer – Bristol Times and Mirror – Bromsgrove & Droitwich Messenger – Burnley Express – Burnley Gazette – Chester Chronicle – Civil & Military Gazette (Lahore) – Clarion – Clifton Society – Coatbridge Express – Cotton Factory Times – Coventry Evening Telegraph – Cricket and Football Field – Daily Citizen (Manchester) – Daily Citizen (Manchester) – Daily Herald – Daily Mirror – Daily News (London) – Daily Telegraph – Dartmouth & South Hams Chronicle – Dundee Courier – Dundee Evening Telegraph – Edinburgh Evening News – Empire News & The Umpire – Evening Despatch – Evening Star – Evesham Journal – Exeter and Plymouth Gazette – Football Gazette (South Shields) – Football News (Nottingham) – Fulham Chronicle – Glasgow Herald – Glossop-dale Chronicle and North Derbyshire Reporter – Gloucestershire Echo – Hackney and Kingsland Gazette – Halifax Evening Courier – Hampshire Independent – Hampshire Telegraph – Harborne Herald – Hereford Journal – Hull Daily Mail – Illustrated Sporting and Dramatic News – Irish Independent – Kenilworth Advertiser – Kent & Sussex Courier – Kinematograph Weekly – Lancashire Evening Post – Lancaster Standard and County Advertiser

– Leamington Spa Courier – Leeds Mercury – Leicester Evening Mail – Liverpool Daily Post – Liverpool Echo – Liverpool Evening Express – Lloyd's Weekly Newspaper – London Evening Standard – Louth Standard – Manchester City News – Manchester Courier – Manchester Evening News – Manchester Times – Morning Post – Nantwich Chronicle – Nantwich Guardian – Newcastle Daily Chronicle – North Star (Darlington) – North Wales Weekly News – Northern Daily Telegraph – Northern Whig – Northwich Chronicle – Northwich Guardian – Nottingham and Midland Catholic News – Nuneaton Observer – Pall Mall Gazette – Penistone, Stocksbridge and Hoyland Express – Portadown Times – Preston Herald – Reading Observer – Reynolds's Newspaper – Ripley and Heanor News – Rochdale Observer – Rochdale Times – Runcorn Examiner – Sandwell Evening Mail – Scottish Referee – Sheffield Daily Telegraph – Sheffield Evening Telegraph – Sheffield Independent – Shields Daily Gazette – Shields Daily News – Smethwick Telephone – South Yorkshire Times – Sport-Vilåg – Sporting Chronicle – Sporting Life – Sports Argus – Staffordshire Sentinel – Star Green 'Un – Sunday Independent (Dublin) – Sunday Mirror – Sunday Post – Sunday Sun (Newcastle) – Sunday World (Dublin) – The Bioscope – The People – The Referee – The Scotsman – The Sportsman – Topical Times – Ulster Football and Cycling News – Warrington Examiner – Waterford Standard – Weekly Dispatch (London) – Western Mail – Wigan Observer and District Advertiser – Wolverhampton Express and Star – Worcester Herald – Workington Star – Wrexham Advertiser – York Herald – Yorkshire Evening Post – Yorkshire Post and Leeds Intelligencer

BOOKS

Barclay, Paddy, *Sir Matt Busby: The Definitive Biography* (London: Ebury Press, 2017).

Belton, Brian, *Red Dawn: Manchester United in the Beginning* (London: Pennant, 2009).

Blakeley, Georgina, and Brendan Evans, *The Regeneration of East Manchester: A Political Analysis* (Manchester: Manchester University Press, 2013).

Blundell, Justin, *Back From the Brink* (Manchester: Empire Publications, 2006).

Boujaoude, Charbel, *Green & Gold, Newton Heath 1878–1902* (Manchester: Empire Publications, 2010)

Cannadine, David, *Victorious Century* (London: Allen Lane, 2017).

Carnevali, Francesca, and Julie-Marie Strange, eds., *20th Century Britain: Economic, Cultural and Social Change* (London: Routledge, 2014).

Clarke, Alf, *Official History of Manchester United* (London: Newservice Ltd., 1948).

Crafts, Nicholas, ed., *Work and Pay in Twentieth-Century Britain* (Oxford: Oxford University Press, 2007).

Dobbs, B., *Edwardians at Play* (London: Pelham, 1973).

Doherty, John, *The Insider's Guide to Manchester United* (Manchester: Empire Publications, 2005).

Dunning, Eric et al, *The Roots of Football Hooliganism – An Historical & Sociological Study* (London: Routledge, 1988).

Dunphy, Eamon, *A Strange Kind of Glory* (London: William Heinemann, 1991).

Dykes, Garth, *The United Alphabet* (Leicester: ACL & Polar Publishing, 1994).

Gardiner, Ean, *Harry Stafford: Manchester United's First Captain Marvel* (Manchester: Empire Publications, 2018).

Gibson, Alfred, and William Pickford, *Association Football & The Men Who Made It* (London: Caxton, 1905).

Harding, John, *Behind the Glory, 100 Years of the PFA* (Derby: Breedon Books, 2009).

Harding, John, *Football Wizard: The Billy Meredith Story* (Manchester: Empire Publications, 2014).

Harrington, Peter, *Gibson Guarantee: Saving of Manchester United* (Imago, 1994).

Inglis, Simon, *League Football and the Men Who Made it* (London: Willow, 1983).

James, Gary, *Manchester: A Football History* (Halifax: James Ward, 2008).

James, Gary, *The Emergence of Footballing Cultures: Manchester, 1840–1919* (Manchester: Manchester University Press, 2019).

Mangan, James, *Athleticism in the Victorian and Edwardian Public School: The Emergence and Consolidation of an Educational Ideology* (London: Frank Cass, 2000).

Mason, Tony, *Association Football & English Society, 1863–1915* (Brighton: Harvester Press, 1980).

McCartney, Iain, *Building the Dynasty: Manchester United 1946–1958* (Durrington: Pitch, 2015).

McCartney, Iain, *Old Trafford: 100 Years at the Theatre of Dreams* (Manchester: Empire, 2010).

Metcalf, Mark, *Manchester United, 1907–11: The First Halcyon Years* (Stroud: Amberley Publishing, 2014).

Metcalf, Mark, *Manchester United's First Championship* (Derby: DB, 2010).

Midwinter, Eric, *Red Shirts and Roses: The Tale of Two Old Traffords* (Manchester: Parrs Wood Press, 2005).

Newburn, Tim, and Elizabeth Stanko, eds., *Just Boys Doing Business? Men, Masculinities and Crime* (London: Routledge, 1994).

O'Neill, Joseph, *Crime City, Manchester's Victorian Underworld* (Preston: Milo Books, 2008).

Rea, Anthony, *Manchester's Little Italy: Memories of the Italian Colony of Ancoats* (Manchester: Neil Richardson, 1988).

Shury, Alan, *The Definitive Newton Heath* (Nottingham, SoccerData Publication, 2002).

Taw, Thomas, *Manchester United's Golden Age, 1903-1914* (Westcliffe-on-Sea: Desert Island Books, 2004).

Thornton, Eric, *Manchester United: Barson to Busby* (London: Hale, 1971).

Tyrell, Tom, *The Illustrated History of Manchester United, 1878-1999* (London: Hamlyn, 1999).

Pearson, Geoffrey, *Hooligans: A History of Respectable Fears* (London: Macmillan Press, 1983).

Vincent, David, *Bread, Knowledge and Freedom: A Study of Nineteenth-Century Working-Class Autobiography* (London: Routledge, 1981).

White, Jim, *Manchester United: The Biography* (London: Sphere, 2009).

Wilson, Jonathan, *Behind the Curtain: Football in Eastern Europe* (London: Orion, 2006).

Young, Percy, *Manchester United* (London: Heinemann, 1962).

ARTICLES/JOURNALS/CHAPTERS IN BOOKS

Dyhouse, Carol, 'Working-Class Mothers and Infant Mortality in England, 1895–1914,' *Journal of Social History* 12.2 (1978), 248–267.

Huggins, Mike, 'Oop for t' coop: sporting identity in Victorian Britain', *History Today*, May 2005.

Jouannou, Paul, and Alan Candlish, 'The Early Development of a Football Hotbed: The Onset of the Game in Tyne and Wear, 1877–82', *Soccer & Society* (2017).

McLeod, Hugh, 'The "Sportsman" and the "Muscular Christian": Rivals Ideas in Nineteenth-Century England', *Gender and Christianity in Modern Europe* (Leuven: Leuven University Press, 2012), 85–106.

Millwall, Robert and Frances Bell, 'Infant Mortality in Victorian Britain: The Mother as Medium', *The Economic History Review*, 54.4 (2001), 699–733.

Porter, Andrew, 'The South African War and the Historians', *African Affairs*, 99.397 (2000), 633–648.

Reynolds, Ernest, 'An Epidemic of Peripheral Neuritis Amongst Beer Drinkers in Manchester and District', *British Medical Journal*, 24 November 1900.

Springhall, John, 'Building Character in the British Boy: the Attempt to Extend Christian Manliness to Working-Class Adolescents, 1880–1914', in *Manliness and Morality: Middle-class Masculinity in Britain and America, 1800–1940* (New York: St Martin's Press, 1987), 52–74.

Tate, Stephen, 'James Catton, "Tityrus" of The Athletic News (1860 to 1936): A Biographical Study', *Sport in History*, 25.1 (2005), 98–115.

Tate, Stephen, 'The Sporting Press,' *Volume 3: The Edinburgh History of the British and Irish Press*, (Edinburgh: Edinburgh University Press, 2020).

Tosh, John, 'Masculinities in an Industrializing Society: Britain, 1800–1914', *Journal of British Studies*, 44.2 (2005), 330–342.

PRIMARY SOURCES

1861–1921 Census Data (via ancestry.com and findmypast. co.uk – and other similar registers).

FA Council Minutes – held by the National Football Museum Archives, Deepdale Stadium, Preston.

FA Emergency Committee Reports – held by the National Football Museum Archives, Deepdale Stadium, Preston.

Kelly Directory.

The Lancet.

Report of the Inter-Departmental Committee on Physical Deterioration (London: Wyman & Sons, 1904).

Slater's Guide to Manchester & Salford.

Slater's Directory of Birmingham.